AF560147

ENGLISH LITERATURE IN EIGHTEENTH CENTURY

ENGLISH LITERATURE IN EIGHTEENTH CENTURY

By

Dr. Lopa Sanyal, *Ph.D.*

Associate Professor

Dyananda College of Science & Arts

Bangalore

Published by:
Namit Wasan

DISCOVERY PUBLISHING HOUSE PVT. LTD.
4383/4B, Ansari Road, Darya Ganj
New Delhi-110 002 (India)
Phone : +91-11-23279245; 23253475; 43596065
E-mail : discoverybooksindia@gmail.com
discoverypublishinghouse@gmail.com
namitwasan9@gmail.com
web : www.discoverypublishinggroup.com

Edition: **2020**

ISBN: 978-81-8356-136-5

English Literature in Eighteenth Century

Printed at:
Infinity Imaging Systems
Delhi

Preface

This book aims to provide a general manual of English Literature in Eighteenth century for students in colleges and universities and others. The first purposes of every such book must be to outline the development of the literature with due regard, and to give appreciative interpretation of the work of the most important authors. This volume combines satisfactory accomplishment of various ends with a selection of authors sufficiently limited for clearness and with adequate accuracy and fullness of details, biographical and other. A book, it seems to us, should supply a systematic statement of the important facts, so that the greater part of the student's time, in class and without, may be left free for the study of the literature itself.

We hope that the book may prove adaptable to various methods and conditions of work. Experience has suggested the brief introductory statement of main literary principles, too often taken for granted by teachers, with much resulting haziness in the student's mind. This volume offers readers the entire range of literary expression from the Restoration to the end of the eighteenth century.. Forgotten or neglected authors and themes as well as new and emerging genres within the expanding market place for printed matter during the eighteenth century receive special attention and emphasis. The volume's guiding purpose is to examine the social and historical circumstances within which literary production and imaginative writing take place in the period and to evaluate the enduring verbal complexity and cultural insights they articulate so powerfully.

It is hoped that this volume not be regarded as merely another summary of English literature. The volume covers the field, we believe, with an eclectic adequacy not attempted by any other book. In matters of selection and interpretation the authors always have remembered the probable and the practical needs of both the undergraduate college student making his first long excursion into

English literature. To make the volume primarily usable it has been found necessary to deviate from the conventional plan of most textbooks.

It is a cause for regret that we cannot discharge completely our indebtedness to earlier source-studies. Were one able to ferret out the borrowed ideas and to assign to each scholar his particular contribution to the field, such citation of authorities would still be prohibitive because of a number of considerations, chiefly the limitation of space. On the one hand, our general plan of stating matters of common knowledge without recording our indebtedness has meant that in not a few cases outstanding sources of information are mentioned only scantily, or not at all. But it is that very restriction that has made possible a fuller acknowledgment of our obligations in the more specialized instances.

Author

Contents

The Eighteenth Century: Pseudo-Classicism and The Beginnings of Modern Romanticism

POLITICAL CONDITIONS

During the first part of the eighteenth century the direct connection between politics and literature was closer than at any previous period of English life; for the practical spirit of the previous generation continued to prevail, so that the chief writers were very ready to concern themselves with the affairs of State, and in the uncertain strife of parties ministers were glad to enlist their aid. On the death of King William in 1702, Anne, sister of his wife Queen Mary and daughter of James II, became Queen. Unlike King William she was a Tory and at first filled offices with members of that party. But the English campaigns under the Duke of Marlborough against Louis XIV were supported by the Whigs.

THE GENERAL SPIRIT OF THE PERIOD

The writers of the reigns of Anne and George I called their period the Augustan Age, because they flattered themselves that with them English life and literature had reached a culminating period of civilization and elegance corresponding to that which existed at Rome under the Emperor Augustus. They believed also that both in the art of living and in literature they had rediscovered and were practicing the principles of the best periods of Greek and Roman life. In our own time this judgment appears equally arrogant and mistaken. In reality the men of the early eighteenth century, like those of the Restoration, largely misunderstood the qualities of the classical spirit, and thinking to reproduce them attained only a superficial, pseudo-classical, imitation. The main characteristics of the period and its literature continue, with some further development, those of the Restoration, and may be summarily indicated as follows:

1. Interest was largely centered in the practical well being either of society as a whole or of one's own social class or set. The majority of writers, furthermore, belonged by birth or association to the upper social stratum and tended to overemphasize its artificial conventions, often looking with contempt on the other classes. To them conventional good breeding, fine manners, the pleasures of the leisure class, and the standards of 'The Town' (fashionable London society) were the only part of life much worth regarding.

2. The men of this age carried still further the distrust and dislike felt by the previous generation for emotion, enthusiasm, and strong individuality both in life and in literature, and exalted Reason and Regularity as their guiding stars. The terms 'decency' and 'neatness' were forever on their lips. They sought a conventional uniformity in manners, speech, and indeed in nearly everything else, and were uneasy if they deviated far from the approved, respectable standards of the body of their fellows. Great poetic imagination, therefore, could scarcely exist among them, or indeed supreme greatness of any sort.

3. They had little appreciation for external Nature or for any beauty except that of formalized Art. A forest

seemed to most of them merely wild and gloomy, and great mountains chiefly terrible, but they took delight in gardens of artificially trimmed trees and in regularly plotted and alternating beds of domestic flowers. The Elizabethans also, as we have seen, had had much more feeling for the terror than for the grandeur of the sublime in Nature, but the Elizabethans had had nothing of the elegant primness of the Augustans.

4. In speech and especially in literature, most of all in poetry, they were given to abstractness of thought and expression, intended to secure elegance, but often serving largely to substitute superficiality for definiteness and significant meaning. They abounded in personifications of abstract qualities and ideas ('Laughter, heavenly maid,' Honor, Glory, Sorrow, and so on, with prominent capital letters), a sort of a pseudo-classical substitute for emotion.

Although the 'Augustan Age' must be considered to end before the middle of the century, the same spirit continued dominant among many writers until near its close, so that almost the whole of the century may be called the period of pseudo- classicism.

DANIEL DEFOE

English novelist, pamphleteer, and journalist, is most famous as the author of *Robinson Crusoe* (1719), a story of a man shipwrecked alone on an island. Along with Samuel Richardson, Defoe is considered the founder of the English novel. Defoe was born as the son of James Foe, a butcher of Stroke Newington. He studied at Charles Morton's Academy, London. Although his Nonconformist father intended him for the ministry, Defoe plunged into politics and trade, traveling extensively in Europe. In the early 1680s Defoe was a commission merchant in Cornhill but went bankrupt in 1691. In 1684 he married Mary Tuffley; they had two sons and five daughters. Defoe earned fame and royal favor with his satirical poem "The True born Englishman" (1701). In 1702

Defoe wrote his famous pamphlet *The Shortest Way With Dissenters* . Himself a Dissenter he mimicked the extreme attitudes of High Anglican Tories and pretended to argue for the extermination of all Dissenters. Nobody was amused; Defoe was arrested and pilloried in May 1703. While in prison Defoe wrote a mock ode, "Hymn To The Pillory" (1703). The poem was sold in the streets, the audience drank to his health while he stood in the pillory and read aloud his verses. When the Tories fell from power Defoe continued to carry out intelligence work for the Whig government. In his own days Defoe was regarded as an unscrupulous, diabolical journalist. Defoe was one of the first to write stories about believable characters in realistic situations using simple prose. He achieved literary immortality when in April 1719 he published *Robinson Crusoe,* which was based partly on the memoirs of voyagers and castaways, such as Alexander Selkirk. During the remaining years, Defoe concentrated on books rather than pamphlets. Among his works are *Moll Flanders*(1722), *A Journal Of The Plague Year* (1722) and *Captain Jack*(1722) His last great work of fiction, *Roxana,* appeared in 1724. In the 1720s Defoe had ceased to be politically controversial in his writings, and he produced several historical works, a guide book and *The Great Law Of Subordination Considered* (1724), an examination of the treatment of servants. Phenomenally industrious, Defoe produced in his last years also works involving the supernatural, *The Political History Of The Devil* (1726) and *An Essay On The History And Reality Of Apparitions*(1727). He died on 26 April 1731, at his lodgings in Ropemaker's Alley, Moorfields.

JONATHAN SWIFT

Famous Irish poet, pamphleteer, satirist and wit of Augustan Age. He was educated (more or less) at Trinity College, Dublin. In the aftermath of the 1689 Jacobite rebellion in Ireland, Swift found shelter in England, under the auspices of Sir William Temple, a prominent diplomat and statesman. Swift served as secretary to Temple for the next ten years. In the process, he earned his M.A. at Oxford, was ordained into the Episcopalian Church of Ireland and was charged with the tutorship of Temple's young ward, Esther Johnson, a.k.a. "Stella".

After Temple died in 1699, Swift moved back to Ireland, working at various posts in the Church. In 1704, two satirical pieces – *Tale of the Tub* and *Battle of the Books* – earned him some renown (and some enemies). Returning to England intermittently, he became intimate with the Augustan wits and literary men of the day – Addison, Steele, Pope and Congreve.

Although a lifelong supporter of the Whigs, the growing chasm between Whigs and the Church led Swift, in 1708, to launch a series of pamphlet attacks on the Whigs. By 1710, Swift had switched over the Tories completely and put his skills at their disposal. Swift took over *The Examiner*, a Tory rag, and, with a couple of 1711 pamphlets, helped turn to the tide of English public opinion against the "Whig" War of Spanish Succession.

With the death of Queen Anne in 1714, the Tories fell from favor and Swift returned to Ireland. He would serve as Dean of St. Patrick's Cathedral in Dublin for the rest of his life. He remained bitter but quiet for several years.

In 1720, he roused himself from his perch and got busy again. His 1720 *Irish Manufacture* essay attacked English economic policy towards Ireland and suggested a boycott of English goods. The pamphlet was later declared seditious by the British government. His *Swearer's Bank* (1720) was his proposition for the setting up a bank to help small tradesmen in Ireland. His visceral series of 1724-5 pamphlets, known as *Drapier's Letters* led to the downfall of Wood's half-pence, the Whig government's plan to make up for the shortfall of coinage in Ireland by minting copper coins. His 1727 and 1728 pieces on the state of Ireland explains how British economic policies are keeping Ireland in a state of underdevelopment and poverty. This series of works on the state of the Irish economy culminated in the wickedly delicious *A Modest Proposal* (1729). His bitterness against

British policy came out most fully in his *Injured Lady* (1746). Oh, incidentally, he also found time to write that masterpiece of satire, *Gulliver's Travels* (1726).

After the death of his beloved Stella, Swift began to drop off and gradually grew mentally unstable in the years before his death in 1745. Having served his role as an Irish patriot and Tory critic of Whig policies, Swift is duly celebrated in William Butler Yeats's poem "The Seven Sages" and in "Swift's Epitaph".

RICHARD STEELE

English essayist and playwright, b. Dublin. After studying at Charterhouse and Oxford, he entered the army in 1694 and rose to the rank of captain by 1700. His first book, a moral tract entitled The Christian Hero, appeared in 1701. The same year saw a production of his first play, The Funeral, a sentimental comedy, which he followed with two more comedies, The Lying Lover (1703) and The Tender Husband (1705). In 1722 he produced his last and most important play, The Conscious Lovers. A year after the death of his first wife in 1706, he married Mary Scurlock, the "dear Prue" of his famous letters. Steele, however, was not made for a domestic life, and much of his time was spent carousing with his companions. He held several minor government positions before beginning his famous periodical, the Tatler (1709–11), the writing of which was soon joined by his close friend Joseph Addison. This was followed by the Spectator (1711–12), the Guardian (1713), and later periodicals of lesser importance. The partnership of Steele and Addison was one of the most successful in the history of English letters. Although they differed greatly in temperament, their aims and tastes were in the main united. They were Whig partisans, and sympathetic with the moral attitude of the rapidly growing middle class. Although Steele's prose lacks the polished grace of Addison's, his writing reflects his charm, spontaneity, wit, and imagination. In 1713, Steele carried on a celebrated political controversy with Swift, the chief Tory spokesman, in the course of which he wrote his pamphlet

The Crisis. He became a Whig member of Parliament in 1713, was expelled by his political enemies the following year, but returned under the Hanoverians, and was knighted in 1715. His opposition to the Peerage Bill in his weekly, the Plebeian (1719), involved him in a quarrel with Addison, and Steele's attempt at reconciliation was frustrated by his friend's death. He founded the first theatrical paper, the Theater, in 1720. His improvidence and free-living finally caught up with him, and debts forced his retirement to Wales in 1724, where he spent his remaining years in obscurity.

ALEXANDER POPE

Alexander Pope was an English poet who, modeling himself after the great poets of classical antiquity, wrote highly polished verse, often in a didactic or satirical vein. In verse translations, moral and critical essays, and satires that made him the foremost poet of his age, he brought the heroic couplet, which had been refined by John Dryden, to ultimate perfection. Pope was the son of a London cloth merchant. His parents were Roman Catholics, which automatically barred him from England's Protestant universities. Until he was 12 years old, he was educated largely by priests; primarily self-taught afterward, he read widely in English letters, as well as in French, Italian, Latin, and Greek. A devastating illness, probably tuberculosis of the spine, struck him in childhood, leaving him deformed. He never grew taller than 4 ft 6 in and was subject to violent headaches. Perhaps as a result of this condition, he was hypersensitive and exceptionally irritable all his life.

In 1717 Pope moved to a villa in Twickenham, west of London on the Thames River, where he lived for the rest of his life. The most celebrated personages of the day came to visit him there. He was a bitterly quarrelsome man and attacked his literary contemporaries viciously and often without provocation. To some, however, he was warm and affectionate; he had a long and close friendship with the English writers Jonathan Swift and John Gay.

Pope's literary career began in 1704, when the playwright William Wycherley, pleased by Pope's verse, introduced him into the circle of fashionable London wits and writers, who welcomed him as a prodigy. He first attracted public attention in 1709 with his Pastorals. In 1711 his Essay on Criticism, a brilliant exposition of the canons of taste, was published. His most famous poem, The Rape of the Lock (first published 1712; revised edition published 1714), a fanciful and ingenious mock-heroic work based on a true story, established his reputation securely. In 1713 Pope published Windsor Forest, which endeared him to the Tories by referring to the Peace of Utrecht. In 1714 his work The Wife of Bath appeared, which, like his The Temple of Fame (1715), was imitative of the works of the same title by the 14th-century English poet Geoffrey Chaucer. In 1717 a collection of Pope's works containing the most noteworthy of his lyrics was published. Pope's translation of Homer's Iliad was published in six volumes from 1715 to 1720; a translation of the Odyssey followed (1725-1726). He also published an edition of Shakespeare's plays (1725).

Pope and his friend Swift had for years written scornful and very successful critical reviews of those whom they considered poor writers; in 1727 they began a series of parodies of the same writers. The adversaries hurled insults at Swift and Pope in return, and in 1728 Pope lampooned them in one of his best-known works, The Dunciad, a satire celebrating dullness. He later enlarged the work to four volumes, the final one appearing in 1743. In 1734 he completed his Essay on Man. Pope's last works, Imitations of Horace (1733-1739), were attacks on political enemies of his friends.

Pope used the heroic couplet with exceptional brilliance, giving it a witty, occasionally biting quality. His success made it the dominant poetic form of his century, and his poetry was translated into many languages.

THE ROMANTIC MOVEMENT

The reaction which was bound to accompany the triumph of Pseudo-classicism, as a reassertion of those instincts in human nature which Pseudo-classicism disregarded, took the form of a distinct Romantic Revival. Beginning just about as Pope's reputation was reaching its climax, and gathering momentum throughout the greater part of the eighteenth century, this movement eventually gained a predominance as complete as that which Pseudo-classicism had enjoyed, and became the chief force, not only in England but in all Western Europe, in the literature of the whole nineteenth century. The impulse was not confined to literature, but permeated all the life of the time. In the sphere of religion, especially, the second decade of the eighteenth century saw the awakening of the English church from lethargy by the great revival of John and Charles Wesley, whence, quite contrary to their original intention, sprang the Methodist denomination. In political life the French Revolution was a result of the same set of influences. Romanticism showed itself partly in the supremacy of the Sentimental Comedy and in the great share taken by Sentimentalism in the development of the novel, of both of which we shall speak hereafter; but its fullest and most steadily progressive manifestation was in non-dramatic poetry. Its main traits as they appear in the eighteenth century are as clearly marked as the contrasting ones of Pseudo-classicism, and we can enumerate them distinctly, though it must of course be understood that they appear in different authors in very different degree and combinations.

1. There is, among the Romanticists, a general breaking away not only from the definite pseudo-classical principles, but from the whole idea of submission to fixed authority. Instead there is a spirit of independence and revolt, an insistence on the value of originality and the right of the individual to express himself in his own fashion.

2. There is a strong reassertion of the value of emotion, imagination, and enthusiasm. This naturally involves some reaction against the pseudo-classic, and also the true classic, regard for finished form.

3. There is a renewal of genuine appreciation and love for external Nature, not least for her large and great aspects, such as mountains and the sea. The contrast between the pseudo-classical and the romantic attitude in this respect is clearly illustrated, as has often been pointed out, by the difference between the impressions recorded by Addison and by the poet Gray in the presence of the Alps. Addison, discussing what he saw in Switzerland, gives most of his attention to the people and politics. One journey he describes as 'very troublesome,' adding: 'You can't imagine how I am pleased with the sight of a plain.' In the mountains he is conscious chiefly of difficulty and danger, and the nearest approach to admiration which he indicates is 'an agreeable kind of horror.' Gray, on the other hand, speaks of the Grande Chartreuse as 'one of the most solemn, the most romantic, and the most astonishing scenes.... I do not remember to have gone ten paces without an exclamation that there was no restraining. Not a precipice, not a torrent, nor a cliff, but is pregnant with religion and poetry.'

4. The same passionate appreciation extends with the Romanticists to all full and rich beauty and everything grand and heroic.

5. There is a strong tendency to melancholy, which is often carried to the point of morbid ness and often expresses itself in meditation and moralizing on the tragedies of life and the mystery of death. This inclination is common enough in many romantic-spirited persons of all times, and it is always a symptom of immaturity or lack of perfect balance. Among the earlier eighteenth century Romanticists

there was a very nourishing crop of doleful verse, since known from the place where most of it was located, as the 'Graveyard poetry.' Even Gray's 'Elegy in a Country Churchyard' is only the finest representative of this form, just as Shakespeare's 'Hamlet' is the culmination of the crude Elizabethan tragedy of blood. So far as the mere tendency to moralize is concerned, the eighteenth century Romanticists continues with scarcely any perceptible change the practice of the Pseudo-classicists.

6. In poetic form, though the Romanticists did not completely abandon the pentameter couplet for a hundred years, they did energetically renounce any exclusive allegiance to it and returned to many other meters. Milton was one of their chief masters, and his example led to the revival of blank verse and of the octo-syllabic couplet. There was considerable use also of the Spenserian stanza, and development of a great variety of lyric stanza forms, though not in the prodigal profusion of the Elizabethan and Jacobean period.

THE OTHER SENTIMENTALISTS AND REALISTS

Richardson and Fielding set in motion two currents, of sentimentalism and realism, respectively, which flowed vigorously in the novel during the next generation, and indeed (since they are of the essence of life), have continued, with various modifications, down to our own time. Of the succeeding realists the most important is Tobias Smollett, a Scottish ex-physician of violent and brutal nature, who began to produce his picaresque stories of adventure during the lifetime of Fielding. He made ferociously unqualified attacks on the statesmen of his day, and in spite of much power, the coarseness of his works renders them now almost unreadable. But he performed one definite service; in 'Roderick Random,' drawing on his early experiences as a ship's surgeon, he inaugurated the out-and-out sea story, that is the story which takes place not, like 'Robinson Crusoe,' in small part, but mainly, on board ship. Prominent, on the other hand, among the sentimentalists is Laurence Sterne, who, inappropriately enough, was a clergyman, the author of 'Tristram Shandy.' This book is quite unlike anything else ever written. Sterne published it in nine successive volumes during almost as many years, and he made a point of almost complete formlessness and every sort of whimsicality. The hero is not born until the third volume, the story mostly relates to other people and things, pages are left blank to be filled out by the reader—no grotesque device or sudden trick can be too fantastic for Sterne. But he has the gift of delicate pathos and humor, and certain episodes in the book are justly famous, such as the one where Uncle Toby carefully puts a fly out of the window, refusing to 'hurt a hair of its head,' on the ground that 'the world surely is wide enough to hold both thee and me.' The best of all the sentimental stories is Goldsmith's 'Vicar of Wakefield' (1766), of which we have already spoken. With its kindly humor, its single-hearted wholesomeness, and its delightful figure of Dr. Primrose it remains, in spite of its artlessness, one of the permanent landmarks of English fiction.

HISTORICAL AND 'GOTHIC' ROMANCES

Stories which purported to reproduce the life of the Past were not unknown in England in the seventeenth century, but the real beginning of the historical novel and romance belongs to the later part of the eighteenth century. The extravagance of romantic writers at that time, further, created a sort of subspecies called in its day and since the 'Gothic' romance. These 'Gothic' stories are nominally located in the Middle Ages, but their main object is not to give an accurate picture of medieval life, but to arouse terror in the reader, by means of a fantastic apparatus of gloomy castles, somber villains, distressed and sentimental heroines, and supernatural mystery. The form was inaugurated by Horace Walpole, the son of the former Prime Minister, who built near Twickenham (Pope's home) a pseudo-medieval house which he named Strawberry Hill, where he posed as a center of the medieval revival. Walpole's 'Castle of 'Otranto,' published in 1764, is an utterly absurd little story, but its novelty at the time, and the author's prestige, gave it a great vogue. The really best 'Gothic' romances are the long ones written by Mrs. Ann Radcliffe in the last decade of the century, of which 'The Mysteries of Udolpho,' in particular, was popular for two generations. Mrs. Radcliffe's books overflow with sentimentality, but display real power, especially in imaginative description. Of the more truly historical romances the best were the 'Thaddeus of Warsaw' and 'Scottish Chiefs' of Miss Jane Porter, which appeared in the first decade of the nineteenth century. None of all these historical and 'Gothic' romances attains the rank of great or permanent literature, but they were historically important, largely because they prepared the way for the novels of Walter Scott, which would hardly have come into being without them, and which show clear signs of the influence of even their most exaggerated features.

NOVELS OF PURPOSE

Still another sort of novel was that which began to be written in the latter part of the century with the object of exposing some particular abuse in society. The first representatives of the class aimed, imitating the French sentimentalist Rousseau, to improve education, and in accordance with the sentimental Revolutionary misconception which held that all sin and sorrow result from the corruptions of civilization, often held up the primitive savage as a model of all the kindly virtues. The most important of the novels of purpose, however, were more thorough-going attacks on society composed by radical revolutionists, and the least forgotten is the 'Caleb Williams' of William Godwin (1794), which is intended to demonstrate that class-distinctions result in hopeless moral confusion and disaster.

SUMMARY

The variety of the literary influences in eighteenth century England was so great that the century can scarcely be called a literary unit; yet as a whole it contrasts clearly enough both with that which goes before and with that which follows. Certainly its total contribution to English literature was great and varied.

Eighteenth-Century Thought

INTRODUCTION

The seventeenth century had been a period of epoch making scientific discovery, the building of great philosophical systems on the basis of reason, and the settlement of violent conflicts in Church and State. The eighteenth century did not make comparable scientific discoveries or undertake to build new systems; it tried to cash in on the speculative profits of the seventeenth century and to put ideas to work. The great German thinker Leibniz carried into the eighteenth century the ideals of the seventeenth: he constructed a bold and speculative system on the idea that reality must be reason in action, leading to the conclusion that God has necessarily made this "the best of all possible worlds" (*Théodicée*, 1710); and as a rational reformer he sought to bring about the actual unification of science, religion, and society. But it has already been said that the dominant strain in eighteenth-century English thought derives from Newton plus Locke. Under the influence of Locke, English philosophy tends to break up into the practical discussion of questions of education, morals, psychology, sociology, and economics. Newton's system was interpreted as vindicating the great principle of harmony or rational order in morals, society, politics, and religion. The brilliant achievements of Newtonian physics led men to expect that simple laws could be found which would be valid for these fields also, and Locke's sober program of descriptions and analyses was continued. The conclusions which would emerge would not be radical or revolutionary; they would give a rational description of things as they are, and would thus appeal to "reasonable" men.

The line of thought in which philosophers are most interested often differs from the line of popular thought. To consider the first briefly, both Newton and Locke assumed a principle of causality which established the existence of matter as the cause of sensation and likewise the existence of God as the cause of the order of nature. The greatest English philosophers of the eighteenth century, Berkeley and Hume, centered attention on the problem of knowledge formulated by Locke, particularly the question of our knowledge of causes. Locke had said that all our knowledge of the external world is by way of sensation, content of consciousness; Berkeley went on to say that since this is so, since all our knowledge is of ideas, the conception of material substance is meaningless, and God remains the sole guarantor of an external world. Hume took the last step and reduced human knowledge to a mere series of impressions, with no certain reference to what is outside the content of consciousness at a given moment, and thus landed in complete theoretical skepticism. Whereas Berkeley had argued against the existence of matter, on the ground that we have no knowledge of such a cause, Hume extended the argument to mind and to God. This conclusion if consistently maintained meant the destruction of the vision of world-order and world-harmony. But things did not go so far; even in Hume, skepticism in action meant a shrewd limitation of knowledge to what is actually found in experience. The wider influence of the empirical philosophy popularized a psychology based on the association of ideas and a hedonistic ethics. The Scottish common sense school (notably Thomas Reid) which set about refuting Hume did not contribute much to the advance of technical philosophy, but long dominated the widely influential Scottish universities and to a large extent the minds of educated men in Great Britain and America.

The thinkers who rely on critical reason in the mid-century are often grouped under the term *Enlightenment* (from the German *"Aufklärung"*). With its emphasis on propaganda to spread the light of reason, the term applies to Voltaire and Diderot and many others, not so closely to Rousseau, and with varying degrees of appropriateness to Hume. Adam Smith, Franklin, and Jefferson.

DEISM

Deism may be described as an attempt to base religion on truth discovered in nature and by reason. In the spirit of the age, the deists appeal from arbitrary authority to reason, but since they are largely concerned with weakening or discrediting the Christian revelation, they differ from the rationalizing divines and the Newtonian physico-theologists who likewise seek and find God's plan in nature. The deists were often treated as moral and social outcasts, and the bitter hostility of the orthodox obscured the fact that the basic distinction was one of emphasis, and that almost all were agreed in exalting reason and reducing the irrational, mysterious, and supernatural elements in religion. This should be kept in mind when we read the attacks on deists or "freethinkers" by Swift, Addison, Steele, Fielding, and others.

Outside this field of controversy, deistic tendencies blended with cool rational orthodox views, with the current emphasis on Christianity as a system of moral behavior, as in the influential sermons of the latitudinarian Archbishop Tillotson. Deism also stimulated biblical scholarship) by insisting on a critical examination of texts. As a philosophy it lacked imaginative color and emotional depth, and may be said to represent the impoverished side of neo-classicism. Its shallow optimism lacked the "tragic sense of life" which we find in more somber minds like Butler and Johnson. Its conception of a rigid reason which does not admit of progress lost out in an age which was becoming interested in the changing perspectives of history. It appealed to the head rather than the heart, and never reached the masses who were moved by the evangelical revival. But its position in liberal thought, its coherence and utility as a program of life, may be seen in the careers of two great American deists, Franklin and Jefferson, and in the history of Unitarianism in Old and New England.

ETHICS

The turn away from metaphysical speculation, the weakening of purely supernatural sanctions in religion, the interest in man as a social animal and in the useful ends of literature—all these and related causes fill the period with discussion of morals. Many literary types are developed or modified to suit this interest—the essay in verse or prose, the satire in verse or prose, the novel, the drama, the descriptive-reflective poem. The work of the moralists carries over with unusual directness into literature, and into fields which we now think of as distinct from ethics-psychology, sociology, political science, economics, and aesthetics. It was, of course, traditional to apply moral standards to the presentation of human character, but it was a new thing to pay so much attention to the problem of identifying and defining the good as actually found in the individual and in society. This interest was now shared as never before by the professional philosopher and the popular writer.

Does the good have its ultimate basis outside individual interest or desire? Is it absolute or relative? The answers were given partly in terms of inherited philosophies and religions, Christianity, Platonism, Stoicism, adjusted to newer conceptions of reason or natural law, and partly in terms of the new interest in psychology, in what man finds actually happening in his mind. Both the love of simple order and the respect for tradition sought to identify the good with some universal ideal like reason; at the other extreme, a factual report on human nature might show man to be selfish and sensual. Thus in the philosophy of Hobbes, a materialistic world-view was associated with a picture of man as a predatory animal restrained from an unbridled exercise of his selfish will only by the police power of the state. Moreover, Hobbes taught, the state exercises this power not in the realization of an ideal or by virtue of divine or natural right, but because of a selfish calculation of advantage. Hobbes raised two issues sharply: (*a*) Is the good absolute, or relative to human desire? (*b*) If relative to human desire, is it approved on selfish or unselfish grounds? His clean-cut position came into direct conflict with established tradition and with the English tendency to compromise. The chief task of the typical English moralist of the next century was to answer Hobbes. The age was reluctant to think of the good as arbitrarily willed by the individual, the state, or even God himself.

The Cambridge Platonists upheld an absolute standard based on divine reason and congruous with human nature. Emphasis on man's natural participation in and approval of this world-plan made for an optimistic view of human nature, and at the same time the good was described as having useful and pleasant consequences for man. Thus the good is absolutely valid, and from the point of view of man's interests it is also vindicated by an en-product of happiness. Richard Cumberland in his *De Legibus Naturae* (I672) took this position in reply to Hobbes. Locke the compromiser is on both sides of the main issues; with his emphasis on the test of experience he can say, "Things are good or evil only in respect to pleasure or pain." Yet sensations and feelings point to a world ordered by God according to law, and Locke is rationalist enough to argue that moral laws may be deduced with mathematical certainty. In his practical exposition of morals, however, God rather than mathematical certainty gives the guarantee. In spite of his rationalistic vein, Locke fathers the hedonistic and the utilitarian in English morals—the doctrine that the good is what is "good for" something in the sense of ultimately producing pleasure. Let the late seventeenth and early eighteenth centuries also harbored the other tendency, to equate morals with mathematics, to think of social relations as logical relations, and to deduce morals a priori from the fitness or congruity of things. This appears in the theologian Samuel Clarke and was expounded in popular form in William Wollaston's *Religion of Nature Delineated.* (There were busts of Clarke, Wollaston, Newton, and Locke in Queen Caroline's famous Hermitage at Richmond.) Both deists and orthodox divines showed considerable interest in thus trying to explain morality in terms of identity, equivalence, proportion, and consistency.

LATER ETHICS

A more subtle psychology would show both self-regarding and altruistic elements in human nature, though the facile contrast between selfishness and benevolence appears constantly in the popular thought of the time. The ethics of the theologian Butler balanced the observed facts of selfishness and benevolence, and set over the passions a monitor conscience representing not only reason but moral compulsion of divine authenticity. But the general trend was away from absolute doctrines and toward empiricism and utilitarianism, a description of the good in terms of actual human experiences and desires. Religion continued to color thinking about morals, and God was invoked by the pleasure-pain moralists, first, because as the Creator he gave his sanction to such a scheme, and second, because in case the virtuous man suffers more pain than pleasure in this life, the balance will be redressed in a future life. This was orthodox doctrine; we often find it in the authors of the time (Young, Richardson), and it was restated by the late eighteenth-century theologian William Paley, whose books were generally used in British and American colleges. Leaving heaven and hell out of account, other ways were devised of explaining how the moral life was based on pleasurable and painful sensations. The principle of the association of ideas was used by Hartley and others to show how moral judgments, like Locke's compound ideas, were built up out of simple elements of sense experience. Studying results rather than origins, Jeremy Bentham (*Principles of Morals and*

Legislation, 1780, 1789) tried to determine the exact value of acts and policies by ascertaining the quantity of pleasure or pain produced. This calculation of results was associated in the later British utilitarian school with a practical reform movement in legislation. In the mid-century Hume, the consistent empiricist, could find no rational standard of the good, merely a "sentiment" which approved the good, and so carefully did he keep to the findings of experience that he could not fully explain the sentiment in terms of utility (pleasure and pain); in Hume, as for his age, the instinctive social and altruistic quality of human nature is a central fact, on which the great structures of society must be based. The same is true for his countryman Adam Smith (*Theory of Moral Sentiments*, 1759), whose teachings moreover show, in combining an ethics of sympathy with the economic doctrine of laissez faire, free action in the economic world for individual profit (*The Wealth of Nations*, 1776), that the basic assumption of the age is "that true self-love and social are the same."

Type of Literature in Eighteenth Century

What kind of literature was required and produced by this age? Without elaborate critical campaign or controversy, change occurred in response to a felt need in the field of prose. Sprat, we have seen, speaks of the plain style required by the new science; Burnet and many others speak of the new plain style favored by Restoration preachers. The widening of the reading public had much to do with this important change: popularization encouraged simplification, and this tendency had already appeared in the style of the Puritan preachers and in much utilitarian and popular writing. The change of prose style extended to literary criticism, journalism, and political and philosophical discussion. The pamphlet and the essay were in favor, small units of prose calculated to enlighten and persuade. If the appeal was to tradition and prejudice, it must still be clothed in the garb of reason; the reader must be taken to be a sensible man, not a fanatic, enthusiast, radical, or pedant.

Poetry was more easily classified by type than prose, and established types remained. The great symbols of the Renaissance imagination still persisted. *Paradise Lost* (1667) promptly won admiration even among Restoration courtiers, but of course it was the product of the preceding age. When the Restoration tried to attain sublimity, as in the heroic plays and in attempts at epic, its voice became hollow and its style bombastic. The same insincerity appeared in the most pretentious lyric form cultivated during the period, the Pindaric ode developed by Abraham Cowley, which aspired to enthusiasm and inspiration. In the prefatory note to *Gondibert* (I651) Hobbes and Davenant had already said that an epic poem should be clear and rational and should avoid the supernatural. Cowley said the same thing in his lines in praise of this poem:

Methinks heroic poesy till now Like some fantastic fairy-land did show, Gods, devils, nymphs, witches' and giants' race, And all but man in man's chief work had place.

Thou like some worthy knight with sacred arms Dost drive the monsters thence, and end the charms. Instead of those dost men and manners plant,

The things which that rich soil did chiefly want.

Enthusiasm and heroism gave way before the study of men and manners, of human nature operating within the limits of a fixed literary and social code. This was already the direction of French classicism, and the early residence of Charles II in France and the vogue of French fashions and standards in his reign have been taken to indicate a decisive influence. It may be noted that the height of classicism in France was reached from 1660 to 1685; that is, the first quarter-century of the reign of Louis XIV corresponds exactly to the reign of Charles II. Cases of direct influence appear: Corneille is of importance for dramatic criticism, Boileau for criticism and satire. Yet at most the French influence only gave articulation and color to a change already under way in England. There was already a neo-classical tradition in western Europe derived ultimately from the Italian critics of the Renaissance. France was doing far more than England to develop this tradition, and had assumed leadership, but after all one literature takes from another only what it is predisposed to take. We must not therefore consider

Restoration literary types and theories as mere derivatives of the French, though there was a considerable debt to French criticism. And of course French remained the international language of diplomacy, society, and culture for over a century to come.

Somewhat similar though not identical reasons underlie the development of burlesque literary forms, the deliberate cultivation of incongruity between subject and style, a pretentious style being used for low matter or high matter being treated in undignified style. This might be done for the purpose of expressing a cynical or satirical view of mankind, as in Butler *Hudibras,* or it might be a playful campaign against extravagant literary projects and pretensions, or merely a light exercise in technique and style. Every literary form had its burlesque antitype—epic, tragedy, opera, pastoral, lyric, romance,—and the process was extended during the eighteenth century.

The interest in analysis and exposition, fortified by the traditional idea that poetry ought to teach as well as delight, led to the development of the group of types included under the terms verse-essay or verse-treatise, the georgic (conceived broadly as a poem telling how to do something), and later the descriptive-didactic poem. If the age had rigid ideas about poetic form and diction, it sometimes seemed to have curiously indiscriminate ideas about poetic subject matter. The maintenance of the right attitude and style on the part of the poet, it was felt, could make any subject eligible for the appropriate type of poetry. Of course a somewhat similar attitude marked the masters of the new prose also, but prose was less hampered than verse by traditional requirements of genre and style. The new attitude was sober yet flexible, moderately strict without sacrificing geniality and good manners, relatively plain in style and light in touch, and disposed to assume easily accessible common ground between writer and reader.

Drama in Eighteenth Century

THE BEGINNINGS OF RESTORATION DRAMA AND OPERA

The formal opening of the period of modern English drama may be dated from the issuing by Charles II, on 21 August, 1660, of letters patent conferring upon Thomas Killigrew and Sir William D'Avenant the right to 'erect' two companies of players. The advent of Charles II to the throne meant the restoration of drama, as well as of monarchy. The grant of 21 August was of large significance. It restored to English drama, with the seal of royal authority, rights and privileges of which it has never subsequently been deprived. Yet the act that thus conferred larger liberty upon the drama marks, in fact, the creation of a theatrical monopoly from whose shackles the London stage was not wholly freed for almost three centuries. For the moment, however, it was enough that the ban on English drama was formally lifted.

The way, indeed, had already been opened for the resumption of theatrical activity. D'Avenant's productions at Rutland House had been followed by the performances of his operas, in 1658 and 1659, on the public stage at the Cockpit Theatre, in Drury Lane. In early February, 1660,

General Monck entered London, and soon afterward a license for acting was given to John Rhodes, a London bookseller, said to have been previously connected with the Blackfriars Theatre as wardrobe-keeper. Before the issue of the patent of 21 August, three companies of actors had begun to be assembled—at the Cockpit, at the Red Bull, and at Salisbury Court, in Whitefriars.

The reopening of the theatres brought the revival of numerous Elizabethan plays. John Downes, prompter at Lincoln's Inn Fields Theatre during practically the entire Restoration period, gives a list of fifteen ' Principal Old Stock Plays' acted during the earlier years of the Theatre Royal, later known as the Drury Lane. Two plays are by Dryden, three by Shakespeare, three by Jonson, seven by Beaumont and Fletcher. A supplementary list of old plays which 'were Acted but now and then; yet being well Performed, were very Satisfactory to the Town' consists largely of works by Shakespeare, Jonson, Beaumont and Fletcher, and Shirley. Adaptations of still other Shakespearean plays gave them at least counterfeit presentment on the stage. Though his romantic comedies were denied the favor shown to The Merry Wives of Windsor, Shakespeare's tragedies were reanimated by the genius of Betterton. Blurred and imperfect as was the Restoration vision, it was never blind to Elizabethan achievement. The interregnum had weakened, but not broken, the continuous chain of English drama.

Though the opening years of the Restoration theatres seem largely devoted to the revival of earlier dramas and to the novelty of political dramatic satire, there were early indications of more significant dramatic progress. In the work of John Wilson (I627-1696), Recorder of Londonderry, Restoration comedy is at once quickened by Elizabethan impulse and shown to be capable of genuine comic achievement. The comedies of Ben Jonson were speedily installed as favorites on the Restoration stage. Pepys saw The Silent Woman, 7 January, 1661, and Downes mentions it, together with Volpone and The Alchemist, as among the principal old stock plays at the Theatre Royal. John Wilson, though too vigorous to be dismissed merely as an imitator, fell naturally under Jonson's influence. In the Preface to The Cheats (written 1662) he says: 'Comedy, either is, or should be, the true Picture of Vertue, or Vice; yet so drawn, as to shew a man how to follow the one, and avoid the other.' The Cheats is preëminently a 'humour comedy,' with deception, in its various forms, as the vice depicted. Bilboe and Titere Tu usurp the titles of Major and Captain, though they are but common bullies; Runter is a pretended legal authority; Scruple is a hypocrite—a Nonconformist who conforms for a living of £ 300, but goes back to his flock for £ 400 by 'natural affection'; Mopus is a quack astrologer. The strength of the comedy lies rather in characters and in dialogue than in plot. In The Projectors (printed 1665) the influence of Jonson shows in characters like Sir Gudgeon Credu- lous, the miser, Suckdry, the usurer, and Leanchops, the servant. The very names of the characters reveal the habit which Jonson popularized in 'humour comedy.'

As the decade advanced, nevertheless, alien influences asserted themselves with increasing power. In The Siege of Rhodes D'Avenant had already introduced English opera, using recitative music which he declared to be 'unpractis'd here; though of great reputation amongst other Nations.' His words raise at once the question of foreign influence upon English opera. Too much stress should not be laid on D'Avenant's chance phrase. The facile assumption that early English opera is the product of French influences is dangerous. Under the protection of Mazarin, Italian opera had been carried into France as early as 1645. The real development of French opera, however, dates only from the decade of the seventies, a period subsequent to the operas of D'Avenant and other English writers. As operatic tendencies became accentuated in France, dramatists like Corneille, Molière, and Quinault had more or less to do with its libretti. All three, in fact, contributed to Psyché (I671), whose success turned Quinault to writing for Lulli, its composer, libretti which thoroughly established the popularity of French opera. The first French opera has been recently declared to be the Pomone (I671) of Cambert and Pierre Perrin, and the popular collaborations of Lulli and Quinault begin only in the very year, 1673, when Shadwell turned The Tempest into an opera. Unquestionably the popularity of opera in France, and its occasional actual transfer to the English stage, stimulated operatic activity in England, especially in the decade which produced Matthew Locke's music to Psyche and the earliest of Purcell's operas, Dido and Aeneas (1680). Yet a score or so of years had already elapsed since the production of The Siege of Rhodes. Without attempting to disprove wholly the foreign influence upon early English opera which D'Avenant's own words imply, it would seem that the case should not rest here. Two reasons naturally suggest themselves to account largely for D'Avenant's introduction of English opera—his previous practice in the masque and his desire to cloak, under a novel disguise, the real nature of his dramatic efforts. His early operas are not an alien Continental product. In a word, French influence was more potent in the later development of Restoration opera than at its outset.

The slender thread of Spanish weave which is thus apparent in the fibre of early Restoration drama is discernible from time to time in the texture of later English drama. Wycherley, Mrs. Behn, and Crowne, in the later seventeenth century, and Steele, Cibber, and Mrs. Centlivre in the early eighteenth century may serve as sufficient examples of the continuance of Spanish influence, however faint at times, upon English dramatists. In general, however, Spanish drama, or even Spanish literature, made but minor contribution to English drama of the Restoration. Apart from its occasional suggestions for plot, Spanish drama may have somewhat stimulated early Restoration tendency toward the comedy of intrigue. In a familiar passage, Scott declared that 'the Spanish comedy, with its bustle, machinery, disguise, and complicated intrigue, was much more agreeable' to the taste of Restoration audiences than 'regular comedy . . . depending upon delicate turns of expression, and nicer delineations of character.' Yet this must not be mistaken for proof of the dominance of Spanish influence over Restoration comedy. From Etherege onward, the 'artificial' Restoration comedy of manners is largely characterized by a grace and fluency of prose dialogue which, in Congreve, is carried even to indifference toward dramatic action. The bustle and machinery of Spanish comedy actually affected but slightly the course of English dramatic development. The indebtedness of Restoration playwrights to Spanish sources is neither considerable in extent nor potent.

Far more significant in its bearings upon Restoration drama was French influence. French drama, French dramatic theory, and French romance affected English writers of the period so notably that it was once almost habitual to regard Restoration drama as an essentially Gallicized product. In its simplest form, this theory held that Charles II and his followers returned from Cavalier exile on the Continent dominated by French dramatic standards which forthwith gave to English drama its primary stimulus and determined its content, form, and general character. The ease with which proofs may be amassed of direct Gallic influence upon Restoration plays doubtless contributed to the wide acceptance of this facile theory. Its fault lies not in its underlying elements of partial truth, but in its gross exaggeration. It would be an equal error to belittle evidences of French influence upon English drama, some of which are too obvious to escape even a superficial reader. Translations, adaptations, and imitations of French drama are numerous and important. Molière was despoiled by English writers of comedy; Corneille, and later Racine, left indubitable marks upon English tragedy. Potent, especially, was the force of French dramatic theory. Yet not even the multiple proofs of Gallic graftings on the stock of Restoration drama can obscure the contention that its roots lie in English soil. The stage which D'Avenant helped to reëstablish owed neither its origin nor its initial progress to Gallic masters. Throughout the interregnum the Elizabethan dramatic tradition persisted. With the reopening of the theatres, the managers of the Patent Houses turned to Shakespeare, Jonson, Beaumont and

Fletcher, and other early English dramatists, and in them Restoration playwrights found models to imitate and materials to refashion. Even the novelty of English opera seems chiefly attributable to native influences. Subsequent discussion of the later development of Restoration drama will frankly recognize its large indebtedness to Gallic models, yet even when French authority seems most dominant it never fully imposed its yoke upon the English theatre. The rigid conventions of the classical Continental dramas were, again and again, abated on the freer English stage. In a word, Restoration drama is not to be dismissed as an essentially foreign product. It is the resultant of English and Continental forces.

EIGHTEENTH-CENTURY DRAMA

Christopher Rich and his associates carried on at Drury Lane while the group who seceded under Betterton in 1695 acted first at Lincoln's Inn Fields and from 1705 with little success at the new theater which Vanbrugh built in the Haymarket. The normal situation was to have competing companies at two principal houses, and this prevailed in the long run; but in the first quarter of the century the most important competition was between the legitimate drama on the one hand, and Italian opera and pantomime on the other. There was a strong incentive either to reserve one theater for plays and the other for opera, or overambitiously to try to make one house dominate both fields. Rich was the first manager to exploit the taste of the public for spectacular musical entertainments, but no manager succeeded in permanently controlling both drama and opera. A new group of actor-managers at Drury Lane after 1710 (Cibber, Wilks, Doggett, later Booth) got into serious financial and legal trouble, which was somewhat relieved when Steele joined them in 1715. The Haymarket never became a house of the first importance, and was given over to opera. In the 1720's Drury Lane found its chief competitor in John Rich, who was at Lincoln's Inn Fields and after 1732 at Covent Garden. John Rich inherited his father's flair for spectacular and novel entertainments, and succeeded with pantomime and balladopera. A new period of glory began for Drury Lane when Garrick, the greatest of actormanagers, took over in 1747, and ruled until his retirement in 1776. His immediate successor was Sheridan, who for a few years prolonged the ascendancy of Drury Lane. Covent Garden also prospered under Rich until his death in 1761, though it had to take second place. From 1767 to 1777 George Colman was the most important patentee at Covent Garden. Minor houses were of importance at times—the little theater in the Haymarket, where Fielding had his brief and brilliant dramatic career, a house of some later importance under the management of Foote and Colman, and Giffard's theater in Goodman's Fields, which brought popular (drama to the City after 1729 and saw Garrick's first appearance on the London stage. The Licensing Act of 1737, intended to restrict the production of plays to Drury Lane and Covent Garden, was not completely enforced, but no doubt narrowed the field. Provincial theaters and strolling companies became more common in the second half of the century.

The physical theater and the methods of production changed very slowly. What has been said of the structure of the Restoration theater largely holds good for the following century. Characters were often "discovered" by opening flat sets, but the curtain was not regularly used between acts. The fashionable members of the audience sat in the boxes, side or front, on the stage itself, or even at times in the orchestra-pit ("music room"), and the gallants went behind the scenes into the "green room." Garrick finally succeeded in getting the spectators off the stage in 1763, except for benefit performances. After-money, reduced admission for the last two acts, was taken until the 1780's, and stimulated the development of the after-piece. The audiences slowly grew better behaved. Attempts were made to exclude masked prostitutes early in the century. There were the usual complaints about the behavior of the fashionable part of the audience, but more serious trouble usually started among the occupants of the pit and among the servants in the upper gallery. Garrick's importation of French dancers for his unsuccessful Chinese Festival led to bad disturbances in 1755, and the attempt to abolish aftermoney in 1763 led to one of the worst outbreaks of the century.The pit gradually became more fashionable, and was thought to contain the most discriminating part of the audience. In the middle gallery (pit balcony) were average middle-class citizens, in the upper gallery the unruly rabble and the servants. Prologues and epilogues sometimes addressed the different parts of the house: *You* relish satire [to the pit]; *you* ragouts of wit [the boxes]; *Your* taste is humor, and high season'd joke [first gallery]; *You* call for hornpipes, and for Hearts of Oak [second gallery]! (Garrick Epilogue to Murphy *All in the Wrong,* 1761)

Performances regularly began at six; since places were not reserved in advance, the gentry and well-to-do citizens sent footmen early to hold their seats. Others came early themselves and scrambled for places. Both theaters were remodeled near the end of the century to accommodate larger audiences.

The emergence of great actors, their careers and their rivalries, largely determined dramatic history and stimulated dramatic criticism. The stage inherited from the Restoration a heavy and declamatory style of acting in tragedy, and a genteel and sophisticated or else broadly farcical style in comedy. Different styles seem to be indicated for actors and actresses; the most popular serious plays called for gravity and pomp in the masculine rôles, for elevated pathos in the feminine. Betterton was the great exponent of the established style for the tragic actor at the beginning of the century, and Booth and Quin carried on the tradition. But a more natural and realistic style came to be favored. Thus Aaron Hill *Prompter* (I734) attacked Quin's formality, and called for a more delicate and sensitive expression of the passions; and similarly Churchill *Rosciad* (I761) satirically described Quin:

His eyes, in gloomy socket taught to roll, Proclaimed the sullen habit of his soul. Heavy and phlegmatic he trod the stage, Too proud for tenderness, too dull for rage.

Garrick brilliantly realized the new style and applied it to both tragedy and comedy, ranging from a new interpretation of the serious rôles in the Elizabethan and Restoration repertory to polite comedy and broad farce. An admiring contemporary remarked that other actors were much the same in all their parts: Booth was always the philosopher, Cibber always the fop, but Garrick realized a different personality in each rôle. Macklin *Shylock* and Garrick *Richard III* marked the advent of this imitation of nature by the actor. This meant emphasis on gesture and impersonation rather than declamation. Yet interest in declamation persisted, indicated in the mid-century by Thomas Sheridan's teaching of rhetoric and elocution, and eventually a more formal grand style was favored, exemplified in the late eighteenth century by John Philip Kemble and his sister Mrs. Siddons.

TRAGEDY

The theory of tragedy was a principal part of the neoclassical critical heritage, but tragedy, like the other grand form epic, failed in practice. The swelling rhetoric of the heroic play established a strong tradition: "Declamation roared while passion slept." Young *Busiris* (I719) and *The Revenge* (I721) show how far a respectable poet could go in this direction, which easily lent itself to the burlesque of Carey and Fielding. Nor could tragedy be saved by the disciplinary power of neo-classical controls. Ambrose Philips *Distrest Mother* (I712), adapted from Racine *Andromaque,* and Addison *Cato* have more dignity than vitality. *Cato* observes the classical rules, though not with extreme strictness; its regularity makes it almost unique among successful English plays. Thompson *Sophonisba* (I730), following *Cato,* reduces a love and honor theme to a somewhat tame interplay of reason and passion.

The pathetic vein of Otway and Rowe was associated with Shakespearean imitation and with developing sentimentalism. Tragedy fostered sentimentalism when it put a stronger emphasis on the appeal to pity and on the response to such an appeal as a test of virtue. As Pope's prologue to

Cato puts it, the tragic muse commands "tears to stream through every age," and Britons are adjured to "show you have the virtue to be moved." Sentimentalism found a less exacting mode of expression in comedy, yet it did produce an important innovation in serious drama, the prose bourgeois tragedy of Lillo, Johnson, and Moore, with later important results on the Continent in the work of Lessing and Diderot.

Nicholas Rowe (1674-1718)

Rowe, a young barrister of the Middle Temple, appeared in 1700 as a likely successor to Dryden and Otway in tragedy. He was not a needy bohemian playwright but a dignified man of letters, a friend of the Augustan wits. His *Tamerlane* (produced 1710, published 1702) was a vehicle of Whig sentiment, and was long played on the anniversary of William's landing. Rowe's politics won him patronage under George I, and he was made poet laureate in 1715. He wrote only one unsuccessful comedy; all his important contributions are in serious drama. Heroic trappings were being exchanged for domestic themes and rhetorical moralizing, a more direct appeal to the sympathies of a middle-class audience, and sentimental moods and effects found their way at first more easily into tragedy than into comedy. In the dedication to his first play, *The Ambitious Step-Mother* (I700), Rowe argues that tragedy, while it should arouse terror, should make its chief appeal to pity, "a sort of regret proceeding from good nature," and adds, "It was this passion that the famous Mr. Otway succeeded so well in touching." In *The Fair Penitent* (I703), an adaptation of Massinger and Field *Fatal Dowry*, he scored his first great success. Like Otway *Orphan*, this play deals with the woes of a private family instead of "the fate of kings and empires"; in the seduction of the fair Calista by the "gay Lothario," whose name became proverbial, he presented the first of his "she-tragedies." This play and its most important successor *Jane Shore* (I714), "written in imitation of Shakespeare's style," provided favorite rôles for eighteenth-century actresses, and remained in the standard repertory. A less important shetragedy was his *Jane Gray* (I715). Dr. Johnson explains that Rowe's popularity came from "the reasonableness and propriety of some of his scenes, from the elegance of his diction, and the suavity of his verse." Rowe was also the first modern editor of Shakespeare and his translation of Lucan *Pharsalia* (I718) was widely read.

George Lillo (1693-1739)

Lillo was a London jeweler of Dutch extraction who had some small part of the gift of Defoe and Richardson for putting pedestrian bourgeois matter into significant literary form. He evidently acquired some literary background; he had considerable familiarity with earlier English drama, and an adaptation of *Arden of Feversham* shows that he was interested in Elizabethan domestic tragedy. After a trivial ballad-opera *Silvia* (I730), he scored a great success with *The London Merchant*, or *The History of George Barnwell* (I731). In stiff prose dialogue which still shows the influence of blank verse Lillo here tells the story of the apprentice who was driven by his infatuation for the harlot Millwood to rob his master and kill his uncle, and was finally led repentant to the gallows. He took this traditional city theme from a broadside ballad. Hogarth *Industry and Idleness* tells a parallel story, and not long afterwards a contemporary moralist, almost certainly Samuel Richardson, praised the play as the only instance "where the stage has condescended to make itself useful to the City youth." For many years *The London Merchant* was regularly acted at Christmas or Easter as a warning to the young. Lillo's middle-class setting and his clumsy moralizing went straight to the heart of his public. With no poetry or subtle psychology, he made a sentimental appeal by dwelling on Barnwell's youthful innocence and edifying repentance. His crude originality appears also in his remarkable verse-tragedy *Fatal Curiosity* (I736), the story of the return of young Wilmot, who is entertained as an unrecognized guest by his poverty-stricken parents, and murdered by them for his money. The bitterness of poverty and the somber pride of the elder Wilmot are well portrayed; the atmosphere is gloomy and fatalistic, Stoic rather than

Christian. Lillo was admired by Richardson and Fielding, and imitated on the Continent by Diderot (*Le Père de Famille*), Lessing (*Miss Sara Sampson*), and others. Though he had followers in England (Charles Johnson, *Caelia*, 1732), and Edward Moore (*The Foundling*, 1748; *The Gamester*, 1753), his influence tends either to revert to the sub-literary level of the chapbook and broadside ballad, or to be taken up into the more elaborate sentimental effects of the novel.

COMEDY

The age was disposed to view man, not in his ultimate struggle with the world as presented by the imagination and the will, but in his transaction of everyday affairs in a social context. When a great writer like Swift takes both points of view, the result is puzzling. The effect was to favor comedy, and to further the attempt to make comedy edifying. At the same time stage tradition was strong; Restoration modes persisted; rakes continued to swagger and fine ladies to coquet; much of the surface play of life in town encouraged at least the affectation of cynicism and flippancy. Under these conditions, the rate of progress of the reformation of manners in comedy is stated differently by different historians. If we classify Farquhar as a Restoration dramatist, we find that his work is softened by moral scruples. If we call Cibber a moral reformer, we find that his attitude toward sex relations is often flippant. Mrs. Susanna Centlivre's comedies of intrigue (*The Busy Body*, 1709; *A Bold Stroke for a Wife*, 1718) set forth farcical complications with Restoration irresponsibility, though not with intellectual keenness. Thus Belair exclaims in her *Love at a Venture* (1706): "Oh, the pleasure of intrigue; it finds employment for every sense, sharpens the wit, and gives a life to all our faculties." Even when she writes about the evil of gambling (*The Gamester*, 1705; *The Basset Table*, produced 1705, published 1706) she deals with a situation, not a moral. She may be taken as illustrative of the interest in varied, realistic, and amusing episode which appears strongly in Vanbrugh, Farquhar, and Steele. The devices of humors, complicated intrigue, broad farce (with abundant gags by popular comedians), satirically exaggerated comment on the life of the town—all could still be used. But in seeking pure entertainment, "making an audience merry," comedy lost a controlling idea or purpose. In the long run the chief form of control came to be the moralizing and sentimental. To get a balanced view, however, we should consider all the current entertainments, and avoid the idea that the stage was given over mainly to the triumph of sentiment.

Fielding's dramatic career is interesting in this connection. He was the most active writer of comedy from 1728 to 1737; he did pieces in the man-about-town Restoration style (*Love in Several Masques*, 1728; *The Temple Beau*, 1730; *The Modern Husband*, 1732; *The Universal Gallant*, 1735), but also turned to farce from Molière (*The Mock Doctor*, 1732; *The Miser*, 1733), and to plays of specific satiric purpose (*The Coffee House Politician*, 1730; *The Old Debauchees*, 1732). His most characteristic work, however, was in the short piece devoted to burlesque of current drama and to political satire. Such were *The Author's Farce* (1730), the popular *Tom Thumb* (1730), and *The Covent-Garden Tragedy* (1732). For the three act enlargement of *Tom Thumb is The Tragedy of Tragedies* (1731), Fielding added elaborate annotation, a device taken from Swift and Pope. The tradition of Buckingham *Rehearsal* lies back of this work, and, in the foreground, the success of *The Beggar's Opera* had stimulated burlesque. Henry Carey's *Chrononhotonthologos* (1734) is another amusing burlesque of pompous tragedy. From 1736 Fielding had his own company at the Haymarket, and here appeared his daring anti-Walpole burlesques, *Pasquin* (1736) and *The Historical Register* (1737). The government then passed the Licensing Act of 1737; Fielding company was put out of business, and he had to turn to law, journalism, and prose fiction. No one can tell whether Fielding's unwritten comedies would have gained in depth and significance, but his career as it stands shows the divergence between popular dramatic entertainment and serious literature. His work is also important for the history of the after-piece: there was an increasing demand for short pieces to end the evening's entertainment—pantomime, satirical burlesque, or farce. In the next generation Samuel

Foote's after-pieces and David Garrick's were notable. James Townley *High Life below Stairs* (1759) is an excellent example. In Garrick's programs a still shorter piece, the interlude, might come between the principal play and the after-piece. From 1728, the year of *The Beggar's Opera* and Fielding's first piece, ballad opera, burlesque, farce, and pantomime threw regular comedy into the shade. But the chief reason for the decline of the comic spirit is usually said to be the rise of the drama of sentiment or sensibility. Here Cibber and Steele occupy key positions.

PANTOMIME AND OPERA

The favor of the public was easily won by entertainments other than dramatic—by opera, ballad-opera, pantomime, ballet, sub-literary farce, and other performances as miscellaneous as vaudeville acts. The Restoration had enjoyed productions in which song, dance, and scenic effect overshadowed dramatic interest, and called these pieces "operas." But from the time of Queen Anne Italian opera took the taste of the town, and singers and composers (Handel and Buononcini) were serious rivals of actors and dramatists. There are many contemptuous references to Italian opera by such writers as Dennis, Addison, and Steele. Handel Rinaldo (1711) made him the leading figure in the field. Grand opera did not occupy so important a place later in the century, though Arne Artaxerxes (1762) was a great success, and the operas of Metastasio, from whom Arne took this piece, were very popular. It would be almost impossible to exaggerate the effect of The Beggar's Opera (1728). For ten years numerous imitations appeared, checking the production of regular drama, but no one repeated Gay's success. Isaac Bickerstaffe, however, inaugurated a new period of light opera in the 1760's with Love in a Village, The Maid of the Mill, and Lionel and Clarissa. Sheridan Duenna (1775) was a last great hit of this kind, but that quarter of the century saw innumerable operettas, burlettas, and the like, with varied combinations of comedy, music, dancing, and scenery. Charles Dibdin's popular songs were an important part of this chapter in the history of musical entertainment.

The public enjoyed "turns" between the acts and afterpieces following the regular play. We have noted that the demand for after-pieces put a premium on burlesque and farce, and thus modified the development of comedy. A similar demand stimulated the development of pantomime. This was the specialty of John Rich at Lincoln's Inn Fields from 1724 and at Covent Garden from 1732. The vogue began in 1723, when Thurmond produced Harlequin Dr. Faustus at Drury Lane, and Rich a rival Necromancer, or Harlequin Dr. Faustus. A typical pantomime was in two parts, one treating a historical or mythological theme, the other centering about the comic pranks of Harlequin. Both parts had dancing, music, and spectacular scenic effects, especially "transformations," sudden changes wrought by Harlequin as magician. This kind of entertainment was so popular that admission prices were raised on pantomime nights. Arthur Murphy gives a good brief description of the pantomime:

> A Gothic taste has taken possession of the public. Nature is banished. We give credit to the magician's wand, and harlequin's wooden sword. The seasons are confounded together. . . . all climates are presented before us; heaven and hell appear; good angels and evil demons meet; the trap doors open; Pluto rises in flame-colored stockings; and this monstrous chaos makes the supreme delight of an enlightened nation.

LATER TRAGEDY

In tragedy dull formal plays were accepted and produced by both houses, no doubt because they were thought to give actors important opportunities in serious parts. Voltaire's tragedies were popular, especially as translated by Aaron Hill (Zara, 1736; Alzira, 1736; Merope, 1749). Remote classical and foreign themes prevailed; in spite of the example of Lillo and Moore, a direct treatment of contemporary life did not develop in tragedy. Moore Gamester (I753) has a somber power superior to Lillo, but is crude in its contrast of villainy and virtue. The treatment of the somewhat similar situation of erring husband and forgiving wife in Fielding Amelia shows how the novel was coming to surpass the drama. Middle-class tragedy could go no farther than Richardson Clarissa. The fine acting of Shakespearean rôles by Garrick and some of his best contemporaries no doubt gave the mid-century its truest experience of stage tragedy.

John Home Douglas (produced at Edinburgh 1756, at London 1757, published 1757) aroused much excitement because it was written by a Scottish Presbyterian clergyman; historically it marks the point where tragedy is directly affected by pre-romantic poetry; the ballad source (Child Maurice), the localized setting, the pervasive pathos and sentimental treatment of fate give this play some poetic as well as dramatic value. But the romantic coloring of the serious play was later connected with the growing interest in spectacular scenery and in what was called the "Gothic": here we may put Walpole Mysterious Mother (1768), Jephson Count of Narbonne (1781, a dramatization of The Castle of Otranto), and numerous other stage versions of the Gothic novels in the 1790's. This kind of play, combined with music and scenic effects, came to be called *melodrama* or *melodrame* from about 1802. It was of more theatrical than literary importance.

LATER COMEDY

Comedy failed to amuse and to offer important characterization at the same time. This appears even in the successful comic pieces of Fielding and Garrick. Serious characterization in comedy came to be the province of the sentimentalists. As we have seen, the drama of sensibility had a mixed inheritance from Cibber and Steele. In Cibber there was an attempt to blend virtue with the genteel and the witty; in Steele virtue was blended with the humane, the pathetic, and the bourgeois. The Cibberian blend persisted, and was important both for comedy and prose fiction, but there is deeper significance in what Steele had to offer. As Mr. F. W. Bateson puts it, the real center of gravity in this movement is humanitarian, a new interest in a sympathetic and vivid presentation of character.1 This was fully realized in the *Spectator* essay and the novel rather than in comedy. The novel accustomed the public to more vivid characterization and more elaborate moralizing, and then exerted a reflex influence on the drama, eventually producing extreme examples of sensibility on the stage. Meanwhile, under English influence, the work of Destouches appeared in France in the 1720's and the fully developed *comédie larmoyante* of La Chaussée in the 1730's. The genial treatment of character as it appears in eighteenth-century literature at its best was here sacrificed to a didactic cult, as it had before been sacrificed to the cynical Restoration code.

There were almost no important new English comedies from the middle 1730's to about 1760; most notable were Hoadly Suspicious Husband (I747), with the rake Ranger as one of Garrick's principal parts, and Moore Foundling (I748), directly influenced by Richardson. The dominant comic type was a refined or softened play on the Restoration model, or else a short piece dependent for its effect on mimicry and farce. Aside from Garrick, Samuel Foote and Arthur Murphy were chief exponents of the short piece. Foote was a remarkable mimic who unscrupulously caricatured individuals on the stage. His farces are of little literary value, but they hit many current fads and modes (Taste, 1752; The Author, 1757; The Patron, 1764; The Englishman in Paris, 1753; The Minor, 1760; The Mayor of Garratt, 1763). Important full-length comedies, not serious, appear about 1760: Macklin Love à la Mode (I759), and The True-Born Scotchman (produced at Dublin 1764, prohibited at that time in England, later produced as The Man of the World, 1781), and two admirable comedies by George Colman, The Jealous Wife (1761) and The Clandestine Marriage (I766, in collaboration with Garrick), the latter one of the great hits of the period. Colman's short pieces, beginning with Polly Honeycombe (I760), are often fresh and effective. The workmanlike Arthur Murphy showed competence both in short pieces (The Apprentice, 1756; The Upholsterer, 1758; The Citizen, produced 1761, published 1763), and in full-length comedies (The Way to Keep Him, 1760; Know Your Own Mind, 1777).

Evidently the public was not insisting on the tearful and the edifying, but a turn in that direction appeared in the 1760's, when we have Whitehead School for Lovers (I762), a superior comedy which owes something to Richardson's novels and to the refined analysis of sentiment in French drama, and Mrs. Sheridan The Discovery (I763). These markedly sentimental plays were produced by Garrick, even though he protested against the mode. Hugh Kelly False Delicacy (I768), which Garrick brought out in opposition to Goldsmith's Good Natured Man, shows the movement reaching its peak; the play has the ambiguity of much sentimental moralizing; false delicacy or sentimental over-refinement is dangerous, and characters are introduced to warn against it, but the charms of true delicacy are also presented. Here, as in Kelly School for Wives (I773), sentimentalism criticizes itself. Its influence is felt in the cultivation of scrupulous and fastidious characters, "self-tormentors," even in plays not classed as sentimental, notably Beverley in Murphy All in the Wrong (I761) and Faulkland in Sheridan's Rivals (I775).

In the drama, however, sentimentalism did not lead to sustained analysis, but to facile emotionalism and the quest for quick and easy effects. Richard Cumberland first comedy, The Brothers (I769), combines this vein of sentiment (extreme benevolence versus foiled and finally repentant villainy) with a tangled plot. In The West Indian (I771) he presents a good rake or corrigible libertine in connection with a varied presentation of social types. He undertook to show the good side of the nabob, and later of the Scot (in The Fashionable Lover) and the Jew, in the play of that name. In Cumberland the analytical power of sentimentalism is lost; he goes in for emotional short-cuts and rapid action; hence a type of play develops which we should now call melodrama, in Holcroft pieces and the translations from the German of Kotzebue—The Stranger, Lovers' Vows, and Sheridan Pizarro. The true comedy of manners was thus eclipsed.

It is against this background that the brilliant comedies of Goldsmith and Sheridan should be considered. It had long been Goldsmith's view that nature and humor, unjustly stigmatized as "low," should override the refinements of sensibility; his was the humane realism of Steele. This did not exclude a touch of sentimental sympathy for the errors of a generous heart, as in The Good Natured Man (I768). In 1773 Goldsmith gave his views in the Essay on the Theatre; or, a Comparison between Laughing and Sentimental Comedy, and put them into practice in She Stoops to Conquer. If Goldsmith is opposed to sentimental excess he also keeps clear of the Restoration vein of satire and drawing-room wit; like Steele, he shows a personal enjoyment of his own fun and a preference for homely circumstance. Goldsmith's great contemporary in comedy, Richard Brinsley Sheridan, is much closer to the Restoration; indeed, in his brilliant early years (The Rivals, 1775; The School for Scandal, 1777) he moved rapidly toward the ideal of a Restoration comedy purged of offense. This program is further illustrated by his remaking of Vanbrugh Relapse as A Trip to Scarborough (I777) and his brilliant reapplication of the methods of The Rehearsal in The Critic (I779). His work can be described in terms of the Cibberian ideal, not hitherto fully realized on the stage, of polite virtue and triumphant wit reconciled with the reformation of manners. He was also affected though not infected by the mode of extreme delicacy and sensiblerie, especially in the Faulkland-Julia plot of The Rivals. By the end of the decade he dominated Drury Lane and the London stage. His success was unchallenged, yet the forces allied with sentimentalism were too strong to make a prolongation of this triumph possible. The social poise represented by the comedies of Goldsmith and Sheridan could not be maintained, and the framework of the best eighteenth-century comedy could not sustain the strains and stresses of the age of the French and the American revolutions.

Primitivism in Eighteenth Century

PRIMITIVISM

The notion of primitivism gained new significance in the eighteenth century because of the popularity of certain allied notions with which it was compatible. One of these was the doctrine of the so-called natural goodness of man, expounded in the first decade of the century by Shaftesbury and later by Rousseau. Obviously if man is inherently good, he must certainly be so in the primitive state before he is exposed to corrupting influences of any sort. Exponents of man's natural virtue such as Lord Shaftesbury and Richard Steele blamed defective education for acquired vices, and others such as Rousseau found science and civilization at fault.

Primitivism also merged with deism in a type of rationalism which implied, that the truths of "reason" or "nature," since they are universal, must be at least as well known to uncivilized men as to those in society and that since the unsophisticated man is protected from the corrupting forces of society, his insight into God and nature will be all the more direct and certain.

In 1700 a Swedish missionary delivered a sermon to a tribe of Indians in Pennsylvania. A native spokesman in reply exposed Christian doctrine to such searching questions that the episode was reported in a history of the Swedish church in America printed in Uppsala in 1731. An enterprising American deist translated literally the reasoning of the Indian orator, who among other points had asserted that since he and his ancestors had always believed that a good life would be pleasing to God, this opinion must have come to them directly from heaven; and that although it may be possible that the Christians have superior knowledge, it is at the same time certain that their morals are depraved. When this colloquy appeared as a deistical essay in several American newspapers, it inspired Benjamin Franklin's Remarks Concerning the Savages of North America (1784), in which an Indian replies to a doctrinal sermon on original sin, "What you have told us ... is all very good. It is indeed bad to eat apples. It is better to make them all into cyder."

A further major impetus to primitivism consisted in the accounts of travels, real or imaginary, to uncivilized regions of the world. By far the most influential were those concerning North America and the Pacific Islands, especially the sentimental romances of Chateaubriand, and the sociological speculations induced by the discoveries of Captain Cook.

The first major philosopher to rely extensively on evidence concerning primitive tribes, John Locke, actually used it to refute suppositions of natural goodness and wisdom. In order to destroy the doctrine of innate ideas in his Essay Concerning Human Understanding, Book I, Ch. III, Sec. 9 (1960) he cited a variety of monstrous beliefs and religious customs existing among savage tribes in Africa. At the same time Locke anticipated modern anthropology in recognizing that the crude superstitions of backward peoples represent definite stages in the evolution of thought. "Doctrines that have been derived from no better original than the superstition of a nurse, or the authority of an old woman, may, by length of time and consent of neighbors, grow up to the dignity of principles in religion or morality" (ibid., Book I, Ch. XI, Sec. 22). Shaftesbury, however, attacked

Locke's credulity, without attributing the least glamour or superiority to primitive society as later thinkers would do. He charged that books of travel were to people of his day what books of chivalry had been to their ancestors. Their leisure hours were filled with "Barbarian customs, savage manners, Indian wars, and wonders of the *terra incognita*." According to Shaftesbury, "they have far more pleasure in hearing the monstrous accounts of monstrous men, and manners; than the... lives of the wisest and most polish'd people." Rather than the accounts of diversity in religious observances which Locke had used to attack innate ideas, Shaftesbury advised philosophers "to search for that simplicity of manners, and innocence of behaviour, which has been often known among mere savages; ere they were corrupted by our commerce"(Advice to an Author, Part III, Sec. III). Shaftesbury was not praising the savage, but arguing that his example could be used to support uniformitarianism just as well as diversitarianism. He thus prepared the way for later authors who cited the savage to prove natural goodness and the universality of belief in God.

One of the most remarkable of the author-travelers who drew upon personal experience to promote primitivism was the Jesuit Father Joseph François Lafitau, who had lived in North America and who wrote his Manners of the American Natives Compared with the Manners of Earliest Times (*Moeurs des sauvages amériquains, comparées aux moeurs des premiers temps,* 1724) in order to protest against travelers who spoke of barbaric people as though they had no notion of religion. Lafitau affirmed that both the barbarians of the times of ancient Greece and Rome and the savages of his time had the concept of God. He denied the possibility that these nations, widely separated in their customs and manners of thinking, would concur in the same opinion if God had not "engraved the sentiment in the heart of all men at the same time that it is depicted without by the beauty of his works." This, he affirmed is what Lactantius calls "the evidence of peoples and nations" (*De falsa religione,* Book I, Ch. 2). After citing the aphorism of Cicero and Seneca that the universal belief in the truth of something is an assured and infallible evidence that it is indeed true, Lafitau quoted an earlier deistical work, Guedeville's Dialogues or Conversation of a Native and the Baron de la Hontan (*Dialogues ou Entretiens d'un sauvageet du baron de la Hontan,* 1704) to prove the existence of religion among the Hurons.

Giambattista Vico also believed in the existence of "universal and eternal principles," including the belief in God "on which all nations were founded and still preserve themselves." He lashed out, therefore, in his Principles of the New Science (*Principi di scienza nuova,* 1725, 1744) at "the modern travelers who narrate that peoples of Brazil, South Africa, and other nations of the New World... live in society without any knowledge of God." Vico argued simply that "these are travelers' tales, to promote the sale of their books by the narration of portents."

One of the major literary works of the century, Swift's Gulliver's Travels (1726), provides a convincing example of the pervasiveness of primitivistic conceptions even though Swift himself was highly mundane and sophisticated. His ridiculing of the passion for precious metals—represented by the odious Yahoos digging for days to extract them from the earth and then hiding them by heaps in their kennels—had been preceded in Gueudeville's Dialogues by a passage in which a Huron Indian condemns the prizing of precious metals and characterizes money as "the demon of demons." Swift's concept that only vicious nations have words to express the vices of humanity, that the vocabulary of the Houyhnhnms is totally inadequate to portray "the desire of power and riches, of the terrible effects of lust, intemperance, malice and envy,"had been applied by Montaigne to the Brazilians: "The very words that signify lying, treachery, falsehood, avarice, envy, detraction and pardon were unheard of among them" ("Of Cannibals"). Swift's most fundamental concept that the natural reason which the Houyhnhnms possess penetrates directly to the truth, that it strikes with immediate conviction, "as it must needs do where it is not mingled, obscured, or discoloured by passion and interest," had been previously suggested by Lafitau in *Moeurs des sauvages amériquains:* "They think precisely about their concerns, and better than the masses among us: they go immediately to their ends by direct routes."

Rousseau, who was generally considered during the century as being almost fanatical in his dedication to the natural man, actually depicted man in the primitive state as little better than a brute or animal in his first two major works. His primary doctrines, nevertheless, supported primitivistic suppositions. In his Discourse on the Sciences and Arts (*Discours sur les sciences et les arts,* 1749), in which he gave a negative answer to the query whether the development of the sciences and arts has helped to purify morals, Rousseau paradoxically argued that the achievements of man's intellect have brought about a corresponding decline in man's happiness. This decline he attributed to the failure of man's passions to adjust to his intellectual progress. Man's inherent flaw consists in his perpetual need to elevate himself above his peers. In his Discourse on Inequality (*Discours sur l'inégalité,* 1755), which traces social imbalance to the establishment of the concept of property, Rousseau touched on an argument frequently used to vindicate primitivism in economic theory—that luxury is an evil of mundane society productive of most of its vices. Otherwise he portrayed man in a struggle for self-preservation so fierce that, had he remained in the savage state, the human race would have been in danger of extermination. In common with Lord Monboddo, he wondered whether the orangutang should be considered a savage man. The only difference between man and brute animals, he declared, was man's faculty of perfecting himself, a concept obviously antiprimitivistic.

Rousseau vigorously denied, however, that human perfection consisted in science or belles-lettres. In the preface to a comedy, Narcissus or the Lover of Himself (*Narcisse ou l'amant de lui-même,* 1752), he emphasized the doctrines of his first discourse: that the taste for the refinements of society leads to idleness and vainglory and that science corrupts the mental processes.

Although it is true that Rousseau did not exalt the mythical state of nature, he nevertheless almost constantly portrayed the advantages of life removed from society. The famous opening sentence of his Émile or Concerning Education (*Émile ou de l'éducation,* 1762) epitomized his confidence in nature as the strongest force in education: "Everything is good in leaving the hands of the creator of things; everything degenerates in the hands of man."

The classical concept of the Golden Age continued to flourish, particularly in England. James Thomson, in The Castle of Indolence (1748), described the idyllic state of the biblical patriarchal age.

Toil was not then. Of nothing took they heed,
But with wild beasts the silvan war to wage,
And o'er vast plains their herds and flocks to feed:
Blest sons of nature they! true golden age indeed!
(Canto I, Stanza 37)

Pope in An Essay on Man (1733-34) stressed the benevolence of life in a mythical prehistorical period.

Nor think, in Nature's State they blindly trod:
The state of Nature was the reign of God:.

(III, 149-50)

Thomson in "Spring" (1730) gave essentially the same portrayal of the prime of days before injurious acts or surly deeds were known among the "happy sons of Heaven." Reason and benevolence were law, and manners were pure, white, and unblemished lines. Joseph Warton in The Enthusiast: or, The Lover of Nature, (1744) paraphrased Lucretius' *De rerum natura V* to produce the same effect.

Happy the first of Men, ere yet confin'd
To smoaky Cities; who in sheltering Groves,
Warm Caves, and deep-sunk Vallies liv'd and lov'd,
By Cares unwounded (lines 78-81).

Closely related to the Golden Age is another classical concept that even in one's own day a richer way of life may be found in rural retirement than in urban centers, a concept which may be called domestic primitivism. In English its best expression is the poem The Choice (1700) by John Pomfret. The Georgic tradition in English verse similarly celebrates agricultural life for its wholesomeness, simplicity, and virtue. Examples are John Philips' Cyder (1708) and John Dyer's The Fleece (1757).

The transition from the Golden Age of fable to a state of nature in modern times is well illustrated in the poem The Alps (*Die Alpen,* 1729) by Albrecht von Haller in praise of his native Swiss mountains. He described first of all the "happy golden age, gift of the first good," when wheat grew of its own accord, honey and milk ran in the streams, and lambs lay down with the wolves. But most to be prized in this idyllic existence which might be called soft primitivism was the absence of superfluous luxury and lust for wealth. In the modern world as well, according to Haller, the state of nature (represented by life in the country or the mountains) is to be preferred to urban conditions because of its simplicity and even its hardship. Life in the Alps provides bodily health and inculcates virtues of independence, self-reliance, courage, and fortitude, the same virtues extolled by the Stoics.

Die Arbeit füllt den Tag and Ruh besetzt die Nacht.
("Work filled the day, and rest possessed the night.")

A humble Swiss peasant later attained considerable celebrity for rising to the "sublime heights of philosophy" entirely by devoting his genius to agricultural pursuits. This unlearned but shrewd farmer named Jacob Kleinjogg had turned a debt-ridden property into a profitable enterprise. His achievements were heralded by Hans Caspar Hirzel in *Die Wirthschaft eines philosophischen Bauers* (1761) which was later translated into English as The Rural Socrates (1770). Herzel argued that "in the country, humanity presents itself to our view, in a state of innocent simplicity, resembling in some degree, the state of nature." The older Mirabeau together with the physiocrats regarded Klein-jogg as a modern hero, and Benjamin Franklin's disciple Benjamin

Vaughan edited an American edition of The Rural Socrates in 1800. No doubt a considerable amount of the homage accorded to "the ploughboy poet," Robert Burns, as well as to such pedestrian versifiers as Stephen Duck can be traced to this vogue for living close to nature in the domestic environment.

An English novel of revolutionary tendencies in education Sandford and Merton (1783-89), by Thomas Day, contrasts a young farm boy, Sandford, a British counterpart of Jacob Kleinjogg, with a wealthy scion of an aristocratic family, Merton. The tutor of the two boys, the Reverend Mr. Barlow, a disciple of Rousseau's Émile, instructs them according to a pattern of close contact with nature, and inculcates lessons through practical experience. Day complements the domestic primitivism of the English farm with innumerable moral tales celebrating the virtues of faraway Negroes, Laplanders, and Indians.

A more famous panegyric of the virtues of English country life is Oliver Goldsmith's The Deserted Village (1770) which celebrates "Sweet Auburn, loveliest village of the plain." Thomas Gray in similar vein drew attention in his Elegy Written in a Country churchyard (1750) to the virtues and unrealized talents of the rural dweller, "Far from the madding crowd's ignoble strife."

Other English poets recognized that the rugged life of the soil which may be called hard primitivism is not always idyllic, but they found it nevertheless admirable and salutary because of the Spartan character it developed. William Collins in his Ode on the Popular Superstitions of Scotland, written about 1749, described the "bleak rocks" and "rugged cliffs" of the Hebrides which contribute to the "sparing temp'rance" of the inhabitants.

Thus blest in primal innocence they live,
Suffic'd and happy with that frugal fare
Which tasteful toil and hourly danger give,
Hard is their shallow soil, and bleak and bare.

These lines are based on Martin Martin's Voyage to St. Kilda (1698), an influential treatment of domestic primitivism.

Even Warton in The Enthusiast tempered his rhapsodic portrayal of nature by recognizing that the fierce north wind often smites the shivering limbs of shepherds and that wild animals may fright them from their caves to rove "houseless and cold in dark, tempestuous Nights." But these rigorous conditions were, nevertheless, to be prized because they develop corresponding virtues.

The primitivism based on the appeal of a simple life in far away places may be termed exotic, the chief characteristic of which is praise of "the noble savage," a phrase which seems to have been introduced into the English language by Dryden in The Conquest of Granada, Part I (1669).

I am as free as Nature first made man,
Ere the base laws of servitude began,
When wild in woods the noble savage ran.

This is, of course, a description of the assumed political state of nature rather than a portrayal of actual faraway lands. The latter Dryden had earlier supplied in a reference to the discoveries of Columbus in To My Honour'd Friend Dr. Charleton (1663).

The fevrish aire fann'd by a cooling breez,
The fruitful Vales set round with Shady Trees;
And guiltless Men, who danc'd away their Time,
Fresh as their Groves and Happy as their Clime.

The Spanish conquest of Mexico and Peru does not seem to have inspired any depiction of the noble savage in Spanish literature, with a single exception, a treatise on the Virtues of the Indian (*Virtudes del Indio*), by Juan de Palafox first printed secretly around 1650 in the town of Puebla, Mexico. It was republished in Spain in 1661 and translated into French in 1666. The work, written for the purpose of extolling the qualities and virtues of the Indians of New Spain, stressed their contentment with poverty, their frugality, modesty, piety, and innocence. The Indian nevertheless did not play a major role in Spanish or Spanish-American literature until he was introduced in the nineteenth century under the influence of Chateaubriand. In France and England, however, translations of Spanish chronicles of the conquistadores led directly to several eighteenth-century dramatic and fictional representations of noble Aztecs and Incas. Most important was Marmontel's philosophical novel, The Incas, or The Destruction of Peru (*Les Incas, ou la destruction del'empire du Pérou,* 1779), which affirmed the moral superiority of the state of nature.

The first influential work of prose fiction devoted to exotic primitivism was an English work, Oroonoko; or, The Royal Slave (1688) by Aphra Behn, which concerns the stoic sufferings of a princely African Negro brought by trickery to Surinam in Dutch Guiana. The author not only extols the handsome looks, intelligence, and courage of Oroonoko, but also lauds the Indians of Surinam.

These people represented... an absolute Idea of the first State of Innocence, before man knew how to sin: and 'tis most evident and plain, that simple Nature is the most harmless, inoffensive, and virtuous Mistress. 'Tis she alone, if she were permitted, that better instructs the World, than all the Inventions of Man: Religion would here but destroy that Tranquillity they possess by Ignorance; and Laws would but teach 'em to know offenses, of which they have no notion.

Undoubtedly the most famous literary savage of all times is Friday of Daniel Defoe's, Life and... Adventures of Robinson Crusoe (1719), a work which Rousseau considered the best textbook of the natural sciences in print and the only book which he allowed Émile to read during the period of developing reason, from 12 to 16 years. Crusoe, who in the novel is described as living alone for twenty-five years on an island near the mouth of the Oroonoko River, had no high opinion of the natives of the area, who were cannibals, but he acquired a strong affection for Friday whom he had saved from death at the hands of two other natives.

Crusoe himself may not have appeared to Defoe as a happy child of nature, but he was considered in this light by the Yverdon Encyclopédie. "After four years, this European felt himself eased of the great burden of social life, when he had the good fortune of losing the habit of reflection and thought which used to take him back to the past or torment him with the future" (article "Sauvages").

Most of the noble savages who appear as characters in literature are masculine, but a notable exception appears in Richard Steele's story of "Inkle and Yarico" which appeared in the Spectator (No. 11, 1710/1711).Based on Richard Ligon's True and Exact History of the Island of Barbados (1657), the story concerns the sacrificial love of a beautiful native princess, Yarico,for an avaricious English trader, Inkle. Fleeing a partyof hostile Indians on the American mainland, Inkle is befriended by the nude and innocent Yarico. For several months she shelters him in the woods and finally leads him to the coast, where he embarks on an English vessel along with the protectress, promising faithfully to take her with him to England. At Barbados, however, Inkle sells her into slavery despite her tearful revelation that she is carrying his child. For the benevolent Steele, the story illustrated the pernicious effects of the love of gain overcoming natural impulses. The sentimental overtones of the story were developed in over forty- five imitations or variants in poetry and drama in English, German and French produced before 1830.

An entirely new element was added to exotic primitivism when the French explorer Louis Antoine de Bougainville touched at Tahiti in 1768, followed shortly thereafter by an English scientific expedition, including in its personnel, Joseph Banks, Daniel Carl Solander, and Captain James Cook. Tahiti offered to the delighted Europeans a beneficent climate with food in abundance, a race of natives extremely handsome even by European standards, an apparent community of property, and sex habits which approached free love. In addition, the Tahitians followed a religion rich in fertility rites. All this contrasted sharply with the various Indian tribes of America, who for the most part lived in difficult climates, were hostile and cruel toward foreign tribes, and aroused very little sex interest in each other or in their European visitors.

Bougainville gave Tahiti the French name "Nouvelle Cythère" because of the sexual appetites of its inhabitants as well as "the beauty of its climate, its soil, its situation and its produce".

When Diderot reviewed Bougainville's report on his expedition, Voyage Around the World (*Voyage autour du monde,* 1771), he affirmed that this was the only account of a voyage which had given him the taste for any country other than his own. Aware of the dangers of corrupting the island paradise of Tahiti, he implored Bougainville to leave the innocent and fortunate natives in peace and happiness, free to follow their way of life based on "the instinct of nature." For Diderot, this meant that they had no conception of "the baleful distinction between yours and mine" and that their wives and daughters were shared in common without the furors of love and jealousy which existed in European society. Changing any of this, according to Diderot, would be equivalent to forging the chains of their future slavery.

The voyage of the English scientists was described first of all in a work in French, Supplement to the Voyage of Bougainville, or Journal of a Voyage Made Around the World by Messrs. Banks and Solander (*Supplément au voyage de M. de Bougainville, ou Journal d'un voyage autour du monde fait par MM. Banks et Solander,* 1772) by de Fréville. The author described the South Sea islands as "a happy land," with "the best built and most handsome inhabitants one could ever see. The women especially seemed to have been embellished with all the graces." More important, de Fréville also found among these islanders "humanity, rectitude, and the frankness of the Golden Age." In 1773 John Hawkesworth compiled and adapted the observations of Cook, Banks, and Solander in a single narrative, New Voyage Round the World. In describing the happiness of the natives of Tahiti, he formulated the essential dilemma of the theory of progress. "If we admit that they are upon the whole happier than we, we must admit that the child is happier than the man, and that we are losers by the perfection of our nature, the increase of our knowledge, and the enlargement of our views."

Bougainville brought back to France with him a native of Tahiti, Aotourou, whom a minor social critic, Nicolas Bricaire de La Dixmerie, used as an instrument for satirizing French culture and the ideas of Rousseau in The Native of Tahiti to the French People; with a message to the philosopher, friend of the natives (*Le Sauvage de Taiti aux Français; avec un envoi au philosophe ami des sauvages,* 1770). Another Tahitian, Poutaveri, was described poetically by Jacques Delille in The Gardens (*Les Jardins,* 1782), as visiting the royal gardens and breaking out in tears at seeing a tree which reminded him of his own land.

Les champs de Taiti si chère à son enfance,
Où l'amour sans pudeur n'est pas sans innocence.

("The fields of Tahiti so dear to his childhood,Where love without bashfulness is not withoutinnocence.")

The English similarly brought back to London a handsome and agreeable young man, Omai, who was lionized and portrayed in several poems, dramatic performances, and paintings.

Diderot took advantage of the vogue of Tahiti to publish a Supplement to the Voyage of Bougainville (*Supplément au voyage de Bougainville,* 1796) in which he unequivocally denounced the evils of private property and the restraints of the Christian religion. He attributed to Tahiti the concept which a century earlier Aphra Behn had applied to the Indians of South America, that "Religion would here but destroy that Tranquillity they possess by Ignorance; and laws would but teach 'em to know offenses of which they have no notion." Diderot's Supplément, bearing the subtitle, On the Inconvenience of Attaching Ethical Concepts to Certain Physical Actions to which They are not Appropriate, enlarges the erotic and exotic elements suggested by Bougainville. The notions of jealousy, fidelity, chastity, and modesty associated with sexual gratification represent, according to Diderot, moral concepts improperly attached to a physical act. In protesting against the taint of vice being associated in civilized societies with the sexual act, Diderot wrote caustically: "Bury yourself, if you wish, in the dark forest with the perverse companion of your pleasures, but allow the good and simple Tahitians to reproduce without shame in the sight of heaven in broad daylight"

Like Rousseau, Diderot attributed all violent sex passions to the restraints placed on indiscriminate lovemaking in society.For both authors, the limitation of one man to one woman was a type of unhealthy restraint. The moral principle of Diderot's subtitle, however, certainly does not apply to any work of Rousseau. Indeed, it represents an opinion which Shaftesbury in his Characteristics (1711) had particularly condemned travel writers for affirming: "That all actions are naturally indifferent; that they have no note or character of good, or ill, in themselves; but are distinguish'd by mere fashion, law or arbitrary decree." In the dialogue itself, Diderot comes to no conclusion concerning whether a distinction exists between vice and virtue—or whether some vices may also appear in a state of nature as well as in artificial society. Taking just the opposite position to Saint Paul's in the dichotomy between the natural man and the spiritual man, Diderot described the inner conflict raging within each man in society between his natural impulses and his moral prejudices. "There existed a natural man; inside this man an artificial man has been introduced, and there takes place in the cavern a civil war which lasts throughout life." By extolling the sexual freedom existing in Tahiti, Diderot gave his answer to a question which Hawkesworth had raised in his New Voyage...: "Whether the shame attending certain actions, which are allowed on all sides to be in themselves innocent, is implanted in Nature, or superinduced by custom?" Diderot pro vided a further answer to this question by inserting in the midst of his dialogue on Tahitian sexual rites a translation of Benjamin Franklin's hoax, The speech of Polly Baker (1747). Franklin's mythical Polly had supposedly been tried in New England on charges of bearing five bastard children. In defending herself before the court, she pleaded that she had merely been performing her religious duty—"the Duty of the first and great Command of Nature, and of Nature's God, Encrease and Multiply." The story combines two of Franklin's favorite themes, rational religion and philo-progenitiveness, the latter of which is a theme of Diderot's Supplément as well.

Before the discovery of Tahiti, Lafitau had merged the concepts of chronological and cultural primitivism by drawing a parallel between the Greeks and Hebrews of the ancient world and the American Indians of the modern. A traveler to Africa, Michel Adanson in his Natural History of Senegal (*Histoire naturelle du Sénégal,* 1758) saw the blacks in the same light. Their "ease and indolence" together with "the simplicity of their dress and manners" brought to his mind the concept of "the first man," and he "seemed to see the world at its birth." After Cook's voyages, Lord Monboddo similarly observed in his Origin and Progress of Language (1774) that the "golden age may be said yet to exist... in the South Sea, where the inhabitants live, without toil or labour, upon the bounty of nature in those fine climates."

At the turn of the century, Chateaubriand's sentimental romances Atala (1800) and René (1802) concerning incredibly noble Indians of North America left an indelible impression on his readers and kept the stream of primitivism alive in literature until it was later again replenished by James Fenimore Cooper's Leatherstocking Tales. The portrayal in René of "happy savages," seated tranquilly under their oaks, letting their days pass without counting them, is idealized and sentimental. According to Chateaubriand, the rational activity of the happy Indians is limited to satisfying their needs, and they "arrive at the result of wisdom, like a child, between play and sleep." Their excess of happiness occasionally induces a transitory melancholy, from which they are diverted by looking toward the sky for God. Despite this idyllic portrayal, Chateaubriand admitted in his later account of his travels in the United States (*Voyage en Amérique,*

1827) that the American Indian had passed the savage state long before the eighteenth century and that European civilization had, therefore, not been brought to bear upon "the pure state of nature," but upon a native American civilization then beginning. For Chateaubriand as well as for Rousseau and most eighteenth-century authors, no matter how rhapsodically they pursued the themes of primitivism, exotic or domestic, the pure state of nature was largely myth.

Novel in Eighteenth Century

APPROACH TO THE NOVEL

The most important development in English prose of the eighteenth century was the emergence of the modern novel. This is to be explained partly in terms of numerous antecedent and contributory literary forms, and partly also in terms of the new reading public created by the growing influence and literacy of the middle class. People whose grandparents had read little or nothing except a few religious works and popular chapbooks were now ready to buy and read prose fiction.

The antecedent forms may be roughly divided intc *romantic* and *realistic*. Prose romance, derived ultimately from the medieval code of chivalry and courtly love, was still accessible to readers; Sidney *Arcadia* and the French heroic romances of the seventeenth century (the works of Gomberville, La Calprenède, and Scudéry) were familiar before and after 1700. But such works were out of line with the tastes of an unheroic and increasingly bourgeois age. Shorter romances, purporting to be closer to real life and high life, were written by Mrs. Behn, Mrs. Aubin, and others. Mrs. Behn famous *History of the Royal Slave, or Oroonoko* (1688) is an heroic and exotic piece of this kind. Stories on this scale were called "novels," and were often mere pieces of complicated intrigue and scandal. The reaction against over-artificial romance often leads writers into burlesque and anti-romance, one of the commonest roads to realism. There was some work of this kind at the end of the seventeenth century, but, falling far short of *Don Quixote*, it was too clumsy to lead far. Again, one might expect the refined analysis of motive and conduct in the romantic tradition to lead to psychological realism, and this actually happens in Mme de Lafayette famous *Princesse de Clèves* (1678), but England shows no such turn toward fiction at once analytic and aristocratic.

At the other end of the scale, realistic fiction, associated with the life of the lower classes, tended to remain coarse and sub-literary. An exception must be made of the intensely vivid realism of Bunyan's great allegories, yet Bunyan's work is in part an anticipation of rather than an influence on the later novel. Allied with anti-romance, the Spanish picaresque tradition, the fiction of roguery, was coherent and well established, but English imitation of this form (Kirkman and Head, *The English Rogue*, 1665-71) lacks humor and humanity. About on the same level were the criminal biographies so popular during this period. The central picaresque theme had undergone developments on the Continent which were to be of great importance for English fiction; the original scheme setting forth the adventures of a *picaro* (servant-rogue) might be modified to present the travel experiences of a young man, perhaps of good family, seeking his fortune, and this brings us close to Fielding and Smollett.

Without undertaking a formal definition of the novel, we can say that it entails a critical or analytical attitude toward characters represented under actual or conceivable social conditions. The critical attitude is directed toward both individual character and the social situation. As it appears in eighteenth-century fiction, it does not derive simply from the commentary on life to be found either in earlier romance or in low-life realism; it does not have the artificiality and fastidiousness of the one or the social irresponsibility of the other, but the sober practical outlook of the middle class.

This outlook had a religious tinge and a strongly moral turn, but it was not daringly imaginative or intensely pious, as we see when we pass from Bunyan to Defoe. In other words, eighteenth-century fiction had to be didactic and secular, not only to win the approval of middle-class readers but to develop its own characteristic criticism of life. For the development of this criticism, the methods afforded by other literary forms were of great importance. Tragedy and comedy offered an analysis of character in action more powerful and penetrating than almost anything earlier fiction had to show. The eighteenthcentury novel took the predominant place occupied by the drama in earlier periods. The character-sketch extensively practiced in the seventeenth century, the new type of periodical essay perfected by Steele and Addison, the letterform applied to fiction—all afforded means of combining a formulation of social and moral standards with an analysis of character in action. This combination yields the novel. It is perhaps unprofitable to argue just when the type appears. If Defoe does not seem to us to be writing novels, it is perhaps because he does not develop an elaborate analysis by means of the contributory forms. The origins of Defoe's fiction are not entirely clear, but evidently he works on the model of fictional biography, the "life and adventures" formula, with some indebtedness to the picaresque, the criminal biography, and the travel narrative, at the same time substituting for other possible points of view (the irresponsibility of the picaresque, the wonder and excitement of the travel story) a sober moralizing attitude derived from bourgeois conduct-books. He does not seem to take lessons from drama, essay, or character-sketch in developing his characters. The greater preoccupation with the inner life of the characters, the finer shades of personality, and the personal and social overtones of episode to be found in Richardson and Fielding twenty years later marks a step of crucial importance.

THE LATER NOVEL

Though the minor fiction of the second half of the century can be roughly classified as epistolary, feminine, and sentimental, of the school of Richardson, or robust and humorous, of the school of Fielding and Smollett, there was much interweaving and combination. A dominantly Richardsonian novel of merit, such as Frances Sheridan *Sidney Bidulph* (I761, revised and expanded 1767) is exceptional. Tom Jones and Clarissa were too long and complex to serve as practicable models. Stereotyped characters and situations were presented in more facile style and were expected to call forth stock responses; the reader could instantly identify the suffering heroine, the seducer, the harsh parent, the selfish rich man, the deserving poor man, the faithful servant. Plots and devices from Richardson and Fielding were repeated on a smaller scale. The influence of Marivaux' Marianne was especially clear in the minor feminine novel. Prévost's pervasive influence will be considered later. Most of this fiction was written by obscure hackwriters or sometimes by mediocre amateurs, read indiscriminately by patrons of circulating libraries, and viewed with contempt by the critics.

THE NOVEL OF SENTIMENT

Sentimentalism, we have seen, was closely tied up with the moral purpose which was necessary to get analytical fiction under way. The novel gave a fuller opportunity for this analysis than the drama, and in the hands of great writers like Richardson, Fielding, and Sterne, sentimentalism led to a subtler psychology, but no sooner were sentimental views widely diffused than they encouraged novelists, dramatists, and poets to take short cuts to quick and easy effects. As has been said, it was not generally felt that social and rational controls could be abandoned for the charms of sensibility. Sterne's position is extreme, and yet his playful exaltation of impulse and feeling is an artistic device rather than a program for life; we get the impression that sensibility is a mood or tone which colors the mind and society. The system is given, and then sensibility plays over it. Though Goldsmith did not admire Sterne, we may say the same thing of the free play of humor and sentiment in *The Vicar of Wakefield* (I766). The novels of the young Scottish advocate Henry Mackenzie (*The Man of Feeling*, 1771; *The Man of the World*, 1773; Julia de

Roubigné , 1777) are considered the most sentimental in the language, a reputation which he earned by his first and most successful book. Though he imitates Sterne's methods, he swings from delicately sentimental effects to violent melodrama. Yet Mackenzie is capable of pointing out the dangers of an over-sensible heart. This ambiguity of sentimentalism, its disposition to dwell on both the dangers and delights of feeling, is one of its most characteristic features. It appears in the great continental novels of sensibility, in Rousseau *Nouvelle Héloïse* (I761), which begins by presenting sympathetically the claims of passion in the account of the love affair of Julie and her tutor St. Preux, and then, after marrying Julie to the philosophic Wolmar, dwells on the merit of restraint and renunciation; and in Goethe *Werther* (I774), which describes sympathetically the hopeless passion of the hero and his suicide, but which could be interpreted also as an example of the evils of excessive sensibility. The various applications of the sentimental doctrine of natural goodness to the problems of education (Rousseau, *Emile*, 1762; Henry Brooke, *The Fool of Quality*, 17651770; Thomas Day, *Sandford and Merton*, 1783- 1789) criticize the rich and fashionable, and develop natural piety and altruism by carefully planned devices. To assert in earnest the rights of the sentimental rebel, the man who pits his intuitions against tradition, is to be a revolutionary. A few English novelists, notably William Godwin and Thomas Holcroft, came close to this point in the last decade of the century, in the heated atmosphere created by the French Revolution, but underlying English conservatism checked this development, and English sentiment did not find its outlet in political action.

GOTHIC AND HISTORICAL ROMANCE

The new vein of Gothic and historical romance is also connected with sentimentalism in the broad sense of an appeal to the feelings. It tried to get its effects by an appeal to the sense of the sublime and the picturesque, as well as to the softer feelings of pity and sympathy. The theory of the appeal to terror as a source of the sublime had already been formulated in Burke *Enquiry into the Origin of our Ideas of the Sublime and Beautiful* (I757); the association of the marvelous and the supernatural with the Middle Ages was enthusiastically recognized in Hurd *Letters on Chivalry and Romance* (I762) . In Thomas Leland's *Longsword, Earl of Salisbury* (I762), a historical romance of the time of the Crusades, and in Horace Walpole's *Castle of Otranto* (printed 1764, published 1765), which presents supernatural events in a medieval setting in southern Italy, we have examples classified respectively as historical and Gothic. The sub-title of *Otranto* is A *Gothic Story*, and later "Gothic romance" was taken to denote a narrative (devised to arouse terror by suggestion or presentation of the supernatural, but this aspect can scarcely be separated from the historical side of Gothic, and it is not profitable to keep a sharp distinction between two kinds of fiction here. The movement does not begin with *Otranto*, a curious and somewhat special manifestation of Walpole's interest in medieval architecture and Elizabethan drama. Various tendencies which had already appeared in the poetry of the period lie back of the new romance—the interest in ruins, local antiquities, and picturesque landscape, the poetry of night and the tombs, the interest in popular superstition, the great example of the supernatural in Shakespeare, the return to the Middle Ages, the general cult of the sublime and the pathetic. This great complex, which may be called romantic, culminates in Walter Scott. Clara Reeve *Old English Baron* (I777), which has the medieval setting of Walpole and Leland, with more sober realism and reduced use of the supernatural, is hardly rich enough to carry the tradition fully. The later Gothic-historical type develops with the work of Sophia Lee (*The Recess*, 1783-85). Here we find the full effect of the earlier French romance of the Abbé Prévost and his follower Baculard d'Arnaud; Prévost largely followed English drama and poetry in his alternation of tender and violent feelings, his use of gloomy settings, sensational plots, and fatalistic moods. The culmination of this movement in the novels of Anne Radcliffe and the important collateral developments in the work of Mrs. Charlotte Smith lie beyond the limits of this study.

Poem in Eighteenth Century

ORTHODOXY AND CLASSICISM QUIESCENT (1700-1725)

The clearest portrayal of the prominent features of an age may sometimes be seen in poems which reveal what men desire to be rather than what they are; and which express sentiments typical, even commonplace, rather than individual. John Pomfret *Choice* (1700) is commonplace indeed; it was never deemed great, but it was remarkably popular. "No composition in oar language," opined Dr. Johnson, "has been oftener perused,"—an opinion quite incredible until one perceives how intimately the poem harmonizes with the prevalent mood of its contemporary readers. It was written by a clergyman (a circumstance not insignificant); its form is the heroic couplet; its content is a wish for a peaceful and civilized mode of existence. And what is believed to satisfy that longing? A life of leisure; the necessaries of comfort plentifully provided, but used temperately; a country-house upon a hillside, not too distant from the city; a little garden bordered by a rivulet; a quiet study furnished with the classical Roman poets; the society of a few friends, men who know the world as well as books, who are loyal to their nation and their church, and whose conversation is intellectually vigorous but always polite; the occasional companionship of a woman of virtue, wit, and poise of manner; and, above all, the avoidance of public or private contentions. Culture and peace—and the greater of these is peace! The sentiment characterizes the first quarter of the eighteenth century.

The poets of that period had received an abundant heritage from the Elizabethans, the Cavaliers, Dryden, and Milton. It was a poetry of passionate love, chivalric honor, indignant satire, and sublime faith. Much of it they ad mired, but their admiration was tempered with fear. They heard therein the tones of violent generations,—of men whose intensity, though yielding extraordinary beauty and grandeur yielded also obscurity and extravagance; men whom the love of women too often impelled to utter fantastic hyperbole, and the love of honor to glorify preposterous adventures; quarrelsome men, who assailed their opponents with rancorous personalities; doctrinaires, who employed their fiery energy of mind in the creation of rigid systems of religion and government; uncompromising men, who devoted to the support of those systems their fortunes and lives, drenched the land in the blood of a civil war, executed a king, presently restored his dynasty, and finally exiled it again, thus maintaining during half a century a general insecurity of life and property which checked the finer growths of civilization. Their successors trusted that the compromise of 1688 had reduced political and sectarian affairs to a state of calm equilibrium; and they desired to cultivate the fruits of serenity by fostering in all things the spirit of moderation. In poetry, as in life, they tended more and more to discountenance manifestations of vehemence. Even the poetry of Dryden, with its reflections of the stormy days through which he had struggled, seemed to them, though gloriously leading the way toward perfection, to fall short of equability of temper and smoothness of form. To work like Defoe *True-Born Englishman* (I701) and *Hymn to the Pillory* (I703), combative in spirit and free in style, they gave only guarded and temporary approval.

Inevitably the change of mood entailed losses. Sir Henry Wotton's *Character of a Happy Life* (1614) treats the same theme as Pomfret's *Choice;* but Pomfret's contemporaries were rarely if ever visited by such gleams as shine in Wotton's lines describing the happy man as one

Who never understood
How deepest wounds are given by praise,

and as one

Who God doth late and early pray
More of his grace than gifts to lend.

Such touches of penetrative wisdom and piety, like many other precious qualities, are of an age that had passed. In the poetry of 1700-1725, religion forgoes mysticism and exaltation; the intellectual life, daring and subtlety; the imagination, exuberance and splendor. Enthusiasm for moral ideals declines into steadfast approval of ethical principles. Yet these were changes in tone and manner rather than in fundamental views. The poets of the period were conservatives. They were shocked by the radicalism of Mandeville, the Nietzsche of his day, who derided the generally accepted moralities as shallow delusions, and who by means of a clever fable supported a materialistic theory which implied that in the struggle for existence nothing but egotism could succeed:

Fools only strive
To make a great and honest hive.

Obloquy buried him; he was a sensational exception to the rule. As a body, the poets of his time retained the orthodox traditions concerning God, Man, and Nature.

Their theology is evidenced by Addison, Watts, and Parnell. It is a Christianity that has not ceased to be stern and majestic. In Addison *Divine Ode*, the planets of the firmament proclaim a Creator whose power knows no bounds. In the hymns of Isaac Watts, God is as of old a jealous God, obedience to whose eternal will may require the painful sacrifice of temporal earthly affections, even the sacrifice of our love for our fellow-creatures; a just God, who by the law of his own nature cannot save unrepentant sin from eternal retribution; yet an adored God, whose providence protects the faithful amid stormy vicissitudes,—

Under the shadow of whose throne
The saints have dwelt secure.

Spirits as gentle and kindly as Parnell insist that the only approach to happiness lies through a religious discipline of the feelings, and protest that death is not to be feared but welcomed—as the passage from a troublous existence to everlasting peace. In most of the poetry of the time, religion, if at all noticeable, is a mere undercurrent; but whenever it rises to the surface, it reflects the ancient creed.

Traditional too is the general conception of human character. Man is still thought of as a complex of lofty and mean qualities, widely variable in their proportion yet in no instance quite dissevered. To interpret—not God or Nature—but this self-contradictory being, in both his higher and his lower manifestations and possibilities, remains the chief vocation of the poets. They have not ceased the endeavor to lend dignity to life by portraying its nobler features. Addison, in *The Campaign,* glorifies the national hero whose brilliant victories thwarted the great monarch of France on his seemingly invincible career toward the hegemony of Europe, the warrior Marlborough, serene of soul amid the horror and confusion of battle. Tickell, in his noble elegy on Addison, not only, while voicing his own grief, illustrates the beauty of devoted friendship, but also, when eulogizing his subject, holds up to admiration, as a type to be revered, the wise moralist, cultured and versatile man of letters, and adept in the art of virtuous life. Pope, in the most ambitious literary effort of the day, his translation of the *Iliad,* labors to enrich the treasury of English poetry with an epic that sheds radiance upon the ideals and manners of an heroic age. In such attempts to exalt the grander phases of human existence, the poets were, however, owing to their fear of enthusiasm, never quite successful. It is significant that though most critics consider Pope's Homer no better than a mediocre performance, none denies that his *Rape of the Lock* is, in its kind, perfection.

Here, as in the *vers de société* of Matthew Prior and Ambrose Philips, the age was illuminating with the graces of poetry something it really understood and delighted in,- the life of leisure and fashion; and here, accordingly, is its most original and masterly work. *The Rape of the Lock* is the product of a society which had the good sense and good breeding to try to laugh away incipient quarrels, and which greeted with airy banter the indiscreet act of an enamoured young gallant,—the kind of act which vulgarity meets with angry lampoons or rude violence. The poem is an idyll quite as much as a satire. The follies of fashionable life are treated with nothing severer than light raillery; and its actually distasteful features,—its lapses into stupidity, its vacuous restlessness, its ennui,—are cunningly suppressed. But all that made it seem the height of human felicity is preserved, and enhanced in charm. "Launched on the bosom of the silver Thames," one glides to Hampton Court amid youth and gayety and melting music; and for the nonce this realm of "airs, flounces, and furbelows," of merry chit-chat, and of pleasurable excitement, seems as important as it is to those exquisite creatures of fancy that hover about the heroine, assiduous guardians of her "graceful ease and sweetness void of pride." Of that admired world likewise are the lovers that Matthew Prior creates, who woo neither with stormy passion nor with mawkish whining, but in a courtly manner; lovers who deem an epigram a finer tribute than a sigh. So the tender fondness of a middle-aged man for an infant is elevated above the commonplace by assuming the tone of playful gallantry.

The ignobler aspects of life,—nutriment of the comic sense,—were not ignored. The new school of poets, however deficient in the higher vision, were keen observers of actuality; and among them the satiric spirit, though not militant as in the days of Dryden, was still active. The value which they attached to social culture is again shown in the persistence of the sentiment that as man grew in civility he became less ridiculous. The peccadilloes of the upper classes they treated with comparatively gentle humor, and aimed their strokes of satire chiefly against the lower. Rarely did they idealize humble folk: Gay *Sweet William's Farewell to Black-Eyed Susan* is in this respect exceptional. Their typical attitude is seen in his Shepherd *Week*, with its ludicrous picture of rustic superstition and naive amorousness; and in Allan Ramsay *Gentle Shepherd*, where the pastoral, once remote from life, assumes the manners and dialect of the countryside in order to arouse laughter.

The obvious fact that these poets centered their attention upon Man, particularly in his social life, and that their most memorable productions are upon that theme, led posterity to complain that they wholly lacked interest in Nature, were incapable of delineating it, and did not feel its sacred influence. The last point in the indictment,—and the last only,—is quite true. No one who understood and believed, as they did, the doctrines of orthodoxy could consistently ascribe divinity to Nature. To them Nature exhibited the power of God, but not his will; and the soul of Man gained its clearest moral light directly from a supernatural source. This did not, however, imply that Nature was negligible. The celebrated essays of Addison on the pleasures of the imagination (*Spectator*, Nos. 411-414) base those pleasures upon the grandeur of Nature; upon its variety and freshness, as of "groves, fields, and meadows in the opening of the Spring"; and upon its beauty of form and color. The works of Nature, declares Addison, surpass those of art, and accordingly "we always find the poet in love with a country life." Such was the theory; the practice was not out of accord therewith. Passages appreciative of the lovelier aspects of Nature, and not, despite the current preference for general rather than specific terms, inaccurate as descriptions, were written between 1700 and 1726 by Addison himself, Pope, Lady Winchilsea, Gay, Parnell, Dyer, and many others. Nature worshippers they were not. Nature lovers they can be justly styled,—if such love may discriminate between the beautiful and the ugly aspects of the natural. It is characteristic that Berkeley, in his *Prospect of Planting Arts and Learning in America,* does not indulge the fancy that the wilderness is of itself uplifting; it requires, he assumes, the aid of human culture and wisdom,—"the rise of empire and of arts,"—to develop its potentialities.

A generation which placidly adhered to the orthodox sentiments of its predecessors was of course not moved to revolutionize poetical theories or forms. Its theories are authoritatively stated in Pope *Essay on Criticism*; they embrace principles of good sense and mature taste which are easier to condemn than to confute or supersede. In poetical diction the age cultivated clearness, propriety, and dignity: it rejected words so minutely particular as to suggest pedantry or specialization; and it refused to sacrifice simple appropriateness to inaccurate vigor of utterance or meaningless beauty of sound. Its favorite measure, the decasyllabic couplet, moulded by Jonson, Sandys, Waller, Denham, and Dryden, it accepted reverently, as an heirloom not to be essentially altered but to be polished until it shone more brightly than ever. Pope perfected this form, making it at once more artistic and more natural. He discountenanced on the one hand run-on lines, alexandrines, hiatus, and sequence of monosyllables; on the other, the resort to expletives and the mechanical placing of *cæsura*. If his verse does not move with the "long resounding pace" of Dryden at his best, it has a movement better suited to the drawing-room: it is what Oliver Wendell Holmes terms

The straight-backed measure with the stately stride.

Thus in form as in substance the poetry of the period voiced the mood, not of carefree youth, nor yet of vehement early manhood, but of still vigorous middle age,—a phase of existence perhaps less ingratiating than others, but one which has its rightful hour in the life of the race as of the individual. The sincere and artistic expression of its feelings will be denied poetical validity only by those whose capacity for appreciating the varieties of poetry is limited by their lack of experience or by narrowness of sympathetic imagination.

ORTHODOXY AND CLASSICISM ASSAILED (1726-1750)

During the second quarter of the century, Pope and his group remained dominant in the realm of poetry; but their mood was no longer pacific. Their work showed a growing seriousness and acerbity. Partly the change was owing to disappointment: life had not become so highly cultured, literature had not prospered so much, nor displayed so broad a diffusion of intelligence and taste, as had been expected. Pope *Dunciad, Epistle to Dr. Arbuthnot,* and ironic satire on the state of literature under "Augustus" (George II, the "snuffy old drone from the German hive"), brilliantly express this indignation with the intellectual and literary shortcomings of the times.

A cause of the change of mood which was to be of more lasting consequence than the failure of the age to put the traditional ideal more generally into practice, was the appearance of a distinctly new ideal,—one which undermined the very foundations of the old. This new spirit may be termed sentimentalism. In prose literature it had already been stirring for about twenty-five years, changing the tone of comedy, entering into some of the periodical essays, and assuming a philosophic character in the works of Lord Shaftesbury. Its chief doctrines, rhapsodically promulgated by this amiable and original enthusiast, were that the universe and all its creatures constitute a perfect harmony; and that Man, owing to his innate moral and æsthetic sense, needs no supernatural revelation of religious or ethical truth, because if he will discard the prejudices of tradition, he will instinctively, when face to face with Nature, recognize the Spirit which dwells therein,—and, correspondingly, when in the presence of a good deed he will recognize its morality. In other words, God and Nature are one; and Man is instinctively good, his cardinal virtue being the love of humanity, his true religion the love of Nature. Be therefore of good cheer: evil merely appears to exist, sin is a figment of false psychology; lead mankind to return to the natural, and they will find happiness.

The poetical possibilities of sentimentalism were not grasped by any noteworthy poet before Thomson. *The Seasons* was an innovation, and its novelty lay not so much in the choice of the subject as in the interpretation. Didactic as well as descriptive, it was designed not merely to present realistic pictures but to arouse certain explicitly stated thoughts and feelings. Thomson had absorbed some of Shaftesbury's ideas. Such sketches as that of the hardships which country folk suffer in winter, contrasted with the thoughtless gayety of city revelers, and inculcating the lesson of sympathy, are precisely in the vein that sentimentalism encouraged. So, too, the tendency of Shaftesbury to deify Nature appears in several ardent passages. The choice of blank verse as the medium of this liberal and expansive train of thought was appropriate. It should not be supposed, however, that Thomson accepted sentimentalism in its entirety or fully understood its ultimate bearings. The author of *Rule, Britannia* praised many things,-like commerce and industry and imperial power,—that are not favored by the thorough sentimentalist. Often he was inconsistent: his *Hymn to Nature* is in part a pantheistic rhapsody, in part a monotheistic Hebrew psalm. Essentially an indolent though receptive mind, he made no effort to trace the new ideas to their consequences; he vaguely considered them not irreconcilable with the old.

A keener mind fell into the same error. Pope, in the *Essay on Man,* tried to harmonize the orthodox conception of human character with sentimental optimism. As a collection of those memorable half-truths called aphorisms, the poem is admirable; as an attempt to unite new half-truths with old into a consistent scheme of life, it is fallacious. No creature composed of such warring elements as Pope describes in the superb antitheses that open Epistle II, can ever become in this world as good and at the same time as happy as Epistle IV vainly asserts. Pope, charged with heresy, did not repeat this endeavor to console mankind; he returned to his proper element, satire. But his effort to unite the new philosophy with the old psychology is striking evidence of the attractiveness and growing vogue of Shaftesbury's theories.

It was minor poets who first expressed sentimental ideas without inconsistency. As early as 1732, anonymous lines in the *Gentleman's Magazine* advanced what must have seemed the outrageously paradoxical thought that the savage in the wilderness was happier than civilized man. Two years later Soame Jenyns openly assailed in verse the orthodox doctrines of sin and retribution. These had long been assailed in prose; and under the influence of the attacks, within the pale of the Church itself, some ministers had suppressed or modified the sterner aspects of the creed,—a movement which Young's satires had ridiculed in the person of a lady of fashion who gladly entertained the notion that the Deity was too well-bred to call a lady to account for her offenses. Jenyns versified this effeminization of Christianity, charged orthodoxy with attributing cruelty to God, and asserted that faith in divine and human kindness would banish all wrong and discord from the world. In 1735 a far more important poet of sentimentalism arose in Henry Brooke, an undeservedly neglected pioneer, who, likewise drawing his inspiration from Shaftesbury, developed its theories with unusual consistency and fullness. His Universal Beauty voiced his sense of the divine immanence in every part of the cosmos, and emphasized the doctrine that animals, because they unhesitatingly follow the promptings of Nature, are more lovely, happy, and moral than Man, who should learn from them the individual and social virtues, abandon artificial civilization, and follow instinct. Brooke, in the prologue of his Gustavus Vasa, shows that he foresaw the political bearings of this theory; it is, in his opinion, peculiarly a people "guiltless of courts, untainted, and unread" that, illumined by Nature, understands and upholds freedom: but this was a thought too advanced to be general at this time even among Brooke's fellow-sentimentalists.

Though sentimental literature bore the seeds of revolution, its earliest effect upon its devotees was to create, through flattery of human character, a feeling of goodnatured complacency. Against this optimism the traditional school reacted in two ways,—derisive and hortatory. Pope, Young, and Swift satirized with masterful skill the inherent weaknesses and follies of mankind, the vigor of their strokes drawing from the sentimentalist Whitehead the feeble but significant protest, On Ridicule, deprecating satire as discouraging to benevolence. On the other hand, Wesley's hymns fervently summoned to repentance and piety; while Young Night Thoughts, yielding to the new influence only in its form (blank verse), reasserted the hollowness of earthly existence, the justice of God's stern will, and the need of faith in heavenly immortality as the only adequate satisfaction of the spiritual elements in Man.

The literary powers of Pope, Swift, and Young were far superior to those of the opposed school, which might have been overborne had not a second generation of sentimentalists arisen to voice its claims in a more poetical manner.

These newcomers,— Akenside, J. G. Cooper, the Wartons, and Collins,—all of them very young, appeared between 1744 and 1747; and each rendered distinct service to their common cause. The least original of the group, John Gilbert Cooper, versified in *The Power of Harmony* Shaftesbury's cosmogony. More independently, Mark Akenside developed out of the same doctrine of universal harmony the theory of æsthetics that was to guide the school,—the theory that the true poet is created not by culture and discipline at all, but owes to the impress of Nature—that beauty which is goodness—his imagination, his taste, and his moral vision. Though comparatively ardent and free in manner, Akenside pursued the customary, didactic method. Less abstract, more nearly an utterance of personal feeling, was Joseph Warton's *Enthusiast, or the Lover of Nature,* historically a remarkable poem, which, through its expression of the author's tastes and preferences, indicated briefly some of the most important touchstones of the sentimentalism (*videlicet,* "romanticism") of the future. Warton found odious such things as artificial gardens, commercial interests, social and legal conventions, and a formal Addisonian style; he yearned for mountainous wilds, unspoiled savages, solitudes where the voice of Wisdom was heard above the storms, and poetry that was "wildly warbled." His younger brother Thomas, who wrote *The Pleasures of Melancholy,* and sonnets showing an interest in non-classical antiquities, likewise felt the need of new literary gods to sanction the practices of their school: Pope and Dryden were accordingly dethroned; Spenser, Shakespeare, and the young Milton, all of whom were believed to warble wildly, were invoked.

William Collins was the most gifted of this band of enthusiasts. His general views were theirs: poetry is in his mind associated with wonder and ecstasy; and it finds its true themes, as the *Ode on Popular Superstitions* shows, in the weird legends, the pathetic mischance, and the blameless manners of a simple-minded folk remote from cities. Unlike his fellows, Collins had moments of great lyric power, and gave posterity a few treasured poems. His further distinction is that he desired really to create that poetical world about which Akenside theorized and for which the Wartons yearned. Unhappily, however, he too often peopled it with allegorical figures who move in a hazy atmosphere; and his melody is then more apparent than his meaning.

The hopeful spirit of these enthusiasts found little encouragement in the poems with which the period closed,-*Gray's Ode on Eton* and *Hymn to Adversity,* and Johnson *Vanity of Human Wishes.*

Some bold adventurers disdain
The limits of their little reign,

Wrote Gray, adding with the wisdom of disillusion,

Gay hopes are theirs, by fancy fed,
Less pleasing when possessed.

He was speaking of schoolboys whose ignorance is bliss; but the general tenor of his mind allows us to surmise that he also smiled pityingly upon some of the aspirations of the youthful sentimentalists. Dr. Johnson's hostility to them was, of course, outspoken. He laughed uproariously at their ecstatic manner, and ridiculed the cant of sensibility; and in solemn mood he struck in *The Vanity of Human Wishes* another blow at the heresy of optimism. In style the contrast between these poems and those of the Wartons and Collins is marked. Heirs of the Augustans, Johnson and Gray have perfect control over their respective diction and metres: here are no obscurities or false notes; Johnson sustains with superb dignity the tone of moral grandeur; Gray is ever felicitous. Up to the mid-century then, despite assailants, the classical school held its supremacy; for its literary art was incomparably more skillful than that of its enemies.

THE PROGRESS OF SENTIMENTALISM (1751-1775)

During the 1750's sentimental poetry did not fulfill the expectations which the outburst of 1744 had seemed to promise. It sank to lower levels, and its productions are noteworthy only as signs of the times and presages of the future. Richard Jago wrote some bald verses intended to foster opposition to hunting, and love for the lower animals,- according to the sentimental view really the "little brothers" of Man. John Dalton crude *Descriptive Poem* apostrophized what was regarded as the "savage grandeur" of the Lake country; it is interesting only because it mentions Keswick, Borrowdale, Lodore, and Skiddaw, half a century later to become sacred ground. The practical dilemma of the sentimentalist,—drawn toward solitude by his worship of Nature, and toward society by his love for Man,—was described by Whitehead in *The Enthusiast,* the humanitarian impulse being finally given the preference. Though the last of these pieces is not contemptible in style, none of these writers had sufficient ardor to compel attention; and if sentimentalism had not been steadily disseminated through other literary forms, especially the novel, it might well have been regarded as a lost cause.

The great poet of this decade was Gray, whose *Elegy Written in a Country Churchyard,* by many held the noblest English lyric, appeared in 1751. His classical ideal of style, according to which poetry should have, in his words, "extreme conciseness of expression," yet be "pure, perspicuous, and musical," was realized both in the *Elegy* and in the otherwise very different *Pindaric Odes*. The ethical and religious implications of the *Elegy*, its piety, its sense of the frailties as well as the merits of mankind, are conservative. Nor is there in the *Pindaric Odes* any violation of classical principles. Gray never deviates into a pantheistic faith, a belief in human perfection, a conception of poetry as instinctive imagination unrestrained, or any other essential tenet of sentimentalism. Yet the influence of the new spirit upon him may be discerned. It modified his choice of subjects, and slightly colored their interpretation, without causing him to abandon the classical attitude. The *Elegy* treats with reverence what the Augustans had neglected,-the tragic dignity of obscure lives; *The Progress of Poesy* emphasizes qualities (emotion and sublimity) which the *Essay on Criticism* had not stressed; and *The Bard* presents a wildly picturesque figure of ancient days. Gray felt that classicism might quicken its spirit and widen its interests without surrendering its principles, that a classical poem might be a popular poem; and the admiration of posterity supports his belief.

An astounding and epochal event was the publication (1760) of the poems attributed to Ossian. Their "editor and translator," James Macpherson, author of a forgotten sentimental epic, alleged that Ossian was a Gaelic poet of the third century A. D., who sang the loves and wars of the heroes of his people, brave warriors fighting the imperial legions of Rome; and that his poems had been orally transmitted until now, fifteen centuries later, they had been taken down from the lips of Scotch peasants. It was a fabrication as ingenious as brazen. As a matter of fact, Macpherson had found only an insignificant portion of his extensive work in popular ballads; and what little he had found he had expanded and changed out of all semblance to genuine ancient legend. Both the guiding motive of his prose-poem (it is his as truly as *King Lear* is Shakespeare's), and the furore of welcome which greeted it, may be understood by recalling the position of the sentimental school on the eve of its appearance. The sentimentalists were maintaining that civilization had corrupted tastes, morals, and poetry, that it had perverted Man from his instinctive goodness, and that only by a return to communion with Nature could humanity and poetry be redeemed. But all this was based merely on philosophic theory; and could find no confirmation in history or literature: history knew of no innocent savages; and even as unsophisticated literature as Homer was then supposed to be, disclosed no heroes perfect in the sentimental virtues.

Ossian appeared; and the truth of sentimentalism seemed historically established. For here was poetry of the loftiest tone, composed in the unlearned Dark Ages, and answering the highest expectations concerning poetry inspired by Nature only. (Was not a distinguished Professor of Rhetoric saying, "Ossian's poetry, more perhaps than that of any other writer, deserves to be styled the poetry of the heart"?) And here was the record of a nature-people whose conduct stood revealed as flawless. "Fingal," Macpherson himself accommodatingly pointed out, "exercised every manly virtue in Caledonia while Heliogabalus disgraced human nature in Rome." More than fifty years afterwards Byron compared Homer's Hector, greatly to his disadvantage, with Ossian's Fingal: the latter's conduct was, in his admirer's words, "uniformly illustrious and great, without one mean or inhuman action to tarnish the splendor of his fame." The benevolent magnanimity of the heroes, the sweet sensibility of the heroines, their harmony with Nature's moods (traits which Macpherson had supplied from his own imagination), were the very traits that won the enthusiasm of the public. The poem in its turn stimulated the sentimentalism which had produced it; and henceforth the new school contended on even terms with the old.

One of the effects of the progress of sentimentalism was the decline of satire. Peculiarly the weapon of the classical school, it had fallen into unskillful hands: Churchill, though keen and bold, lacked the grace of Pope and the power of Johnson. Goldsmith might have proved a worthier successor;

but though his genius for style was large, his capacity for sustained indignation was limited. Even his *Retaliation* is humorous in spirit rather than satiric. He was a being of conflicting impulses; and in his case at least, the style is not precisely the man. His temperament was emotional and affectionate; by nature he was a sentimentalist. But his inclinations were restrained, partly by the personal influence of Dr. Johnson, partly by his own admiration for the artistic traditions of the classicists. He despised looseness of style, considered blank verse unfinished, and cultivated what seemed to him the more polished elegance of the heroic couplet. The vacillation of his views appears in the difference between the sentiments of *The Traveller* and those of *The Deserted Village*. The former is a survey of the nations of Europe, the object being to discover a people wholly admirable. Merit is found in Italians, Swiss, French, Dutch, and English,—but never perfection; even the free and happy Swiss are disgusting in the vulgar sensuality of their pleasures; happiness is nowhere. One is not surprised to learn that Dr. Johnson contributed at least a few lines to a poem with so orthodox a message.

In *The Deserted Village*, on the other hand, Goldsmith employed the classical graces to point a moral which from the classical point of view was false. His sympathetic feelings had now been captivated by the notion of rural innocence. The traits of character which he attributed to the village inhabitants,—notably to the immortal preacher who, entertaining the vagrants,

Quite forgot their vices in their woe,—

Are those exalted in the literature of sentimentalism, as, for example, in his contemporary, Langhorne *Country Justice*. *The Deserted Village* was in point of fact an imaginative idyll,—the supreme idyll of English poetry; but Goldsmith insisted that it was a realistic record of actual conditions. Yet he could never have observed such an English village, either in its depopulated and decayed state (as Macaulay has remarked), or in its rosy prosperity and unsullied virtue; his economic history and theory were misleading. Like Macpherson, but through self-delusion rather than intent, he was engaged in an effort to deceive by giving sentimental doctrines a basis of apparent actuality. But the world has forgotten or forgiven his pious fraud in its gratitude for the loveliness of his art.

THE TRIUMPH OF SENTIMENTALISM (1776-1800)

Goldsmith's application of sentimental ideas to contemporary affairs foreshadowed what was to be one of the marked tendencies of the movement in the last quarter of the century. Thus in 1777 Thomas Day interpreted the American Revolution as a conflict between the pitiless tyranny of a corrupt civilization and the appealing virtues of a people who had found in sequestered forests and prairies the abiding place of Freedom and the only remaining opportunity "to save the ruins of the human name." At the same time the justification of sentimentalism on historical grounds was strengthened by the young antiquarian and poet, Thomas Chatterton. Like Macpherson, he answers to Pope's description of archaizing authors,—

Ancients in words, mere moderns in their sense.

He fabricated, in what he thought to be Middle English, a body of songs and interludes, which he attributed to a monk named Thomas Rowleie, and which showed that, in the supposedly unsophisticated simplicity of medieval times, charity to Man and love for Nature had flourished as beautifully as lyric utterance. Even more lamentable than Chatterton's early death is the fact that his fanciful and musical genius was shrouded in so grotesque a style.

In 1781 appeared a new poet of real distinction, George Crabbe, now the hope of the conservatives. Edmund Burke, who early in his great career had assailed the radicals in his ironic *Vindication of Natural Society*, and who to the end of his life contended against them in the arena of politics, on reading some of Crabbe's manuscripts, rescued this cultured and ingenuous man from obscurity and distress; and Dr. Johnson presently aided him in his literary labors. In *The*

Library Crabbe expressed the reverence of a scholarly soul for the garnered wisdom of the past, and satirized some of the popular writings of the day, including sentimental fiction. He would not have denied the world those consolations which flow from the literature that mirrors our hopes and dream; but his honest spirit revolted when such literature professed to be true to life. His acquaintance with actual conditions in humble circles, and with hardships, was as personal as Goldsmith's; but he was not the kind of poet who soothes the miseries of mankind by ignoring them. In *The Village* he arose with all the vigor and intensity of insulted common sense to refute the dreamers who offered a rose-colored picture of country life as a genuine portrayal of truth and nature. So evident was his mastery of his subject, his clearness of perception, and his earnestness of feeling, that he attracted immediate attention; and he might well have led a new advance under the ancient standards. But silence fell upon Crabbe for many years; and this proved to be the last occasion in the poetical history of the century that a powerful voice was raised in behalf of the old cause.

The poet who became the favorite of moderate sentimentalists, in what were called "genteel" circles, was William Cowper. He presented little or nothing that could affright the gentle emotions, and much that pleasurably stimulated them. He enriched the poetry of the domestic affections, and had a vein of sadness which occasionally, as in *To Mary*, deepened into the most touching pathos. In *The Task*, a discursive familiar essay in smooth-flowing blank verse, he dwelt fondly upon those satisfactions which his life of uneventful retirement offered; intimated that truth and wisdom were less surely found by poring upon books than by meditating among beloved rural scenes; and, turning his sad gaze toward the distant world of action, deplored that mankind strained "the natural bond of brotherhood" by tolerating cruel imprisonments, slavery, and warfare. Such humanitarian views, when they seek the aid of religious ethics, ought normally to find support in that sentimentalized Christianity which professes the entire goodness of the human heart; but the discordant element in Cowper's mind was his inclination towards Calvinism, which goes to the opposite extreme by insisting on total depravity. Personally he believed that he had committed the unpardonable sin (against the Holy Spirit),—a dreadful thought which underlies his tragic poem, *The Castaway;* and probably unwholesome, though well-intentioned, was the influence upon him of his spiritual adviser, John Newton, whose gloomy theology may be seen in the hymn, *The Vision of Life in Death.* Cowper's sense of the reality of evil not only distracted his mind to madness, but also prevented him from carrying his sentimental principles to their logical goal. What the hour demanded were poets who, discountenancing any mistrust of the natural emotions, should give them free rein. They were found at last in Burns and in Blake.

The sentimentalists had long yearned for the advent of the ideal poet. Macpherson had presented him,—but as of an era far remote; latterly Beattie, in *The Minstrel,* had set forth his growth under the inspiration of Nature,—but in a purely imaginary tale. Suddenly Burns appeared: and the ideal seemed incarnated in the living present. The Scottish bard was introduced to the world by his first admirers as "a heaven-taught ploughman, of humble unlettered station," whose "simple strains, artless and unadorned, seem to flow without effort from the native feelings of the heart"; and as "a signal instance of true and uncultivated genius." The real Burns, though indeed a genius of song, was far better read than the expectant world wished to believe, particularly in those whom he called his "bosom favorites," the sentimentalists Mackenzie and Sterne; and his sense of rhythm and melody had been trained by his emulation of earlier Scotch lyricists, whose lilting cadences flow towards him as highland rills to the gathering torrent. Sung to the notes of his native tunes, and infused with the local color of Scotch life, the sentimental themes assumed the freshness of novelty. Giving a new ardor to revolutionary tendencies, Burns revolted against the orthodoxy of the "Auld Lichts," depicting its representatives as ludicrously hypocritical. He protested against distinctions founded on birth or rank, as in *A Man's a Man for A' That;* and, on the other hand, he idealized the homely feelings and manners of the "virtuous populace" in his immortal *Cotter's Saturday Night.* He scorned academic learning, and protested that true inspiration was rather to be found in "ae spark o' Nature's fire," —or at the nearest tavern:

Leese me on drink! it gies us mair
Than either school or college.

Like Sterne, who boasted that his pen governed him, Burns praised and affected the impromptu:

But how the subject theme may gang,
Let time or chance determine;
Perhaps it may turn out a sang,
Perhaps turn out a sermon.

His Muse was to be the mood of the moment. Herein he brought to fulfillment the sentimental desire for the liberation of the emotions; but his work, taken as a whole, can scarcely be said to vindicate the faith that the emotions, once freed, would manifest instinctive purity. At his almost unrivalled best, he can sing in the sweetest strains the raptures or pathos of innocent youthful love, as in *Sweet Afton or To Mary in Heaven;* but straightway sinking from that elevation of feeling to the depths of vulgarity or grossness, he will chant with equal zest and skill the indulgence of the animal appetites. He hails the joys of life, but without discriminating between the higher and the lower. Yet these exuberant animal spirits which, unrestrained by conscience or taste, drove him too often into scurrility, gave his work that passion—warm, throbbing, and personal-which had been painfully wanting in earlier poets of sensibility. It was his emotional intensity as well as his lyric genius that made him the most popular poet of his time.

In Burns, sentimentalism was largely temperamental, unreflective, and concrete. In William Blake, the singularity of whose work long retarded its due appreciation, sentimentalism was likewise temperamental; but, unconfined to actuality, became far broader in scope, more spiritual, and more consistently philosophic. Indeed, Blake was the ultimate sentimentalist of the century. A visionary and symbolist, he passed beyond Shaftesbury in his thought, and beyond any poet of the school in his endeavor to create a new and appropriate style. His contemporary, Erasmus Darwin , author of *The Botanic Garden,* was trying to give sentimentalism a novel interpretation by describing the life of plants in terms of human life; but, Darwin being destitute of artistic sense, the result was grotesque. Blake, by training and vocation an engraver, was primarily an artist; but, partly under Swedenborgian influences, he had grasped the innermost character of sentimentalism, perceived all its implications, and carried them fearlessly to their utmost bounds. To him every atom of the cosmos was literally spiritual and holy; the divine and the human, the soul and the flesh, were absolutely one; God and Man were only two aspects of pervasive "mercy, pity, peace, and love." Nothing else had genuine reality. The child, its vision being as yet unclouded by false teachings, saw the universe thus truly; and Blake, therefore, in *Songs of Innocence,* gave glimpses of the world as the child sees it,—a guileless existence amid the peace that passes all understanding. He hymned the sanctity of animal life: even the tiger, conventionally an incarnation of cruelty, was a glorious creature of divine mould; to slay or cage a beast was, the *Auguries of Innocence* protested, to incur anathema. *The Book of Thel* allegorically showed the mutual interdependence of all creation, and reprehended the maiden shyness that shrinks from merging its life in the sacrificial union which sustains the whole.

To Blake the great enemy of truth was the cold logical reason, a truncated part of Man's spirit, which was incapable of attaining wisdom, and which had fabricated those false notions that governed the practical world and constrained the natural feelings. Instances of the unhappiness caused by such constraint, he gave in *Songs of Experience,* where *The Garden of Love* describes the blighting curse which church law had laid upon free love. To overthrow intellectualism and discipline, Man must liberate his most precious faculty, the imagination, which alone can reveal the spiritual character of the universe and the beauty that life will wear when the feelings cease to be unnaturally confined. Temporarily Blake rejoiced when the French Revolution seemed to usher in the millennium of freedom and peace; and his interpretation of its earlier incidents in his poem on that theme illustrates in style and spirit the highly original nature of his mind. More than any predecessor he understood how the peculiarly poetical possibilities of sentimentalism might be elicited, namely by emphasizing its mystical quality. Thus under his guidance mysticism, which in the early seventeenth century had sublimated the religious poetry of the orthodox, returned to sublimate the poetry of the radicals; and with that achievement the sentimental movement reached its climax.

Burns died in 1796; Blake, lost in a realm of symbolism, became unintelligible; and temporarily sentimentalism suffered a reaction. The French Revolution, with its Reign of Terror, and the rise of a military autocrat, though supported, even after Great Britain had taken up arms against Napoleon, by some "friends of humanity" who placed universal brotherhood above patriotism, seemed to the general public to demonstrate that the sentimental theories and hopes were untrue to life and led to results directly contrary to those predicted. Once again, in Canning's caustic satires of *The Anti-Jacobin*, conservatism raised its voice. But by this time sentimentalism was too fully developed and widely spread to be more than checked. Under the new leadership of Wordsworth, Coleridge, and Southey, the movement, chastened and modified by experience, resumed its progress; and the fame of its new leaders presently dimmed the memory of those pioneers who in the eighteenth century had undermined the foundations of orthodoxy, slowly upbuilt a new world of thought, gradually fashioned a poetic style more suited to their sentiments than the classical, and thus helped to plunge the modern world into that struggle which, in life and in literature, rages about us still.

Periodicals in Eighteenth Century

EARLY PERIODICALS

The Tatler was a special type of periodical evolved to meet contemporary tastes and requirements, and the *Spectator* was the consummate realization of this type. To understand their success we must consider not only the talents of Addison and Steele, but also the history of English periodicals in the preceding generation. There was comparative freedom of the press after the Licensing Act lapsed in 1695, and a great increase in the publication of small units, such as newspapers and other periodicals, pamphlets, fugitive verse, and small miscellanies. The coffee houses kept a supply of such reading matter for their customers. Much of the political discussion in early newspapers was in dialogue form. But the provision of periodical entertainment was separable from the news, and here we have a main line of origin for the *Tatler*. John Dunton in his *Athenian Gazette* or *Athenian Mercury* (I691-97) used the device of question and answer, queries of all kinds, serious and absurd, being answered by a supposed editorial board called the "Athenian Society," and thus giving rise to an endless series of odd items and brief essays. This periodical was very popular; it combined commonplace moralizing with an appeal to curiosity. In his *Pegasus* (I696) Dunton offered, along with news, an

"Observator" or "Observation," a brief essay on some topic of current interest. The step from the editorial dialogue of the political papers and the question-and-answer box of the Athenians to the essay was natural and important. Other minor periodicals, such as the *Weekly Entertainment* (I700), seem to have realized the single-essay-per-number principle which was to become highly important, but which remained incidental and obscure for a few years. Decidedly literary was Peter Anthony Motteux ' *Gentleman's Journal* (I692-94), with book reviews, verse, essays, popular science, short tales, riddles, even music. Motteux wanted to appeal to the ladies. His project was important, but he scattered his fire too much.

Defoe famous *Review* (I704-13) was largely devoted to editorials on politics and economics, but gave a secondary place to entertaining and moralizing comment on manners. Defoe began by appending to his main article a collection of answers to correspondents called for a time "Advice from the Scandalous Club; being a Weekly History of Nonsense, Impertinence, Vice, and Debauchery." The Scandalous Club, combining miscellaneous comment with moral censorship, derives from Dunton's Athenian Society, though some credit may be due to Henry Care *Pacquet of Advice* from Rome, to which Defoe acknowledges a debt. The transactions of the Club were put into a supplement, and then for a time in 1705 published separately as the *Little Review*. Defoe was not primarily interested in polite entertainment, but he made the important transition from question-and-answer and dialogue form to essay, and a specific contribution of his was the use of the fictitious letter to the editor. The *British Apollo* (I708-11), the last important example of the question-and-answer type, had considerable success under the guidance of a "society of gentlemen" which included Aaron Hill and John Gay. The idea that literary matter was a necessary part of an entertaining periodical was handed on from Motteux' *Gentleman's Journal* to the *Muses Mercury* (I707-08) and the *Monthly Miscellany* (I707-10)- What was now necessary was that topics directly related to the contemporary scene should be treated from a definite point of view in such a way as to give both continuity and variety of interest.

Caption of the first Number of Defoes review

Steele published the *Tatler* three times a week from April 12, 1709, to January 2, 1711. "I own myself of the Society for Reformation of Manners," he wrote in No. 3, but moral reproof was to be part of an entertaining variety.

All accounts of gallantry, pleasure, and entertainment shall be under the article of White's Chocolate-house; Poetry, under that of Will's Coffee-house; Learning, under the title of Grecian; foreign and domestic news you will have from Saint James's Coffee-house; and what else I have to offer on any other subject shall be dated from my own apartment. (No. 1)

My chief scenes of action are coffee-houses, play-houses, and my own apartment. (No. 18)

At first a single number had news and comment under several of these headings, but eventually news items dropped out, and a single short essay develop from the miscellaneous section headed "From my own apartment" comes to occupy an entire number. The topics are varied so as to maintain much of the appeal of the multiple departments. Steele took from Swift's pamphlets against Partridge the pen-name Isaac Bickerstaff, and a Bickerstaff family group is sketched, though this scheme does not dominate the paper. Addison came in early, and contributed about one quarter of the papers, but was never in control of the *Tatler*. Various literary forms are used-character sketches (satirically pointed at individuals in the early numbers), letters with comment, dialogues, allegories, and short tales. The novelty lies in the ingenious slight variations together with the maintenance of an even tone. Extremes were excluded, particularly the extremes of political controversy, though Steele was sometimes partisan in the *Tatler*, and this was perhaps the reason why the paper was rather suddenly dropped and a new start made in the *Spectator*.

The rival *British Apollo* admired the grace and good humor of the *Tatler*. Defoe too admired, though he favored harsher method and asked doubtfully, "Are we to be laughed out of our follies?" Gay in *The Present State of Wit* (I711) praised Bickerstaff for correcting "false sentiments" and "vicious tastes" and presenting "learning" (we should say "good reading") in a form acceptable to town and court. "Lastly, his writings have set all our wits and men of letters upon a new way of thinking." Gay, thus forecast the wide and enduring influence of the periodical essay, an appeal which was due to a reconciliation of morals and manners worked out within the actual framework of society. The courtier was to become virtuous and the solid citizen polite. "The courtier, the trader, and the scholar should all have an equal pretension to the denomination of a gentleman" (No. 207).

The *Spectator* was published six times a week from March 1, 1711, to December 6, 1712, and was revived briefly by Addison in 1714. Addison played a much more prominent part here, though Steele sketched the famous Club and was the creator of Sir Roger de Coverley. Previous periodicals had developed the idea of a club both as a board of editors (Athenian Society or Scandalous Club) and as a fictitious group satirically or humorously described. In the *Tatler* the Bickerstaffs combined the two; the Spectator Club is primarily literary portraiture, though it is occasionally represented as engaging in editorial discussion. Except for Sir Roger, the characters are not highly developed. At times the *Spectator* approaches the novel of manners, but its chief purpose is to formulate in a persuasive and good humored way the matters on which men and women of good sense and good taste can agree. Addison gives a touch of elegance; he is less sentimental and less uneven than Steele, and the famous essays on literary criticism, such as the papers on Paradise Lost, the pleasures of the imagination, and the popular ballads, are entirely his. He prided himself on the success of a periodical which was free from political controversy, cynicism, infidelity, or personal animus (No. 262). Early critics, convinced that Addison had more dignity and weight than Steele, gave him most of the credit for the success of this program; recent students have been inclined to exalt the frankness, charm, and originality of Steele at the expense of the more sedate, reserved, and conventional Addison. At any rate, Steele was justified in saying as the *Spectator* drew to a close: "I claim to myself the merit of having extorted excellent productions from a person of the greatest abilities, who would not have let them appear by any other means" (No. 532). In the *Guardian* (I713) Addison and Steele continued their alliance.

The influence of the periodical essay was important throughout the century. It persisted as an independent periodical, as a unit in a larger periodical, as a collection of essays in book form, and as a formative influence in the development of the novel. In the generation after Steele and Addison periodicals like Fielding *Champion* centered about a principal essay. In the mid-century there was a revival of the independent series expressing the point of view of an individual or a small group of contributors-Johnson *Rambler* (I750-52), Hawkesworth *Adventurer* (I752-54), with aid from Joseph Warton, Johnson, and Bathurst, Fielding *Covent-Garden Journal* (I752), Edward Moore's *World* (I753-56), with important contributions from Chesterfield, Walpole, and others, Colman and Thornton's *Connoisseur* (I754-56). Goldsmith wrote the shortlived *Bee* and contributed *The Citizen of the World* to the *Public Ledger* (I760-61). Henry Mackenzie gave considerable individuality to the *Mirror* (I779-80) and the *Lounger* (I785-87). The form was extensively imitated on the Continent. Meanwhile the *Tatler* and the *Spectator* themselves went through innumerable editions, and the periodical essay became the staple content of readers and anthologies, and influenced the early reading and writing of generations of schoolchildren in England and America.

NEWSPAPERS, MAGAZINES, AND REVIEWS

The Stamp Tax of 1712 imposed a half-penny duty on pamphlets or papers printed on a half-sheet, a penny on those using a half to a whole sheet. This encouraged a six page weekly usually called a "journal," using one and a half sheets and thus avoiding the tax. The typical daily was a half-sheet printed in double columns and carrying only news and a few advertisements, but the journal regularly admitted a political editorial or an essay on the *Spectator* model, and other miscellaneous matter. Though evasion of the tax became impossible, the most influential papers continued to be of this type. They were deeply involved in politics: *Mist's Weekly Journal, or Saturday's Post,* changed to "Fog's" after a prosecution, was the most extreme Tory organ, but from 1726 the *Craftsman* was the principal opposition paper. Walpole subsidized various papers, including the *Daily Gazetteer*. As the century advances, most of the features of the modern newspaper develop—an increase in advertising (notably in the *Daily Advertiser* from 1730), control by proprietors who were not printers, and later the regular reporting of parliamentary debates, and the "leader" (editorial) under a masthead on an inner page. Almon in the *London Evening Post* and William Woodfall in the *Morning Chronicle* were prominent in political reporting in the age of Wilkes and the American Revolution. The London *Chronicle* from 1757 extended its content to include varied material, such as book reviews. The size and circulation of newspapers continued to be very small by modern standards, even though they were prominent and influential. Surviving files often give important evidence in their advertisements for the publication of books and the production of plays. Familiar names such as the *Times* and the *Morning Post* appeal late in the period, though the *Times* did not get its commanding position until early in the next century.

In 1731 Edward Cave, a printer at St. John's Gate, Clerkenwell , began his famous *Gentleman's Magazine*. By "magazine," a new use of the word, he meant a collection or miscellany made up of essays extracted from the weekly journals together with a systematic chronicle of the events of the month. Secondarily he reprinted poetry and began to list new books. While the weekly journals of the 1730's, were largely political, they appealed to literary interests also, as has been said; in this group were the *Universal Spectator*, the *Weekly Miscellany*, and the *Grub-street Journal*, and Cave owed more to them than to more distant precedents for literary entertainment. For a systematic monthly record of the news, Cave's model was a type of monthly publication which gave a comprehensive but dry report of current events, such as Abel Boyer *Political State of Great Britain* (1711-40), and the *Historical Register* (1716-38). The early *Gentleman's* had much political matter. Like other journalists, Cave undertook to print the debates in Parliament, and after 1738 this was largely done for him by Samuel Johnson under the title of "Debates in the Senate of Magna Lilliputia." But Cave always gave space to miscellaneous matter, and interest shifted from public affairs to literature, science, biography, and antiquities. The amount of poetry was increased, though the *Gentleman's* verse was never very high in quality, so that the subscriber got the equivalent of a poetical miscellany. The listing of books was expanded to include brief reviews and notices. The contents were on the level of the well informed though superficial reader, and a bound set of the *Gentleman's* came to be, as the name implies, a necessary part of the gentleman's library in town or country. Cave's success soon called forth many imitators, most important the *London Magazine* from 1732, put out by a syndicate of booksellers, and the *Scots Magazine* at Edinburgh from 1739. The *Universal Magazine* from 1747 was also early and successful, and many others could be named.

From the seventeenth century a well defined type of periodical was devoted to the summarizing and abstracting of books, on the model of the *Journal des Sçavans.* This became standard for the voluminous French periodicals with *Bibliothèque*-titles. Somewhat similarly, though not on the same scale, we have English periodicals variously called *Memoirs of Literature, Present State of the Republic of Letters,* and *History of the Works of the Learned.* The last title is accurate, for the tendency was to make long extracts from learned or technical works. A somewhat similar method was applied by the bookseller Ralph Griffiths to the general field of belles lettres in the *Monthly Review* from 1749; the policy at first was not to write reviews in our sense, but to list every book published, with extracts from or summaries of the most important. In 1756 Archibald Hamilton started the *Critical Review* with Smollett as principal editor. The Tory bias of the *Critical Review* and Smollett's harsh methods provoked much controversy. But there was general resentment of the reviewer in this period, whether he was discussing a play or an art-exhibition in the newspaper, or doing a notice of a book in the *Monthly* or the *Critical*. These two reviews never attained the prestige and power of their early nineteenth-century descendants, the *Edinburgh* and the *Quarterly*. They contained much hack work, but they were widely read, they recorded literary opinion as more fugitive notices did not, and they enlisted the services of some important men, not only Smollett in the *Critical*, but Goldsmith in the *Monthly* (with some contributions to the *Critical* also), and Johnson in the short-lived *Literary Magazine or Universal Review* (I756-58).

John Evelyn (1620-1706)
John Dryden (1631-1700)
Samuel Pepys (1633-1703)
Thomas Otway (1652-1685)

JOHN EVELYN (1620-1706)

John Evelyn (October 31, 1620 – February 27, 1706) was an English writer, gardener and diarist.

Evelyn's diaries are largely contemporaneous with those of the other noted diarist of the time, Samuel Pepys, and cast considerable light on the art, culture and politics of the time (he witnessed the deaths of Charles I and Oliver Cromwell, the last Great Plague in London, and the Great Fire of London in 1666.). Evelyn and Pepys corresponded frequently and much of this correspondence has been preserved.

Born into a family whose wealth was largely founded on gunpowder production, John Evelyn was born in Wotton, Surrey, and grew up in the Sussex town of Lewes. He was educated at Balliol College, Oxford and at the Middle Temple. While in London, he witnessed important events such as the execution of Thomas Wentworth, Earl of Strafford. Having briefly joined the Royalist army, he went abroad to avoid further involvement in the English Civil War and in 1647 married Mary Browne, daughter of the British ambassador in Paris.

In 1652, Evelyn and his wife settled in Deptford, in south-east London. Their house, Sayes Court (adjacent to the naval dockyard), was purchased by Evelyn from his father-in-law Sir Richard Browne in 1653 and Evelyn soon began to transform the gardens. In 1671, he encountered master wood-worker Grinling Gibbons (who was renting a cottage on the Sayes Court estate) and introduced him to Sir Christopher Wren.

It was after the Restoration that Evelyn's career really took off. In 1660, Evelyn was a member of the group that founded the Royal Society. The following year, he wrote the *Fumifugium* (or *The Inconveniencie of the Aer and Smoak of London Dissipated*), the first book written on the growing pollution problem in London.

He was known for his knowledge of trees, and his treatise *Sylva, or Discourse on Forest Trees* (1664) was written as an encouragement to landowners to plant trees to provide timber for England's burgeoning navy.

Following the Great Fire in 1666, closely described in his diaries, he was responsible for controlling the rebuilding of London, in particular for preventing landowners from illegally extending their plots into the new streets. He was closely involved in the reconstruction of St Paul's Cathedral by Wren (with Gibbons' artistry a notable addition). He even designed pleasure gardens, such as those at Euston Hall.

Evelyn was a prolific author and produced books on subjects as diverse as theology, politics, horticulture, architecture and cookery, and he cultivated links with contemporaries across the spectrum of Stuart political and cultural life. Like Pepys, Evelyn was a lifelong bibliophile, and by his death his library is known to have comprised 3,859 books and 822 pamphlets. Many were uniformly bound in a French taste and bear his motto *Omnia explorate; meliora retinete* ('explore everything; keep the best') from I Thessalonians v.21.

His daughter Mary Evelyn (1665-1685) is sometimes acknowledged as the pseudonymous author of the book *Mundus Muliebris* of 1690. *Mundus Muliebris: or, The Ladies Dressing Room Unlock'd and Her Toilette Spread. In Burlesque. Together with the Fop-Dictionary, Compiled for the Use of the Fair Sex* is a satirical guide in verse to francophile fashion and terminology, and its authorship is often jointly credited to John Evelyn, who seems to have edited the work for press after his daughter's death.

In 1694 Evelyn moved to Wotton, Surrey and Sayes Court was made available for rent. Its most notable tenant was Russian tsar Peter the Great who lived there for three months in 1698 (and did great damage to both house and grounds). The house no longer exists, but a public park of the same name can be found in Evelyn Street.

Evelyn died in 1706 at his house in Dover Street, London. His wife Mary died three years later. Both are buried in the Evelyn Chapel in St John's Church at Wotton.

JOHN DRYDEN(1631-1700)

The career of John Dryden shows us the taste and thought of the Restoration, its political, intellectual, artistic, and religious struggles and tensions, variously expressed in the work of a supremely competent writer. His individual genius won him high place, but it was always genius in account with the age. He began as a docile young student under the Commonwealth, taking his political and literary ideas from his surroundings; he ended in opposition, a Catholic and a Tory, but meanwhile he had always been moved to write not only to meet the general taste of the times but to meet special demands and occasions—plays for the fashionable public, poems on current events, complimentary verses, timely satiric and didactic poems, critical essays pointed for self-defense and clarification of current issues. Thus he wrought out literary models and standards which his age accepted, and which were in large part to meet the tastes of the English public for a century to come. The man remains something of a mystery, for biographical facts are meager, but his achievement in letters is of the first importance. The age of Dryden gives the key to the age of Pope and the age of Johnson.

Dryden was born in the parish of Aldwincle All Saints, Northamptonshire, in 1631. His father was a small landed proprietor who took the Puritan side. He was educated at Westminster School and Trinity College, Cambridge, and seems to have had some minor employment with a kinsman in Cromwell's government (1656-58). Aside from some juvenile verses on the death of a schoolfellow Lord Hastings, full of the conceits of the metaphysical school, his first piece was *A Poem upon the Death of his Late Highness Oliver* (1659). Within two years he was hailing the return of Charles II in *Astraea Redux* (1660) and lines *To His Sacred Majesty. A Panegyrick on his Coronation* (1661). He was content, not necessarily in a bad sense, to follow popular opinion. We have little detail about the beginnings of his literary career in London; he may have done hackwork for the bookseller Henry Herringman, and he was already acquainted with Sir Robert Howard (whose sister Elizabeth he married in 1663), an active dramatist and one of the proprietors of the King's Company. Dryden was soon writing regularly for this company; an author seeking the favor of the newly restored court and aristocracy would naturally turn to drama. After an undistinguished beginning in comedy, he collaborated with Howard in *The Indian Queen* (produced 1664, published 1665), and himself wrote the sequel *The Indian Emperor* (produced 1665, published 1667), beginning his notable, though not entirely fortunate, work in the heroic play. The plague closed the theaters in 1665-66, and Dryden retired during this time to Charlton, Wiltshire. Here he wrote of the strange and disastrous events of these months n *Annus Mirabilis* (1667). A more significant work of these years was the essay Of *Dramatic Poesy* (1668), the first notable achievement of the new prose and of Dryden's intellectual power.

For ten years Dryden's energy was divided between comedy and the heroic play. In the *Defence of an Essay of*

Dramatic Poesy (I668) he confesses that he writes what the public wants, and that he does not feel comedy to be his strong point, but there is reason to believe that he took the heroic play more seriously. After *Tyrannic Love* (produce 1669, published 1670) his work in this form reached its height in *The Conquest of Granada* (produced 1670-71, published 1672). These bombastic and artificial rimed plays drew Dryden away for a time from his natural bent. Meanwhile he was defending his work in important prefaces; his vigorous prologues and epilogues, written for his own plays and others too, are also a link between his dramatic practice and his criticism. But the critical current was turning against literary extravagance. The success of the famous burlesque written by Buckingham and others, *The Rehearsal* (produced 1671, published 1672), is a symptom rather than a cause of this change, which appears in the growing sobriety of Dryden *Aureng-Zebe* (produced 1675, published 1676), and in his return to his Shakespearean allegiance in *All for Love* (produced 1677, published 1678). The bombast or "fustian" of the heroic plays went the way of the conceits of metaphysical poetry, but meanwhile these rhetorical exercises had given Dryden final mastery of the heroic couplet.

Dryden was now making a modest living from his plays; he had become a shareholder of the King's Company in 1668. He was appointed poet laureate and historiographer in 1670, the former retroactive to 1668. The literary and social life of the capital involved the writers of the day in quarrels and feuds largely inflamed by the rivalries of the great patrons, such men as Rochester, Mulgrave, Buckingham, and Dorset. Thus Dryden had a tedious controversy with Elkanah Settle, a mediocre writer of heroic plays, whose *Empress of Morocco* was a center of dispute in 1673 and who was backed by Rochester. In December, 1679, Dryden was badly beaten up by hired bullies because of his supposed authorship of some lampoon or satire. It used to be thought that Rochester was responsible; though this is very doubtful, the "Rose Alley Ambuscade" provides us with an ugly glimpse of the Restoration gangster at work.

In the political excitement of the Popish Plot and the Exclusion Bill, bitter personal and partisan controversy was fused with an intense interest in the highest issues of Church and State. Dryden had always had an intelligent layman's interest in ideas; he belonged to the Royal Society and paid some attention to the new science, but probably he had always been more interested in that zone of controversy where religion and politics met. Now the result was twofold: the application of his keen intelligence to the problems of the time led to new achievements in satire and verse-essay, and he was forced as never before to take stock of his own religious and political opinions. *Mac Flecknoe* (probably written about 1678; published 1682) is a purely personal attack on Shadwell, but *Absalom and Achitophel* (1681) and *The Medal* (1682) are supreme examples of satire that combines animus against individuals with what may be called a drama of contending ideas. In siding with the Court against the Whigs led by Shaftesbury Dryden followed his personal inclination and took his color from his associates, but he also came to consider political and religious issues more seriously. A Tory in politics, he was still defending the position of the Church of England in *Religio Laici* (November, 1682), but on the death of Charles II and the accession of the Catholic James II, the poet too became a Catholic, and affirmed this position in *The Hind and the Panther* (April, 1687) In the former poem he defended the Church of England against deists and freethinkers, without extended reference to Dissenters; in the latter, the noble Hind is the Catholic Church, the Panther is the still noble but faulty Church of England, and the hated enemies of both (the Baptist Boar, the Independent Bear, the Presbyterian Wolf) are the dissenting sects. Thus Dryden laid himself open to the charge that he was trying to get on the winning side and keep court favor—a charge constantly repeated by contemporary satirists and later biographers. Recently, however, Bredvold's important study of the history of Dryden's mind and opinions has shown that we must think of him, in his own words, as "naturally inclined to skepticism in philosophy," and that in distrust of man's own power to know and judge aright, he was ;anxious to find an absolute authority in Church and State. Theology calls this position "fideism." His change in 1660, his position in the crisis of 1678-82, his quest for authority in *Religio Laici*—all point toward the Catholic position which he assumed in 1686. His official appointments under Charles were renewed under James, but it cannot be shown that he got much money or prestige from his conversion. Moreover, he appears not to have sympathized with the drastic steps which James took to reëstablish Catholicism; like other moderate English Catholics he would have preferred a conciliatory policy toward the Church of England. It was, of course, impossible for him to change again when Protestantism and limited monarchy triumphed with the Revolution of 1688. He never took the oath of allegiance to William and Mary, lost his official appointments, and resolutely turned again to the business of making his living by his pen.

Though Dryden is not a vivid personality for us, he gains in dignity and mellowness in his later years. His candor appears in his admission of the justice of Jeremy Collier's attack on the viciousness of the Restoration stage. He did not withdraw from the arena, but he no longer thought of himself as a controversialist and fighter. He was by no means a social outcast, and was befriended and admired by men of all parties, particularly by Dorset. From his favorite seat in Will's Coffee House he laid down the law among the wits of the town.

In the last decade of his life he continued to write plays, competently if not with the highest distinction. The turn for rhetorical and eloquent lyric which had appeared in the lines *To the Pious Memory of the Accomplisht Lady Mrs. Anne Killigrew* (1686) and *A Song for St. Cecilia's Day* (1687) reached its height in *Alexander's Feast* (1697). But in the long run his command of verbal harmonies appears to better advantage in his vigorous and resonant heroic couplets. He gave much time and attention to translation, and one of his important achievements was the establishment of standards and methods by which the work of classical and other authors was recast and adapted to the taste of the eighteenth century.

What was wanted, according to Dryden, was something not so free as mere paraphrase or imitation, or so close to the original as word for word translation ("metaphrase"). He had begun work of this sort in the 1680's, in the first volumes of the miscellany called "Tonson's"; he now went on to translate Juvenal and Persius (I693), and, most important of all, Virgil (I697), in a version which itself became a classic and remained for the eighteenth century a model of meter and diction. In the *Fables* (I700) he applied his skill as translator and adapter with brilliance and versatility to Chaucer, Boccaccio, Homer, and Ovid. The famous Preface to the *Fables* shows his final development as a critic, his combination of literary insight and experience with personal power. Thus he could write:

What judgment I had increases rather than diminishes: and thoughts, such as they are, come crowding in so fast upon me that my only difficulty is to choose or to reject, to run them into verse, or to give them the other harmony of prose: I have so long studied and practised both that they are grown into a habit, and become familiar to me.

In the last months of his life he was planning to translate Homer, "a poet more according to my genius than Virgil." He died in 1700, and was buried near Chaucer in Westminister Abbey.

DRYDEN'S SATIRES

Two of the strongest motives in Restoration politics were fear of France and fear of Catholicism. Since Charles II was secretly committed to France and attached to the Catholic faith, while his brother and presumptive heir to the throne, the Duke of York, was openly Catholic, public excitement about the succession to the throne was very great, and led to the formation of an opposition party led by Anthony Ashley Cooper, Earl of Shaftesbury, who played on the nation's fear of popery from the time he went into opposition in 1674. His party backed as Protestant claimant to the throne one of Charles's illegitimate sons, James, Duke of Monmouth. Then in 1678 came the fantastic stories of Titus Oates about a Catholic plot to kill the King and seize the government. The magistrate Sir Edmund Berry Godfrey, before whom he gave his testimony, was mysteriously murdered. The secretary of the Duke of York was executed among others for supposed complicity in the plot. Oates's testimony became more and more sensational. "Scoops," "exposures," and wild rumors were spread by broadsides, pamphlets, and word of mouth as effectively as in the later days of yellow journalism, and the public was swept by a wave of hysteria. Meanwhile something like a two-party system was forming: the Court party got the nickname "Tory"; the opposition "Country" or "Patriot" party was labeled "Whig." The immediate purpose of the Whigs was to pass the Exclusion Bill blocking the succession of the Duke of York, but Charles caught the Whig leaders off guard by suddenly dissolving Parliament at Oxford in March, 1681, and by the end of the year there was a reaction in favor of the Court. In July Shaftesbury was arrested and sent to the Tower. At this point *Absalom and Achitophel I* was published (November, 1681), a partisan utterance perhaps suggested by the King himself and at the same time an immortal satire. Dryden keenly analyzes the characters of the leaders. of the opposition, Achitophel (Shaftesbury) and Zimri (Buckingham), and gives us a classic study of human nature in politics. We may contrast with these analytical portraits Dryden's broad and contemptuous caricatures, such as Shimei (Slingsby Bethel). His treatment of David (Charles) is of course flattering; his attitude toward Absalom (Monmouth) is cautious and conciliatory. His general position is that there must be a loyally accepted authority to keep the state from anarchy; this is Toryism, but not the extreme doctrine of divine right and non-resistance. The versatile satire ranges from savage assault to eloquent discussion of first principles, from invective to verse-essay. To appreciate the quality of Dryden's work we have to compare it with the next best satires of 1681, Oldham's *Satires upon the Jesuits*. The narrative element is slight: Dryden takes from Samuel 2:14-18 the story of Absalom's rebellion against David, abetted by the shrewd old counselor Achitophel, a parallel which had already been used by contemporary writers. There is no dramatic action, and the conspiracy comes to a somewhat abrupt end with the final speech of David, but the whole poem is intended to be a partisan pamphlet rather than a narrative.

Shaftesbury was acquitted by a jury of London Whigs the week after *Absalom and Achitophel I* was published. A medal was struck in honor of this occasion, and Dryden satirized the Whig triumph in *The Medal, A Satire against Sedition* (March, 1682), a short piece notable for its attack on democracy, the tyranny of the crowd. This piece was answered by *The Medal of John Bayes* (May, 1682), probably to be attributed to Shadwell. Mac Flecknoe was published at some time during this year, and was long considered to be a reply to *The Medal of John Bayes*. But a reference in the newspaper *The Loyal Protestant*, February 9, 1681-82, shows that Mac Flecknoe had been written by that time. It is a purely personal attack on Shadwell, seems to refer exclusively to plays produced in or before the 1670's, and may have been written shortly after the death of Richard Flecknoe, whose successor on the throne of Dulness Shadwell is. Thus Dryden inverts the familiar scheme of the "session of the poets" or "assizes of Parnassus," in which various poets contend for Apollo's prize, the laureateship. But here a booby prize is awarded and the poem is centered about the caricature of Shadwell as a dunce, drawn with magnificent unscrupulousness. Dryden's last great fling at personal satire was in the portraits of Og (Shadwell) and Doeg (Settle) in *Absalom and Achitophel II* (November, 1682); the rest of this piece was written by Nahum Tate.

OF DRAMATIC POESY, AN ESSAY

If Dryden's preoccupation with the stage led him to do much second-rate work, we must also remember that it gave the stimulus which made him a great critic. The drama was the chief theme of Restoration criticism, a theme which Dryden made his own. *Of Dramatic Poesy* shows the poise of his temperament, his interest in reconciling the free imaginative drama and robust humor of the Elizabethans with the stricter neo-classical standards largely transmitted from France. The work is truly an essay; that is, it weighs ideas and tries them out. The new classical criticism tended to be dry and mechanical, to apply formulas and catchwords. Dryden pays due attention to formulas and catchwords, but his position is that such things have meaning only as they operate in the judgment and experience of cultivated authors and critics. It is significant that this first important piece of modern English literary criticism is a dialogue with four speakers, Crites (Dryden's brother-in-law Sir Robert Howard), Eugenius (Charles Sackville, Lord Buckhurst, later Earl of Dorset), Lisideius (Sir Charles Sedley), Neander ("New man," Dryden himself). Crites is for the ancients in general against the moderns, Eugenius for the moderns in general against the ancients, with some preference for the English, Lisideius for the French, on the ground that they are stricter in the observance of the classical code than the ancients themselves, Neander for the English drama, whether it be the freedom of Shakespeare or the disciplined regularity of Ben Jonson, as against the more regular French. A subordinate issue, but one which occasioned lively debate between Dryden and Howard before and after the *Essay*, is the question of rime in plays; Crites favors blank verse, Neander rime, which was the mark of the heroic play and was further defended by Dryden against Howard in the Defence of an Essay of Dramatic Poesy (I668). Another opposition which runs through the *Essay* is between the Elizabethan and the Restoration drama, with the balance inclining in favor of the Elizabethan. A little later Dryden came to value contemporary style and wit more highly, but eventually he returned to his underlying belief in the primacy of Shakespeare. The general tone of his criticism is well described by Courthope:

Dryden's Prefaces have all of them, beneath the surface, a parliamentary air; they are the product of active debate in real life. . . . They are also essentially the work of occasion. Some owe their being to innovations on the stage, others to political crises, others again to the enterprise of booksellers; but all imply the existence of a society divided between rival parties, resolved to question, to enquire, to dispute; to give and take blows from opposite sides; an atmosphere, in fact, such as that which prevailed in Will's Coffee-house in the stormy era of the Restoration and the Revolution.

The result is not an authoritarian or dictatorial neoclassicism, but a compromise calculated to appeal to men of moderation and good sense who share the same cultural background.

MAJOR WORKS

- *Astraea Redux*, 1660
- *The Indian Emperor* (tragedy), 1665
- *Annus Mirabilis* (poem), 1667
- *The Tempest* (comedy), 1667, an adaptation with William D'Avenant of Shakespeare's *The Tempest*
- *An Essay of Dramatick Poesie*, 1668
- *An Evening's Love* (comedy), 1669
- *Tyrannick Love* (tragedy), 1669
- *Marriage A-la-Mode*, 1672
- *The Conquest of Granada*, 1670
- *All for Love*, 1677
- *Oedipus*, 1679
- *Absalom and Achitophel*, 1681
- *Mac Flecknoe*
- *The Medal*, 1682
- *Religio Laici*, 1682
- *The Hind and the Panther*, 1687
- *Amphitryon*, 1690
- *Don Sebastian*, 1690
- *Amboyna*
- *The Works of Virgil*, 1697
- *Fables, Ancient and Modern* 1700

SAMUEL PEPYS (1633-1703)

Samuel Pepys was born on February 23rd 1633 in Salisbury Court off Fleet Street. His father, John, was a tailor, his mother Margaret Kite was sister of a Whitechapel butcher and Samuel was fifth in a line of eleven children.

Robert Pepys of Brampton, served in the household of his relatives, the Montagus of Hinchingbrooke. Samuel was sent to Huntingdonshire in 1642 to live with his uncle, because of his health and fears of The Plague (from which several of his brothers died).The house where he lived still stands between Brampton and Hinchingbrooke. Samuel attended the Grammar School at Huntingdon, whose ex-pupils included not only Oliver Cromwell but also Edward Montagu,. the young squire of Hinchingbrooke. Edward, 8 years older than Samuel, inherited the Hinchingbrooke estate from his father, Sir Sydney, in 1644.

Michael Wickes notes

> "The most famous of Huntingdon's medieval buildings was dedicated to John The Baptist. Part of this hospital for the poor, founded around 1160, still stands today as the building which houses the Cromwell Museum. ...the town acquired it to accomodate the Huntingdon Free School. ...it was here that Oliver Cromwell and Samuel Pepys received their elementary education."The Free School later became Huntingdon Grammar School, the forerunner of the present Hinchingbrooke Comprehensive School."

Samuel Pepys returned to London after the civil war and entered St Paul's School. In his diary of November 1st 1660 he recalled how he rejoiced in the execution of Charles I.

His future employer, Edward Montagu, a commander of the parliamentary army, fell out with the Parliamentary side over the execution and left politics for several years, re-emerging as a supporter of the King. Pepys meanwhile attended Magdalene College Cambridge, which today houses his Diary.

He took his bachelor's degree in 1654 and entered the service of Edward Montagu as his secretary and agent in London. By 1655 Pepys had married the fifteen year old daughter of a Huguenot exile, Elizabeth St Michel.

As Mountagu's responsibilities grew, so did Pepys', looking after the Montagu estate and business in London, during absences abroad on naval service and visiting Hinchingbrooke.

In March 1658 he underwent a dangerous operation for the removal of a bladder stone - the recovery from which he celebrated with a banquet for years afterwards.

The late 1650's were turbulent times in England, Oliver Cromwell having died in September 1658 and there being no real successor apart from his son Richard, who was no politician. There was therefore a great deal for Pepys to write about and this was doubtless one of the reasons for beginning his diary.

Pepys' vanity is usually given as the reason for his need to write a diary was . Being proud of his achievements, writing down events involving him gave him great pleasure; re-reading even more so.

His knowledge of shorthand, his political connections through Montagu (now Earl of Sandwich and First Lord of the Admiralty, having brought the King back from exile), and his subsequent government posts as one of the principal officers of the navy administration, gave him power and moderate wealth.

His love of order and efficiency made him a man of some importance and he proudly and successfully addressed the Commons on naval matters. His speech to the Commons on March 5th 1668. pleased him enormously.

By the time the diary ended in the spring of 1669, Pepys' professional success was well established. He was the acknowledged "right hand of the Navy"; master of an elegant household; owner of a coach and a pair of black horses; a man rich enough to retire and live "with comfort, if not in abundance."

He was also recovering from his wife's discovery in October 1668 of his affair with her companion, Deborah Willet (one of a series of dalliances with a variety of women), and was suffering so much from eye strain that he thought he was going blind. In November 1669 his wife Elizabeth died from a fever.

Because his Diary finishes in May 1669 this is the last we read of him in detail, however his life had only reached half way and much of his career lay ahead.

He took on many further administrative and advisory roles, became a member of Parliament (sitting for Castle Rising, Norfolk, 1673-9 and for Harwich in 1679 and 1685-7), serving as Master of Trinity House, gathering a collection of books and manuscripts, became President of the Royal Society in 1684 and had learned friends in many disciplines.

In 1679 he was forced to resign from the Admiralty and sent to the Tower on a charge of selling naval secrets to the French. The charge was subsequently dropped.

In 1685 Charles II died and was succeeded by the Duke of York as James II. Pepys helped to carry the canopy at the Coronation. He was again arrested, in 1690, on suspicion of Jacobite tendencies. Again the charges were dropped, although he was clearly more allied to James II, whom he had worked with and respected when he was at the admiralty, than the incoming William of Orange.

Pepys' Death.

In 1701 he was in failing health and moved in with the faithful Will Hewer in Clapham. He died in Clapham on May 26th 1703 and is buried at St Olave's.

MAJOR WORKS AND THEMES

Pepys dabbled in songwriting and fiction (*Love a Cheat,* manuscript destroyed on January 3, 1664), took Charles II's autobiography down from dictation, wrote many letters and official reports, published *Memoires Relating to the State of the Royal Navy* in 1692, and founded an important library—still intact at Magdalene College, Cambridge—that includes popular ballads, chapbooks, and other "penny merriments." But his significance for literature resides in his million-word diary. Written in shorthand between 1659 and 1669, this private journal is now the most famous diary in the world. An astonishing profusion of vivid details, down to the number of times he ejaculated and the precise kind of cheese he buried during the Great Fire, creates the illusion of a knowable "modern" person, even though he is in fact largely unreflective. With his keen sensuality, feverish metabolism, and passion for all kinds of "telling" and "reckoning, " Pepys seems to combine two characters who are opposed in Wycherley 's *Country-Wife*—Sir Jaspar Fidget, for whom business is pleasure, and Horner, for whom pleasure is business.

Beneath the regularity of the daily diary entries, with their breathless account of shopping, home improvement, masturbation, and other business, we perceive a double construction of time, private and public, subjective and chronometrical. Writing begins with Elizabeth's menstrual period (dispelling hopes for a child, which the journal in a sense replaces), juxtaposed to the momentous state of the nation as it prepared to restore the monarchy. But public and private are intimately related. As his best critics perceive, his narrative is often structured like a virtuoso dramatist's, and his bravura polyglot language implies the scrutiny, even the applause, of an audience. Pepys does not cast himself as the flawless dashing hero or the pious Christian but rather as the rising man who for all his faults gains social recognition.

THE PEPYS LIBRARY

Pepys was a lifelong bibliophile and carefully nurtured his large collection of books, manuscripts, and prints. At his death, there were more than 3,000 volumes, including the diary, all carefully catalogued and indexed; they form one of the most important surviving 17th century private libraries. There are remarkable holdings of incunabula, manuscripts, and printed ballads. Pepys made detailed provisions in his will for the preservation of his book collection; and, when his nephew and heir, John Jackson, died, in 1723, it was transferred, intact, to the Pepys Library, at Magdalene College, Cambridge, where it can still be seen. The bequest included all the original book cases and his elaborate instructions that "the placing as to heighth be strictly reviewed and, where found requiring it, more nicely adjusted".

THE DIARY

Among the most important items in the Library are the original bound manuscripts of Pepys's diary. Although it is clear from the content that they were written as a purely personal record of his life and not for publication, there are indications that Pepys actively took steps to preserve them. Apart from the fact that he wrote his diary out in fair copy from rough notes, he also had the loose pages bound into six volumes, and catalogued them in his library with all his other books, and must have known that eventually someone would find them interesting.

The diary was written in one of the many standard forms of shorthand used in Pepys's time; but, by the time at which the college took an interest in the diary, it was thought to be ciphered. The Reverend John Smith was engaged to transcribe the diaries into plain English; and he laboured at this task for three years, from 1819 to 1822, apparently unaware that a key to the shorthand system was stored in Pepys's library a few shelves above the diary volumes. Smith's transcription (which is also kept in the Pepys Library) was the basis for the first published edition of the diary, released in two volumes in 1825.

A second transcription, done with the benefit of the key, but often less accurately, was completed in 1875 by Mynors Bright, and published in 1875–1879. Henry Wheatley, drawing on both his predecessors, produced a new edition in 1893–

1899, revised in 1926, with extensive notes and an index. The complete and definitive edition, edited and transcribed by Robert Latham and William Matthews, was published in nine volumes, along with separate Companion and Index volumes, over the years 1970–1983. Various single-volume abridgements of this text are also available.

Pepys recorded his daily life for almost ten years in breathtaking honesty; the women he pursued, his friends, his dealings, are all laid out. His diary reveals his jealousies, insecurities, trivial concerns, and his fractious relationship with his wife. It is an important account of London in the 1660s. Included are his personal account of the restoration of the monarchy, the Great Plague of 1665, the Great Fire of London (1666), and the arrival of the Dutch fleet and other events of the Second Anglo-Dutch War (1665–1667). The juxtaposition of his commentary on politics and national events, alongside the very personal, can be seen from the beginning. His opening paragraphs, written in January 1660, begin:

Blessed be God, at the end of the last year I was in very good health, without any sense of my old pain but upon taking of cold. I lived in Axe yard, having my wife and servant Jane, and no more in family than us three. My wife, after the absence of her terms for seven weeks, gave me hopes of her being with child, but on the last day of the year she hath them again.

The condition of the State was thus. *Viz.* the Rump, after being disturbed by my Lord Lambert, was lately returned to sit again. The officers of the army all forced to yield. Lawson lies still in the River and Monke is with his army in Scotland. Only my Lord Lambert is not yet come in to the Parliament; nor is it expected that he will, without being forced to it.

His job required that he meet with many people to dispense monies and make contracts. He often laments over how he "lost his labour" having gone to some appointment at a coffee house or tavern, there to discover that the person he was seeking was not within. This was a constant frustration to Pepys.

The diary similarly gives a detailed account of Pepys's personal life. He liked wine and plays, and the company of other people. He also spent a great deal of time evaluating his fortune and his place in the world. He was always curious and often acted on that curiosity, as he acted upon almost all his impulses.

He was passionately interested in music; and he composed, sang, and played, for pleasure. He taught his wife to sing, and paid for dancing lessons for her (although these stopped when he became jealous of the dancing master).

He had a rather Puritan outlook on life, and periodically would resolve to devote more time to hard work instead of leisure. For example, in his entry for New Year's Eve, 1661, he writes: "I have newly taken a solemn oath about abstaining from plays and wine ...". The following months reveal his lapses to the reader; by February 17, it is recorded, "Here I drank wine upon necessity, being ill for the want of it." His puritanical tendencies did not prevent him from engaging in a number of extra-marital liaisons with various women: these were chronicled in his diary, often in some detail, and generally using a cocktail of languages (English, French and Portuguese) when relating the intimate details. The most dramatic of these encounters was with Deborah Willet, a young woman engaged as a companion for Elizabeth Pepys. On 25 October 1668 Pepys was surprised by his wife whilst embracing Deborah Willet: he writes that his wife "coming up suddenly, did find me imbracing the girl con my hand sub su coats; and endeed I was with my main in her cunny. I was at a wonderful loss upon it and the girl also....". Following this event, he was characteristically filled with remorse but (equally characteristically) this did not prevent his continuing to pursue Willet when she had been dismissed from the Pepys household.

THOMAS OTWAY (1652-1685)

Thomas Otway was born on 3rd March, 1652, in the small village of Milland, Sussex. He was the only son of Humphrey Otway's first marriage but he had a stepsister

Susanna, daughter of Humphrey Otway and his second wife Elizabeth. Nothing is known of Thomas' own mother except that she must have died when he was very young. Humphrey Otway was rector of All Hallows at Woolbedding, Sussex, and the family, though not great, was of some distinction, being of old Yorkshire stock, with the inevitable Irish connections of the English comic dramatist.

At the age of 13 he was entered for Winchester College. Once there, he struck up an acquaintance with Anthony Cary, later Lord Falkland. This friendship was to last all Otway's life; and indeed at Winchester Falkland seemed to have exerted more influence on Thomas than his master, especially urging him "not to be ashamed of idleness". Not surprisingly, Thomas twice missed a scholarship and went to Oxford as a commoner of Christ Church in 1669. His father died in 1671 and at the age of 19 Tom moved on to the more immediate rewards of London.

His first play, "Alcibiades" was published in 1675.

To Britain's great Metropolis I stray'd,
Where Fortune's generall Game is play'd;
I mist the brave and wise, and in their stead
On every sort of Vanity I fed.

His first job in the theatre was as an actor in a play by Mrs. Aphra Behn. She had given up her voluntary services in Continental espionage in order to revive her first play "The Forced Marriage". Betteron, already middle-aged, played the youthful lover while young Otway was cast as the doddering old king. He was a notable failure.

> "Mr. Otway the Poet having an Inclination to turn Actor; Mrs. Behn gave him the King in the Play, for a Probation Part, but he being not us'd to the Stage; the full House put him to such a Sweat and Tremendous Agony, being dash't, spoilt him for an Actor."

Some say that this was his first and last appearance on the stage but it is thought he went on playing bit-parts for two years. However, that particular show resulted in something much more personally disturbing than' the bad notices of his performance.

From A Session of the Poets by the Earl of Rochester, 1647-1680.

Tom Otway came next, Tom Shadwell's, dear Zany;
And swears for Heroicks, he writes best of any;
Don Carlos his Pockets so amply hath fill'd,
That his Mange was quite cur'd, and his Lice, were all kill'd.
But Apollo, had seen his Face on the Stage,
And prudently did not think fit to engage,
The scum of a Play-house, for the Prop of an Age.

The part of Draxilla in that play was played by a 17-year-old girl called Elizabeth Barry, eventually to be the English Theatre's first leading lady. Despite, or possibly because of, a plump, unhandsome appearance and a strong tendency only to speak with one side of her mouth, it is said she did have a considerable presence and was thought a remarkable tragedienne. Thomas fell in love with her; a passion that was to last all his life. She, however, was the mistress of John Wilmot, Earl of Rochester, the poet to whom Otway dedicated "Don Carlos", a heroic tragedy, his first success. But like other poets, Dryden, Settle and Crowne, who had sought the Earl's patronage, Otway was soon to be the object of his ridicule and satire.

Nevertheless, Otway enjoyed a certain popularity especially with the ladies; 5' 7" "but with a thoughtful speaking eye; inclineable to fatness" (a feature later to prove something of an oddity, since the less he had to eat, the fatter he became.) Mrs. Behn said, "Everyone knows Mr. Otway's good nature, which will not permit him to shock any of our sex to their faces." But there were some whose feelings were less warm. Otway and Dryden lived in houses which faced each other and, one night Otway inscribed on Dryden's front door:—

"Here Dryden lives — a poet and wit".

Next evening appeared on his own door:—

"Here Otway lives-exactly opposite".

"Friendship in Fashion", his first comedy, had a small but warm first night at the Duke's Theatre in 1678 but was hissed off the stage at the only known revival in 1708 at Drury Lane. Of the three comedies he wrote, only "The Soldier's Fortune" boasts several revivals and that was last seen in London in 1935 at the Ambassadors Theatre.

Early 1678 sees Otway obtaining a commission through the Earl of Plymouth, one of the natural sons of Charles II and Louise De Querouaille, to whom he dedicated "Venice Preserv'd". With his regiment Otway sets out for military service in Flanders. An unexpected peace treaty soon interrupted the course of the war, causing the troops to be disbanded and Otway's return to England with "naught but drums and trumpets in his head", materially no better off than before. Such a frame of mind brought him into contact with Jack Churchill who was to become the first Duke of Marlborough. "Churchill, for beating an orange wench in the Duke's Playhouse, was challenged by Captain Otway (the poet) and were both wounded, but Churchill most". This pugnacity along with a strong resentment to the general treatment of disbanded troops finally found an outlet in the autumn of 1683 in "The Soldier's Fortune", with Betterton as Beaugard and Mrs. Barry as Lady Dunce.

When the Earl of Rochester died in 1680, he assumed, not unreasonably, that his turn with Elizabeth Barry had come at last. However, Rochester's death only revealed that Elizabeth was also the mistress of Sir George Etherege, who wrote one of the earliest Restoration comedies "The Man of Mode", based on the personality of the Earl of Rochester. Elizabeth, it seemed, preferred her poets to have titles.

Early in 1682 "Venice Preserv'd" was produced for the first time with Mrs. Barry in the lead as Belvidera. It was a huge success; partly due to its bearings on the Popish Plot and because of its portrait of the Earl of Shaftesbury as the kinky old Senator, Antonio. It is the only tragedy of its period to have been played consistently ever since.

On the verge of theatrical and financial prosperity Thomas had a last go with Elizabeth. She promised to meet him in the Mall but, like so many times before in the early years in St. James's Park, she stood him up. He sent her a letter:—

You were pleased to send me word you would meet me in the Mall this evening, and give me further satisfaction in the Matter you were so unkind to charge me with; I was there, but found you not, and therefore beg of you, as you ever would wish yourself to be eased of the highest Torment it were possible for your Nature to be sensible of, to let me see you some time to Morrow, and send me word by this Bearer, where, and at what Hour you will be so just as either to acquit or condemn me; that I may hereafter, for your sake, either bless all your bewitching Sex; or as often as I henceforth think of you, curse Womankind for ever."

Eventually Otway gave up. Desperate want and poverty followed. "The Atheist", a sequel to "The Soldier's Fortune" and his last play, appeared in 1683. He died at the age of thirty-three.

There are many colourful accounts of his death; the most popular, but not necessarily authentic, is that of Theophilis Cibber in Dr. Johnson's "Lives of the Poets". Hiding from his creditors in a pub on Tower Hill, Otway

> "Driven at last to the most grievous necessity, ventured out of his lurking place, almost naked and shivering, and went into a coffee-house on Tower Hill, where he saw a gentleman, of whom he had some knowledge, and of whom he sollicited the loan of a shilling. The gentleman was quite shocked, to see the author of "Venice Preserv'd" begging bread, and compassionately put into his hand a guinea. Mr. Otway, having thanked his benefactor, retired, and changed the guinea to purchase a roll; as his stomach was full of wind from excess of fasting, the first

mouthful choked him and instantaneously put a period to his days."

He is buried in the churchyard of St. Clement Danes.

On King Charles, ascribed to the Earl of Rochester, for which he was banish'd the Court and turn'd Mountebank.

His Scepter and his P— — are of a length,
And she that plays with one may sway the other,
And make him little wiser than his Brother.
I hate all Monarchs and the Thrones they sit on,
From the Hector of France to the Cully of Britain.
Poor Prince, thy P— — like the Buffoons at Court,
It governs thee, because it makes thee sport;
Tho' Safety, Law, Religion, Life lay on't,
'Twill break through all to it's way to C— —.
Restless he rolls about from Whore to Whore,
A merry Monarch, scandalous and poor.

From *Astraea Redux* John Dryden, 1631-1700

Oh Happy Age! Oh times like those alone,
By Fate reserv'd for great Augustus throne!
When the joint growth of Arms and Arts foreshew
The World a Monarch, and that Monarch You.

PLAYS

"Alcibiades" A tragedy, 1675;

"Don Carlos" A tragedy, 1676;

"Titus and Berenice" A tragedy, 1676, adapted from Racine's "Berenice";

"The Cheats of Scapin" Adapted from Moliere's "Les Fourberie de Scapin", 1676;

"Friendship in Fashion" A comedy, 1678;

"Caius Marius" A tragedy, 1679;

"The Orphan" A tragedy, 1680;

"The Soldier's Fortune" A comedy, 1680;

"Venice Preserv'd" A tragedy, 1682;

"The Atheist" or "The Second Part of the Soldier's Fortune", 1683.

John Dennis (1657-1734)
Daniel Defoe (1660-1731)
Matthew Prior (1664-1721)
Jonathan Swift (1667-1745)

DENNIS, JOHN (1657-1734)

Dennis, John (1657-1734), English critic and dramatist, the son of a saddler, was born in London in 1657. He was educated at Harrow School and Caius College, Cambridge, where he took his B.A. degree in 1679. In the next year he was fined and dismissed from his college for having wounded a fellow-student with a sword. He was, however, received at Trinity Hall, where he took his M.A. degree in 1683. After traveling in France and Italy, he settled in London, where he became acquainted with Dryden, Wycherley and others; and being made temporarily independent by inheriting a small fortune, he devoted himself to literature. The duke of Marlborough procured him a place as one of the queen's waiters in the customs with a salary of 20 a year. This he afterwards disposed of for a small sum, retaining, at the suggestion of Lord Halifax, a yearly charge upon it for a long term of years. Neither the poems nor the plays of Dennis are of any account, although one of his tragedies, a violent attack on the French in harmony with popular prejudice, entitled Liberty Asserted, was produced with great success at Lincoln's Inn Fields in 1704. His sense of his own importance approached mania, and he is said to have desired the duke of Marlborough to have a special clause inserted in the treaty of Utrecht to secure him from French vengeance. Marlborough pointed out that although he had been a still greater enemy of the French nation, he had no fear for his own security. This tale and others of a similar nature may well be exaggerations prompted by his enemies, but the infirmities of character and temper indicated in them were real. Dennis is best remembered as a critic, and Isaac D'Israeli, who took a by no means favorable view of Dennis, said that some of his criticisms attain classical rank. The earlier ones, which have nothing of the rancor that afterwards gained him the nickname of " Furius," are the best. They are Remarks. .(1696), on Blackmore's epic of Prince Arthur; Letters upon Several Occasions written by and between Mr Dryden, Mr Wycherley, Mr Moyle, Mr Congreve and Mr Dennis, published by Mr Dennis (1696); two pamphlets in reply to Jeremy Collier's Short View; The Advancement and Reformation of Modern Poetry (1701), perhaps his most important work The Grounds of Criticism in Poetry (1704), in which he argued that the ancients owed their superiority over the moderns in poetry to their religious attitude; an Essay upon Publick Spirit (1711), in which he inveighs against luxury, and servile imitation of foreign fashions and customs; and Essay on the Genius and Writings of Shakespeare in three Letters (1712).

POETIC THEORY OF JOHN DENNIS

The critical writing of John Dennis (1657-1734) participates in the long-standing attempt to appropriate classical aesthetic and philosophical categories in an explicitly Christian framework. His critical project also aims, however, to unite poetry and religion for political ends. His account of poetry is exceptional, in part, because of the ways in which he attempts to base his arguments on a presumed sense of broad political appeal. In offering a poetic theory that purports to unite the aims of Christian religion, imaginative literature, and national politics, Dennis also thus provides a window on what he takes to be the shared assumptions among his English reading public in the early 1700s. In his two main critical works, The Advancement and Reformation of Modern Poetry (1701) and The Grounds of Criticism in Poetry (1704), Dennis argues that the key to English national success is to cultivate an affective poetic synthesis of religious belief that would reform the moral and civic virtue of the nation. Dennis's argument is surprising, however, in its attempt to rehabilitate the term "enthusiasm" by shifting its meaning from a widely used term of abuse toward a positive suggestion of poetic inspiration. At the same time, his broader emphasis upon "passion" as a positive good would make him, through his Romantic readers, one of the most deeply abiding influences upon English culture. The argument here begins by considering the multiple historical contexts upon which Dennis's writings impinge, especially the horizon of expectations that he engages through the term "enthusiasm" and the mixed critical reception of his work. The argument then traces how his appropriation of classical aesthetics, most notably that of Longinus, is shaped by a reductive rationalism whose very effects Dennis aims to overcome. Ultimately, I contend that such a view of reason also determines Dennis's "anti-philosophical" defense of the Christianity. In this way, his quixotic attempt to rehabilitate "enthusiasm" also suggests the extent to which publicly available assumptions at the turn of the eighteenth century could subsume Christianity within an account of modern instrumental rationality.

Dennis's poetic theory thus illuminates the changes in early modern English assumptions about human reason. Understanding the character of such shifts is particularly important for the study of Christianity and imaginative literature. Until there is wider acknowledgement that critical theories, no less than poetic analyses, depend upon presumed historical narratives for their intelligibility, the practice of literary criticism will scarcely move beyond a mere recognition that the deployment of some kind of critical approach is unavoidable. Among the competing master narratives that inform even the least ambitious of postmodern critical theories there is a shared and recurrent two-fold motif regarding Christian faith: the characterization of Christianity as a kind of popular Platonism, and the accompanying reduction of both (Christianity and Platonism) to a species of proto-Enlightenment rationalism in which the use of reason is necessarily a form of coercion. Despite the discrediting of such historical assumptions, they often continue to inform literary analysis and theorizing. The discourse of intersection between Christianity and literature cannot become truly postmodern without the articulation of alternative historical narratives that investigate the rhetorical strategies by which such caricatures came to be presumed. Dennis's writing offers insight into just such an alternative history.

DANIEL DEFOE (1660-1731)

Defoe has the outlook and the style of the plain middleclass Englishman, with a few strong basic religious and social beliefs; in another light he appears as a clever and unscrupulous journalist and propagandist, too clever for his own good; and then at last he appears to be beyond all else a man of genius, the author of one of the world's most famous books. His complex career still baffles biographers at many points; the list of his authenticated works now runs to over four hundred titles, and even this figure does not tell the whole story.

Defoe was the son of a pious dissenting tradesman, James Foe, in the parish of St. Giles Cripplegate. He got a sound practical education at the famous dissenting academy kept at Newington Green by the Reverend Charles Morton, later vice-president of Harvard. His early years were no doubt colored by the austerity, the religious gloom, and the political sufferings of the Dissenters. We know that he fought in Monmouth's rebellion in 1685, and he was always a loyal supporter of the Revolution settlement and William III. He was probably intended for the ministry, but instead went into business. Always a speculator and trader rather than a cautious and thrifty shop-keeper, he was involved in many lawsuits, went bankrupt in 1692, and was saddled with heavy debts. His wide ranging interests appear in his *Essay upon*

Projects (I697), a series of suggestions for improvements and reforms in finance, public works, law, education, and other matters, expressing the new interest in social and economic policy which had begun to appear in such a work as Andrew Yarranton *England's Improvement by Sea and Land* (I677-81).

As a staunch defender of William, Defoe answered a satire by one John Tutchin against the "foreign" king with his famous verses, *The True-Born Englishman* (I701). Who are the mongrel English to complain about being governed by foreigners? He further followed the Whig party line by defending the people's right to petition Parliament (*Legion's Memorial*, 1701), and in *The Mock-Mourners* (I702) he rebuked the Tory partisans who were exulting over William's death. But he wrote with such pungency and dash that he soon got into trouble. The accession of Anne led the extreme Tories to intensify their attacks against Dissent, particularly against the practice of occasional conformity (the taking of communion according to the Anglican form by Dissenters who thereby qualified for public office under the Test Act). Defoe himself denounced the practice, but he also suspected the motives of the Tories who were bringing in a bill against it, and in his famous *The Shortest Way with the Dissenters* (I702) he tried to reduce their position to an absurdity by ironically arguing that Dissent should be extirpated altogether. His irony was at first misunderstood, but soon he felt the full rage of the Tories; he was arrested and sentenced to stand in the pillory, an extremely severe punishment. The Whigs cheered him, but the affair damaged his reputation and, indeed, his character. When he was freed from prison in November 1703, through the somewhat tardy assistance of Robert Harley, he became the secret political agent, of his deliverer. His chief purpose was to keep Whig and dissenting opinion in line for the government. To a certain extent he could rightly disregard party and say that the policy of a moderate Tory like Harley was not far from his own views, but his position was unsound because his secret connection with the government forced him to be evasive and untruthful.

Single handed he went on to write the *Review* (I704-13), one of the most important journals of the day, notable not only for Defoe's political writing but for his sound discussions of business and trade, and of some importance also for the development of the essay-periodical. Much of Defoe's work was done in the form of anonymous pamphlets which cannot always be identified with certainty. As an agent for Harley, he resided for some time in Scotland and had a part in the complicated moves which preceded the union of England and Scotland (I707). When Harley resigned in 1708 Defoe continued to work for the minister Godolphin, and when the Tories came to power in 1710 he went back to work for Harley. Both master and man were compromisers or "trimmers," but Defoe was at least sincere in his support of the Hanoverian succession. Ironical pamphlets against the Jacobites (A *Seasonable Warning,* 1712; *Reasons against the Succession of the House of Hanover,* 1713; *And What if the Pretender Should Come?,* 1713; *What if the Queen Should Die?,* 1713) got him into trouble and into jail again. At the accession of George I Defoe turned his hand to secret work for the new Whig ministry; his devious course cannot be fully followed, but he evidently took government pay for collaborating as editor on Tory journals (*Mist's Journal* and others) with the secret intention of toning down their attacks so as to make them ineffective.

Though his journalistic work continued in the 1720's, his interests now turned in a different direction. In five years (I719-1724) he proceeded to earn for himself a key position in the history of European fiction. The beginnings of his work in prose fiction are obscure; his characteristic interest in specific detail and his plain objective style counted for much. As early as *The Apparition of Mrs. Veal* (I706) his power of manipulating detail had appeared; this famous narrative is not a fabrication of Defoe's, but the effective presentation of a received report. Another important component of his fiction was his didactic purpose, the heavy vein of Puritan middle-class moralizing which appeared in his *Family Instructor* (I715; 1718) and *Religious Courtship* (I722). A familiar form of popular literature at the time was the biographical narrative, whether of the criminal, the adventurer, the traveler, or all these at once. Defoe makes a composite of autobiographical detail, that is, detail said to have been experienced or observed at first hand, for the ostensible purpose of offering useful examples and inculcating morals and warnings. Such a formula covers all his prose fiction— *Robinson Crusoe* (I, II, 1719; III, 1720), *Memoirs of a Cavalier* (1720), *Captain Singleton* (1720), *Moll Flanders* (1722), *Journal of the Plague Year* (1722), *Colonel Jack* (1722), *Roxana* (1724). At the time this amazing series of works was considered popular trash for the humble and the semi-literate. Several were of topical interest: thus Crusoe connects with the recent rescue of Alexander Selkirk, the *Plague Year* with the plague scare of 1720, and *Singleton* with African exploration and piracy. All of them keep to the plain, canny, factual tone, and yet range widely from the piety of Crusoe to the scandalous career of Moll Flanders, and from the familiar life of the London streets to adventure in the heart of Africa or on the high seas. Defoe's travel-and-adventure formula is regularly applied to unscrupulous or vicious people, and owes something to the picaresque, the literature of roguery. But Defoe radically alters picaresque fiction and criminal biography by his sobriety of tone, his middle-class practicality, and his insistence on ways and means and bargains. Whether the story is of low life, or deals, as in *Roxana*, with aristocratic vice, the central characters nonetheless show thrift and moderation, and a certain degree of humane feeling; Defoe's assumed attitude always is that crime, trickery, greed, and recklessness do not pay, however interesting the details may be.

Apparently without realizing the value of his stories, Defoe turned away from this kind of work. *A General History of the Pirates* (1724; enlarged 1726), which has been attributed to him with virtual certainty by Professor John Robert Moore, shows the interest in sea adventure which lies back of some of his fiction; and another probable attribution is *Memoirs of Captain Carleton* (1728). His interest in economics appears in his remarkable *Tour thro' Great Britain* (1724-27), his *Complete English Tradesman* (1725-27), and *Plan of the English Commerce* (1728); his curious interest in the occult in his works *On the*

History and Reality of Apparitions, Political History of the Devil, and *History of Magic;* his abiding zeal for projects and municipal improvements in *Augusta Triumphans.* One of Defoe's chief merits is his firm grasp of social and economic problems, based on sound and careful observation. Here he rose superior to the polite Augustans who despised him. During the last months of his life he evidently went into hiding to escape a creditor; he died in 1731, and was buried in Bunhill Fields.

ROBINSON CRUSOE

This is one of the most famous books in the world, and has been read in innumerable languages by millions of people who never heard of Defoe. Part I gives the island story, Part II Crusoe's further travels in the Orient and Russia, and Part III is merely a collection of devotional and moral essays. The title-page suggests that the island story was from the beginning, as it has remained, the absorbing center of interest. The theme of shipwreck on a desert island was already familiar, and the case of Alexander Selkirk's solitary life on Juan Fernandez had just attracted attention. Many of the details were assembled from travel books. The unparalleled success of the story is due to the complete harmony between Defoe's point of view, the island story itself, and the basic interests of humanity. On the island Defoe's utilitarianism can cover the whole field-his interest in how man manipulates things and gets along as best he can. Defoe does not simply accumulate details for their own sake; though often prolix and trivial, they are such as the central character would be interested in noting under the circumstances. Thus in *Crusoe* we get back to a situation in which the ordinary physical details of life take on a renewed and dramatic significance. At the same time Crusoe's life is not primitive; civilization gives him his ideas and standards as well as the material he salvaged from the wreck; he is man against nature, but he is also a British settler making his way, and also, in thought and action, a plain middle class dissenter. His is a record of progress, a success story couched in universally intelligible terms.

MATTHEW PRIOR (1664-1721)

Prior was known to his contemporaries as an office-holder and diplomat and as an associate of the Tory wits. He is remembered now for some charming light verse. His poetic skill has on the whole been undervalued, though we may not feel that it deserves the elaborate monument which was set up for him in the Poets' Corner in Westminster Abbey. He came of a humble Dorsetshire family, but was born and brought up in London. As a boy he worked in his uncle's tavern, and here, so the story goes, the Earl of Dorset found him reading Horace and sent him to Westminster School. He proceeded to St. John's College, Cambridge. With his school friend Charles Montagu, later Earl of Halifax, he wrote a clever attack on Dryden, *The Hind and the Panther Transversed* (1687). From 1690 he was secretary of the English legation at The Hague, and took part in the negotiations leading to the Peace of Ryswick (I697). He sought political patronage wherever it could be found, and courted Marlborough rather unsuccessfully. In 1710 he was an associate of Harley, St. John, and Swift in the Tory "Brothers." As a diplomat he specialized in French affairs, and did important work in Paris preliminary to the Peace of Utrecht in 1713. After the accession of George I, Prior was arrested and severely examined while the Whigs were trying to get evidence against his superior Harley. He was now out of office and in financial straits. His occasional and scattered verses had been collected in 1709, but now his influential friends arranged for the publication by subscription of his *Poems on Several Occasions*, a sumptuous folio which appeared in 1719 (dated 1718). He made much money by this project and lived out his Epicurean life comfortably, enjoying the friendship of the Earl of Oxford to the last.

In the Preface to the poems of 1709 Prior describes the contents as "amorous odes, serious reflections, or idle tales, the product of his leisure hours, who had business enough upon his hands, and was only a poet by accident." Among "serious reflections" he would later include the heavy didactic poem *Solomon*, and perhaps *Alma*, a piece of rather flippant philosophizing in Hudibrastic couplets, inspired by the skepticism of Montaigne. His "idle tales," such as *An English Padlock* and *Hans Carvel*, are witty and sometimes coarse. The once admired *Henry* and *Emma*, an artificial paraphrase of the sixteenth-century *Nut-Brown Maid*, now fails to please. His "amorous odes" have the imagery of Anacreontic verse (flames, myrtles, Cupid and his bow, Venus and her doves), but this highly conventional mode is skilfully transformed into familiar verse of high quality. Prior is one of the most successful English adapters of the Horatian style, and thus he celebrates his light amours with Cloe (perhaps Anne Durham) and her jealousy of Lisetta (perhaps Elizabeth Cox). The result is often a subtle or playful burlesque of lyric forms. Prior's adroit versification appears in his octosyllabic couplets, adapted from Butler, and also in some highly original pieces in long anapestic lines—*Lines Written at the Hague in 1696, Down Hall* (I723), and the epitaph, not published until 1907, called Jinny the Just. Prior's triviality should not lead us to overlook his versatile talent and the distinctive personal quality of his best work.

JONATHAN SWIFT (1667-1745)

Jonathan Swift was born on November 30, 1667 in Dublin, Ireland, the son of Protestant Anglo-Irish parents: his ancestors had been Royalists, and all his life he would be a High-Churchman. His father, also Jonathan, died a few months before he was born, upon which his mother, Abigail, returned to England, leaving her son behind, in the care of relatives. In 1673, at the age of six, Swift began his education at Kilkenny Grammar School, which was, at the time, the best in Ireland. Between 1682 and 1686 he attended, and graduated from, Trinity College in Dublin, though he was not, apparently, an exemplary student.

In 1688 William of Orange invaded England, initiating the Glorious Revolution: with Dublin in political turmoil, Trinity College was closed, and an ambitious Swift took the opportunity to go to England, where he hoped to gain preferment in the Anglican Church. In England, in 1689, he became secretary to Sir William Temple, a diplomat and man of letters, at Moor Park in Surrey. There Swift read extensively in his patron's library, and met Esther Johnson, who would become his "Stella," and it was there, too, that he began to suffer from Meniere's Disease, a disturbance of the inner ear which produces nausea and vertigo, and which was little understood in Swift's day. In 1690, at the advice of his doctors, Swift returned to Ireland, but the following year he was back with Temple in England. He visited Oxford in 1691: in 1692, with Temple's assistance, he received an M. A. degree from that University, and published his first poem: on reading it, John Dryden, a distant relation, is said to have remarked "Cousin Swift, you will never be a poet."

In 1694, still anxious to advance himself within the Church of England, he left Temple's household and returned to Ireland to take holy orders. In 1695 he was ordained as a priest in the Church of Ireland, the Irish branch of the Anglican Church, and the following year he returned to Temple and Moor Park.

He was proud, sensitive, and discontented, though we must not exaggerate his unhappiness in these early years. Temple initiated him in scholarship and literature, and gave him the distrust of pedantry, scholastic and scientific, expressed in *A Tale of a Tub and The Battleof the Books* of the Books, though the powerful satire is, of course, Swift's own. He was not happy or at ease because he had more than the conventional satirist's scorn of human folly, and because, dependent on favor from the great like other young men in humble place, he was ambitious for power. Temple did not get great things for him; after he took holy orders in 1694, he held the Prebend of Kilroot in Ireland, and later had other unimportant Irish livings and was Chaplain and Secretary to Lord Berkeley (I699). It was during the Moor Park period that he formed his lifelong attachment to Esther or Hester Johnson, known as "Stella." Whether he married her or not—scholars still debate the question—she meant more to him than any other, human being.

Swift's genius thus matured in semi-retirement in the 1690's; during the reign of Queen Anne he entered English politics, spending much time in London and forming friendships with literary and political leaders, notably Addison and Steele. He sided with the Whigs (A *Discourse of the Contests and Dissensions in Athens and Rome,* 1701), but was largely interested in defending the prerogatives of the Church, as in the brilliantly ironical *Argument Against Abolishing Christianity* (written 1708, published 1711), *Sentiments of a Church of England Man* (I708), *A Project for the Advancement of Religion and the Reformation of Manners* (I709) He vehemently opposed deists, Dissenters, and Whigs who wanted to repeal the Test Act. In lighter vein was his humorous campaign against the astrological quack Partridge, whose death he predicted and duly described in spite of the protests of his victim. Here Swift first used the famous pen name "Isaac Bickerstaff."

Swift went over to the Tory government of 1710, and soon became their principal writer, editing the *Examiner* (I710-11) and arguing against the continuance of the war in one of his most powerful anti influential pamphlets, *TheConduct of the Allies* Conduct of the Allies (I711, dated 1712). The famous *Journal to Stella* (written 1710-13, published 1765), set down day by day in playful, even childish style for Stella and her companion Rebecca Dingley in Ireland, gives a minute record of the time when Swift felt himself to be at the height of his political power in London. Politics colored his lit erary friendships; he felt that he was partly estranged from Addison, and he became a bitter opponent of Steele, whom he attacked in *The Importance of the Guardian Considered* (I713) and *The Public Spirit of the Whigs* (I714). The formation of Tory clubs at this time shows shifting personal relationships: Swift belonged to the Saturday Club, which centered about Harley, and to the Brothers, often called by Swift "our Society," founded by Bolingbroke in opposition to the Whig Kit-Cats. He drew closer to Pope, and was admitted to the Scriblerus Club, including, besides Swift and Pope, Gay, Parnell, and Arbuthnot. Scriblerus represented the best Tory genius of the time, but did not engage as a club in politics; its literary pastimes were directed against pedantry, always a favorite target, and eventually had some connection with *Gulliver* and the *Dunciad*. As to politics, Swift was not in Harley's complete confidence, nor did he ever abandon his attitude of proud independence, hard though he labored for the Tory cause. The Tories did not seem to be much more anxious to reward him than the Whigs had been; he did not get the bishopric he wanted, only an appointment as Dean of St. Patrick's Cathedral, Dublin, where he was inducted in June, 1713.

After the collapse of Tory hopes at Queen Anne's death in 1714, Swift made Dublin his permanent residence. He was embittered and disappointed, and to some extent thrown back upon himself and a small circle of Irish intimates. His strange friendship or love affair with Hester Vanhomrigh, who had followed him from London to Dublin—an affair marked by ardent love on her side and puzzling aloofness on his—complicated his private life and came to some sort of crisis before her death in 1723. The poem *Cadenus and Vanessa* (begun about 1713, published 1726) records this relationship. At times he turned his energy to mature and intense writings—Gulliver in the early 1720's, important poems in the early 1730's; these are creative periods scarcely second to the early months of inspiration which had produced *A Tale of a Tub* and *The Battle of the Books*. Swift did his best work in a state of irritated semi-detachment rather than in the depths of savage despair. His power also appears in his brilliant correspondence with such friends as Pope and Bolingbroke. In the political field he conducted a fierce and effective opposition to the policies of the English government in Ireland, and here his achievements surpass anything he did n the last years of Queen Anne. His first loyalty was to the Anglican Church in Ireland, his chief hostility to the Irish Presbyterians; he was far from being in complete sympathy with the oppressed Irish Catholics. Yet his interest in Irish social and economic problems and his indignation at the exploitation of Ireland by the English made him in a sense the spokesman for the whole nation, as in his

Proposal for the Universal Use of Irish Manufactures (1720), in his *Modest Proposal* (1729), with its bitterly ironical suggestion that the children of the Irish poor be used for food, and in the famous *Drapier's Letters* (1724-25), the principal part of a brilliant campaign against the English government's issuance of a patent for a new copper coinage in Ireland. Swift rose to heights of indignation about the inferior currency with which the patentee Wood might flood the country. The excitement was rather artificial, but Swift won the fight and became a national hero. The Dublin populace kindled bonfires on the birthday of the misanthropic Dean.

During visits to England in 1726 and 1727 he renewed his friendships and saw to the publication of Gulliver. After the death of Stella in 1728 his life became more and more lonely, and he suffered from serious attacks of giddiness and deafness, "that old vertigo in my head." He continued to develop his vein of playfulness in verse and prose, notably in the marvellous record of inane everyday talk called *A Complete Collection of Genteel and Ingenious Conversation* (1738). In his latest years he sank into utter gloom and despair. He was declared insane in 1742 and died in 1745. But we must not fix our attention too exclusively on the final tragedy.

Swift always asserted that the good life was the life of reason, by which he meant a life controlled not by hard and (daring thought but by plain common sense. Man's failure to realize this moderate ideal is due to his passions, his unbridled desire for sensual power, pleasure, and success, and worst of all his senseless pride. He has enough reason to see that he is wrong, but does he has enough reason to improve himself? Is he always the dupe of pride and passion? This is the familiar issue raised by Shaftesbury and Mandeville, and by Pope *Essay on Man*. Does Swift despair of mankind altogether, or does he hope that his satire will correct as well as castigate? Of course, like all satirists, he professes to correct. But when we say this we miss something characteristic of Swift, the unmatched intensity with which he attacks the actual ways of mankind. His most famous strokes seem to step up the attack so as to include all human activities. In the *"Digression on Madness"* in *A Tale of a Tub,* happiness is the perpetual pleasure "of being well deceived," human action is based on illusion, to live is to play the lunatic. This is a vision of a world without reason. An ambiguity remains: Is this man as such, or man at his worst? In the fourth voyage of Gulliver, the Yahoos represent the irrational or animal side of man, but Gulliver, not necessarily Swift, identifies them with humanity, and sets them below well-conducted animals, the horses of Houyhnhnmland, who make a reasonable and normal use of their natural powers and thus attain "the perfection of nature." The theme is echoed in the poem called *The Beasts' Confession.*

A famous passage in a letter to Pope, September 29, 1725, connects Gulliver with Swift's general satiric purpose:

The chief end I propose to myself in all my labours is to vex the world rather than divert it, and if I could compass that design without hurting my own person or fortune, I would be the most indefatigable writer you have ever seen. . . . When you think of the world give it one lash the more at my request. I have ever hated all nations, professions, and communities, and all my love is toward individuals; for instance, I hate the tribe of lawyers, but I love Counseller Such-a-one and Judge Such-a-one; so with physicians—I will not speak of my own trade—soldiers, English, Scotch, French, and the rest. But principally I hate and detest that animal called man, although I heartily love John, Peter, Thomas, and so forth. This is the system upon which I have governed myself many years, but do not tell, and so I shall go on till I have done with them. I have got materials toward a treatise proving the falsity of that definition animal rationale, and to show it would be only rationis capax [capable of reason]. Upon this great foundation of misanthropy, though not in Timon's manner, the whole building of my Travels is erected; and I never will have peace of mind, till all honest men are of my opinion.

Man is then capable of reason, and there are honest men, but human life in general, particularly collective action and the working of institutions, justifies a realistic misanthropy. This covers Swift's attitude pretty well, though it does not account for his disgust at the human body and the ferocity of his attack. Swift was after all committed to a party and a church, and was a reformer and a laborer in public causes. This is the comparatively genial view we get in the *Verses on the Death of Doctor Swift* (written 1731, published 1739), lines which every student should compare with the fourth voyage of Gulliver, though the exact truth about Swift is not to be found in either place. It is hard to get a balanced estimate of Swift because his attack on unreason has much greater force than his fence of reason.

While Swift's verse is secondary to his prose, it has been underestimated, possibiy because of the notoriety of a few coarse pieces. In general he works with the octosyllabic couplet of Butler and Prior, and attains memorable plainness and point. Of all eighteenth-century writers he is most hostile to the romantic imagination (*Of Poetry – A Rhapsody*), but this does not keep him from exercising his remarkable powers of statement in verse. His style always conforms to his own standard of simplicity; his prose and verse both keep clear of rhetorical ornament and are intensified by humor and scorn.

A TALE OF A TUB

This first masterpiece is Swift's most exuberant, resourceful, and brilliant work. It was probably written in 1696 and 1697, with additions made in and after 1698, but not published until 1704. The tale itself is a simple parable of a father who leaves coats to three sons, Peter (the Catholic Church), Martin (the Church of England), and Jack (the Dissenters). They change their coats to follow the fashion, finding in their father's will pretexts for everything they do. Peter becomes arrogant and denounces ferociously those who will not accept his dogmas; Jack in a frenzy of reformation tears his coat to tatters and views his father's will with superstitious reverence. Swift's purpose was to defend the

Church of England, but it seemed to many readers that his caricature of ritual and dogma was irreverent. The allegory of the coats suggests Selden's sardonic remark in his *Table Talk* (1689): "Religion is like the fashion; one man wears his doublet slashed, another laced, another plain, but every man has a doublet. So every man has his religion. We differ about trimming."

The Digressions in the *Tale* are brilliant and ingenious burlesques on the absurdities of learning and literature-the vanity of authors, the labor of scholars, the pretensions of critics. Swift's method is to provide grotesque and ignoble physical symbols for the abstract and the spiritual: the pulpit is a wooden device which elevates the preacher, and stands for claims to learning and inspiration; inspiration itself is so much wind. The coats of Peter, Martin, and Jack, the judge's wig, the soldier's uniform, are identified with the institutions and callings they represent. In the same way the process of earning a college degree might be represented as a long period of sitting in uncomfortable chairs for the sake of wearing a cap and gown and getting a piece of parchment. The method is that of Butler *Hu dibras* dibras. The hollow symbols are then taken to be the only reality, and it follows that men spend their lives in pursuit of meaningless shams. This leads to the culminating "Digression on Madness." It should be remembered, however, that Swift here presents, not the universe as seen by a philosopher, but the side of human life which the satirist sees.

Closely related is *The Battle of the Books* (written about 1698, published 1704), Swift's contribution to the famous controversy between the Ancients and the Moderns. Temple had been drawn into this dispute on the side of the Ancients, and Wotton and Bentley were on the other side. Swift, without making any direct contribution to the controversy, represents the two factions joining battle in St. James's Library, and thus presents another satire on literary pretensions and pedantry by a skilful application of the formula of the mock-epic.

GULLIVER'S TRAVELS

Gulliver probably originated in the projects of the Scriblerus Club, particularly in burlesque of travel literature and satire of scientific pedantry. The four parts were substantially written between 1721 and 1725 and published in 1726. The countries Gulliver visits are situated in parts of the Pacific imperfectly known at that time; the South Pacific region of the first and fourth voyages and the North Pacific area of the second were not really put on the map until the second half of the century. *Gulliver* belongs to the familiar type of the imaginary voyage, but instead of a mere recital of travelers' wonders, Swift made it a plain chronicle which is at the same time a sweeping satirical estimate of human nature and society. The first part, Gulliver's sojourn among the tiny Lilliputians, offers an elaborate political allegory, reflecting in some detail the experiences of Swift's fellow Tories at the end of Queen Anne's reign, and also Swift's hostile attitude toward the government of George I; man is here shown in his political pretensions, which carry him from mere selfishness and triviality to bitter malevolence and heartless intrigue. Among the giant Brobdingnagians Gulliver finds magnified the physical grossness of man, but he also finds an admirably simple state superior to the European system. The political satire is centered in Gulliver's professed defense of Euoropean civilization against the criticisms of the king of Brobdingnag. Throughout the first two voyages, and especially in the first, Swift's ingenuity and humor have free play, and make the first half of this powerful satire a universally known children's book. The fourth voyage, to the land of the Houyhnhnms, was written next, and finally the voyage to Laputa and other countries which was published as the third. This is a somewhat scattering satire on the follies of science and scholarship, of economists and projectors ("promoters"). The scorn for speculation is characteristic of Swift, and continues the theme of A Tale of a Tub. There are also many allusions to public affairs of the 1720's, especially to Wood's halfpence. But the third voyage lacks the effective unity which the others gain from a simple central action.

Gulliver is here a passive obesrver, not an active participant. The climax of the voyages, though not Swift's last word on human life, comes in the famous visit to the land of the reasonable horses, the Houyhnhnms, who live a simple sensible life in sharp contrast to the ape-like Yahoos, filthy and degraded creatures with whom Gulliver must reluctantly admit kinship. The misanthropy of this narrative has been discussed above. Gulliver is progressively disillusioned: in the first voyage he discovers social and political malice; in the second, man's full measure of cruelty and wickedness; in the third, the emptiness of the life of the mind; in the fourth, the repulsive effect of man's failure to attain his status as a rational animal—man as a signal illustration of the truth that the corruption of the best is the worst. It is important to remember that Gulliver is not the whole of Swift; he represents only one aspect of a complex personality; but it is a mistake to separate the two completely, to say that Swift has no share in Gulliver's final disgust and bitterness and that he is moved only by reasonable (desire for political and moral reform. There is a utopian element in *Gulliver*—the chapter on education in Lilliput, the peacefulness and simplicity of the Brobdingnagians, and the "horse sense" of the Houyhnhnms; but Swift's ideals, his orthodox views of Church and State and his admiration of colorless good sense, lack the emotional, intellectual, and imaginative power of his satire.

SWIFT'S WORKS

Essays, Tracts, Pamphlets, Periodicals

- A Meditation upon a Broomstick (1703-1710)
- A Tritical Essay upon the Faculties of the Mind (1707-1711)
- The Bickerstaff-Partridge Papers (1708-1709)
- An Argument against Abolishing Christianity (1708-1711)
- *The Intelligencer* (with Thomas Sheridan) (1710-)
- *The Examiner* (1710)

- A Proposal for Correcting, Improving and Ascertaining the English Tongue(1712)
- On the Conduct of the Allies" (1713)
- Hints Toward an Essay on Conversation (1713)
- A Letter to a Young Gentleman, Lately Entered into Holy Orders (1720)
- A Letter of Advice to a Young Poet (1721)
- *The Drapier's Letters* (1724, 1725)
- An Essay on the Fates of Clergymen
- A Treatise on Good Manners and Good Breeding
- On the Death of Esther Johnson
- An Essay On Modern Education

Poems

- "Baucis and Philemon" (1706-1709)
- "A Description of the Morning" (1709)
- "A Description of a City Shower" (1710)
- "Cadenus and Vanessa" (1713)
- "Phillis, or, the Progress of Love" (1719)
- "The Progress of Beauty" (1719-1720)
- "The Progress of Poetry" (1720)
- "A Satirical Elegy on the Death of a Late Famous General" (1722)
- "To Quilca, a Country House not in Good Repair" (1725)
- "Advice to the Grub Street Verse-writers" (1726)
- "The Furniture of a Woman's Mind" (1727)
- "On a Very Old Glass" (1728)
- "A Pastoral Dialogue" (1729)
- "The Grand Question debated Whether Hamilton's Bawn should be turned into a Barrack or a Malt House" (1729)

- "On Stephen Duck, the Thresher and Favourite Poet" (1730)
- "Death and Daphne" (1730)
- "The Place of the Damn'd" (1731)
- "A Beautiful Young Nymph Going to Bed" (1731)
- "Strephon and Chloe" (1731)
- "Helter Skelter" (1731)
- "Cassinus and Peter: A Tragical Elegy" (1731)
- "The Day of Judgment" (1731)
- "Verses on the Death of Dr. Swift, D.S.P.D." (1731-1732)
- "An Epistle To A Lady" (1732)
- "The Beasts' Confession to the Priest" (1732)
- "The Lady's Dressing Room" (1732)
- "On Poetry: A Rhapsody" (1733)
- "The Puppet Show"
- "The Logicians Refuted"

Sermons, Prayers

- Three Sermons and Three Prayers.
- Three Sermons: I. on mutual subjection. II. on conscience. III. on the trinity.
- Writings on Religion and the Church.

Miscellaneous

- *Directions to Servants* (1731)
- *A Complete Collection of Genteel and Ingenious Conversation* (1731)
- "Thoughts on Various Subjects."
- Historical Writings
- Swift Quotations

Joseph Addison (1672-1719) Richard Steele (1672-1729) Edward Young (1683-1765) John Gay (1685-1732)

JOSEPH ADDISON (1672-1719)

Joseph Addison (May 1, 1672 - June 17, 1719) was an English politician and writer. His name is usually remembered alongside that of his long-standing friend, Richard Steele, with whom he founded *The Spectator* magazine.

LIFE AND WRITING

Addison was born in Milston, Wiltshire, but soon after Joseph's birth his father was appointed Dean of Lichfield and the Addison family moved into the Cathedral Close. He was educated at Lichfield Grammar School and Charterhouse School, where he first met Steele, and at Queen's College, Oxford. He excelled in classics, being specially noted for his Latin verse, and became a Fellow of Magdalen. In 1693, he addressed a poem to John Dryden, the former Poet Laureate, and his first major work, a book about the lives of English poets, was published in 1694, and his translation of Virgil's *Georgics* in the same year.

Such first attempts in English verse were so successful as to obtain for him the friendship and interest of Dryden, and of Lord Somers, by whose means he received, in 1699, a pension of £300 to enable him to travel widely in Europe the continent with a view to diplomatic employment, all the time writing and studying politics. Hearing of the death of William III., an event which lost him his pension, he returned to England in the end of 1703. For a short time his circumstances were somewhat straitened, but the battle of Blenheim in 1704 gave him a fresh opportunity of distinguishing himself. The government wished the event commemorated by a poem; Addison was commissioned to write this, and produced *The Campaign*, which gave such satisfaction that he was forthwith appointed a Commissioner of Appeals in the government of Halifax. His next literary venture was an account of his travels in Italy, which was followed by the opera of *Rosamund*. In 1705, the Whigs having obtained the ascendancy, Addison was made Under-Secretary of State and accompanied Halifax on a mission to Hanover. In 1708 he became MP for Malmesbury in his home county of Wiltshire, and was shortly afterwards appointed as Chief Secretary for Ireland and Keeper of the Records of that country. He encountered Jonathan Swift in Ireland, and remained there for a year. Subsequently, he helped found the Kitcat Club, and renewed his association with Steele. In 1709 Steele began to bring out the *Tatler*, to which Addison became almost immediately a contributor: thereafter he (with Steele) started *The Spectator*, the first number of which appeared on March 1, 1711. This paper, which at first appeared daily, was kept up (with a break of about a year and a half when *the Guardian* took its place) until December 20, 1714. In 1713 the drama of *Cato* appeared, and was received with acclamation by both Whigs and Tories, and was followed by the comedy of the *Drummer*. His last undertaking was *The Freeholder*, a party paper (1715-16).

The later events in the life of Addison did not contribute to his happiness. In 1716, he married the Dowager Countess of Warwick to whose son he had been tutor, and his political career continued to flourish, as he served Secretary of State for the Southern Department from 1717 to 1718. However, his political newspaper, *The Freeholder*, was much criticized, and Alexander Pope was among those who made him an object of derision, christening him "Atticus". His wife appears to have been arrogant and imperious; his stepson the Earl was a rake and unfriendly to him; while in his public capacity his invincible shyness made him of little use in Parliament. He eventually fell out with Steele over the Peerage Bill of 1719. In 1718, Addison was forced to resign as secretary of state because of his poor health, but remained an MP until his death at Holland House, June 17, 1719, in his 48th year, and was buried in Westminster Abbey.

Besides the works above mentioned, he wrote a *Dialogue on Medals*, and left unfinished a work on the *Evidences of Christianity*. The character of Addison, if somewhat cool and unimpassioned, was pure, magnanimous, and kind. The charm of his manners and conversation made him one of the most popular and admired men of his day; and while he laid his friends under obligations for substantial favours, he showed the greatest forbearance towards his few enemies. His style in his essays is remarkable for its ease, clearness, and grace, and for an inimitable and sunny humour which never soils and never hurts. The motive power of these writings has been called "an enthusiasm for conduct." Their effect was to raise the whole standard of manners and expression both in life and in literature. The only flaw in his character was a tendency to convivial excess, which must be judged in view of the laxer manners of his time. When allowance has been made for this, he remains one of the most admirable characters and writers in English literature.

CATO

In 1712, Addison wrote his most famous work of fiction, a play entitled *Cato, a Tragedy*. Based on the last days of

Marcus Porcius Cato Uticensis, it deals with, inter alia, such themes as individual liberty vs. government tyranny, Republicanism vs. Monarchism, logic vs. emotion and Cato's personal struggle to cleave to his beliefs in the face of death.

The play was a success throughout England and her possessions in the New World, as well as Ireland. It continued to grow in popularity, especially in the American colonies, for several generations. Indeed, it was almost certainly a literary inspiration for the American Revolution, being well known to many of the Founding Fathers. In fact, George Washington, had it performed for the Continental Army while they were encamped at Valley Forge.

Though the play has fallen considerably from popularity and is now rarely performed, it remains a favorite source of inspiration (and quotations) for proponents of individual rights, free markets, and libertarian values generally. For example, John Trenchard and Thomas Gordon were inspired by the play to write a series of essays on classical liberalism and individual rights, using the name "Cato."

The action of the play involves the forces of Cato at Utica, awaiting the arrival of Caesar just after Caesar's victory at Thapsus (46 B.C.). The noble sons of Cato, Portius and Marcus, are both in love with Lucia, the daughter of Lucius, a senatorial ally of Cato. Juba, prince of Numidia, another fighting on Cato's side, loves Cato's daughter Marcia. Meanwhile, Sempronius, another senator, and Syphax, general of the Numidians, are conspiring secretly against Cato, hoping to draw off the Numidian army from supporting him. In the final act, Cato commits suicide, leaving his supporters to make their peace with the approaching Caesar—an easier task after Cato's death, since he has been Caesar's most implacable foe.

RICHARD STEELE (1672-1729)

Though Addison and Steele are inseparably connected in life and literature, they exhibit wide personal differences. We are sometimes tempted to think that all the Augustan worthies look alike in their periwigs, but Steele's broad good-natured features are in obvious contrast to the conventional oval face of Addison. Steele was born in Dublin; his father was English, his mother possibly Irish. At any rate he shows an impulsiveness and warmth which we may fairly call Irish, and these traits give a touch of pathos and charm to some of his best writing. Thus his personality and work remind us at times of another Anglo-Irishman, Oliver Goldsmith. Steele was educated in London at the Charterhouse, where his lifelong friendship with Addison began. He proceeded to Oxford, being a member first of Christ Church and then of Merton College. Instead of taking a degree, however, he entered the army, where he spent several obscure years as ensign (lieutenant) in one regiment and captain in another. Soon he had also entered into the literary life of the town and was known as a member of the group at Will's. He was probably extravagant and dissipated, though we need not magnify his sins.

His first important publication combines didactic purpose with a naïve personal touch. He had been forced, against his conscience, to fight a duel; and in general he found it hard to be a Christian and a soldier at the same time, so he wrote *The Christian Hero* (I701), "with a design," he tells us, "to fix upon his own mind a strong impression of virtue and religion, in opposition to a stronger propensity towards unwarrantable pleasures." Socially this is a step in the post-Restoration "reformation of manners"; philosophically the tract sets Christian piety above the ideal of pagan and stoical virtue exalted by the admirers of classical antiquity. Steele's early plays, *The Funeral* (I701), *The Lying Lover* (I703), and *The Tender Husband* (I705) illustrate more clearly than those of his contemporary Cibber the movement toward reform of the English stage by avoidance of gross indecency, by the use of gentler and more playful ridicule, and by an appeal to the tender emotions. Steele's interest in the theater was lifelong, but he was soon absorbed in politics. He was always a staunch supporter of Marlborough and the Godolphin ministry, and under that government he held the position of gazeteer (editor of the official newspaper). In 1707 he married Mary Scurlock , the "Prue" to whom he addressed the famous letters which help to confirm the impression that he was always in trouble, involved in debt and given to the careless life of the tavern.

The fall of the Whigs in 1710 put a strain on his relations with Swift. He never withdrew from party strife, but the *Tatler* was largely non-partisan, the *Spectator* almost completely so. It is significant that the success of these two papers came when Steele and Addison were out of office during the Tory régime. Steele had a main hand in several other periodicals, but usually with some controversial purpose. Of these the most important was the *Guardian,* which had many of the qualities of the *Spectator* but took the Whig side and came into conflict with Swift and the *Examiner.* For a political pamphlet called The Crisis the Tories expelled Steele from the House of Commons, though he rightly declared that all he had done was to assert his devotion to the principles of 1688 and his opposition to the Jacobite cause. With the accession of George I and the Whig triumph, Steele was once more in favor; he was knighted, resumed his seat in Parliament, and was given among other things a share in the patent of Drury Lane Theater. Theatrical business complicated Steele's finances and got him into trouble with the Duke of Newcastle, the Lord Chamberlain, who tried to punish him by suspending his patent. In 1722 Steele produced his most successful play, *The Conscious Lovers,* a more markedly sentimental piece than his early plays and one of the most characteristic and influential dramas of the century. Meanwhile he had become partly estranged from Addison for political reasons, but after the death of the latter in 1719 Steele paid generous tribute to his memory and convincingly showed the sincerity of his friendship. His health broke in 1723, and he spent the last six years of his life as a semi-invalid in retirement in Wales.

EDWARD YOUNG (1683-1765)

EDWARD YOUNG was born at Upham, near Winchester, in June, 1681. He was the son of Edward Young, at that time Fellow of Winchester College and Rector of Upham, who was the son of Jo. Young of Woodhay in Berkshire, styled by Wood gentleman. In September, 1682, the Poet's father was collated to the prebend of Gillingham Minor, in the church of Sarum, by bishop Ward. When Ward's faculties were impaired by age his duties were necessarily performed by others. We learn from Wood that, at a visitation of Sprat's, July the 12th, 1686, the Prebendary preached a Latin sermon, afterwards published, with which the Bishop was so pleased that he told the Chapter he was concerned to find the preacher had one of the worst prebends in their church. Some time after this, in consequence of his merit and reputation, or of the interest of Lord Bradford, to whom, in 1702, he dedicated two volumes of sermons, he was appointed chaplain to King William and Queen Mary, and preferred to the deanery of Sarum. Jacob, who wrote in 1720, says "he was chaplain and clerk of the closet to the late Queen, who honoured him by standing godmother to the Poet." His fellowship of Winchester he resigned in favour of a Mr. Harris, who married his only daughter. The Dean died at Sarum, after a short illness, in 1705, in the sixty-third year of his age. On the Sunday after his decease Bishop Burnet preached at the cathedral, and began his sermon with saying, "Death has been of late walking round us, and making breach upon breach upon us, and has now carried away the head of this body with a stroke; so that he whom you saw a week ago distributing the holy mysteries is now laid in the dust. But he still lives in the many excellent directions he has left us, both how to live and how to die."

'The Dean placed his son upon the foundation of Winchester College, where he had himself been educated. At this school Edward Young remained till the election after his eighteenth birthday, the period at which those upon the foundation are superannuated. Whether he did not betray his abilities early in life, or his masters had not skill enough to discover in their pupil any marks of genius for which he merited reward, or no vacancy at Oxford afforded them an opportunity to bestow upon him the reward provided for merit by William of Wykeham; certain it is, that to an Oxford fellowship our Poet did not succeed. By chance, or by choice, New College does not number among its Fellows him who wrote the Night Thoughts.

'On the 13th of October, 1703, he was entered an independent member of New College, that he might live at little expense in the Warden's lodgings, who was a particular friend of his father, till he should be qualified to stand for a fellowship at All-souls. In a few months the Warden of New College died. He then removed to Corpus College. The President of this Society, from regard also for his father, invited him thither, in order to lessen his academical expences. In 1708 he was nominated to a law fellowship at All-souls by Archbishop Tennison, into whose hands it came by devolution. Such repeated patronage, while it justifies Burnet's praise of the father, reflects credit on the conduct of the son. The manner in which it was exerted seems to prove that the father did not leave behind him much wealth.

'On the 23rd of April, 1714, Young took his degree of Batchelor of Civil Laws, and his Doctor's degree on the 10th of June, 1719.

'Soon after he went to Oxford he discovered, it is said, an inclination for pupils. Whether he ever commenced tutor is not known. None has hitherto boasted to receive his academical instruction from the author of the Night Thoughts.

'It is certain that his college was proud of him no less as a scholar than as a poet, for in 1716, when the foundation of the Codrington Library was laid, two years after he had taken his Batchelor's degree, he was appointed to speak the Latin oration. This is at least particular for being dedicated in English "To the Ladies of the Codrington Family." To these Ladies he says "that he was unavoidably flung into a singularity by being obliged to write an epistle-dedicatory void of common-place, and such an one as was never published before by any author whatever; that this practice absolved them from any obligation of reading what was presented to them; and that the bookseller approved of it because it would make people stare was absurd enough, and perfectly right."

'Of this oration there is no appearance in his own edition of his works, and prefixed to an edition by Curll and Tonson in 1741 is a letter from Young to Curll, if Curll may be credited, dated December the 9th, 1739, wherein he says he has not leisure to review what he formerly wrote, and adds, "I have not the Epistle to Lord Lansdowne. If you will take my advice I would have you omit that and the oration on Codrington. I think the collection will sell better without them."

'There are who relate that, when first Young found himself independent and his own master at All-souls, he was not the ornament to religion and morality which he afterwards became.

'The authority of his father, indeed, had ceased some time before by his death, and Young was certainly not ashamed to be patronized by the infamous Wharton. But Wharton befriended in Young, perhaps, the poet, and particularly the tragedian. If virtuous authors must be patronized only by virtuous peers, who shall point them out?

Yet Pope is said by Ruffhead to have told Warburton that "Young had much of a sublime genius, though without common sense; so that his genius, having no guide, was perpetually liable to degenerate into bombast. This made him, pass a 'foolish youth,' the sport of peers and poets; but his having a very good heart enabled him to support the clerical character when he assumed it, first with decency, and afterwards with honour."

They who think ill of Young's morality in the early part of his life may perhaps be wrong; but Tindal could not err in his opinion of Young's warmth and ability in the cause of religion. Tindal used to spend much of his time at All-souls. "The other boys," said the atheist, "I can always answer, because I always know whence they have their arguments, which I have read an hundred times; but that fellow Young is continually pestering me with something of his own."

'After all, Tindal and the censurers of Young may be reconcilable. Young might, for two or three years, have tried that kind of life, in which his natural principles would not suffer him to wallow long. If this were so, he has left behind him not only his evidence in favour of virtue, but the potent testimony of experience against vice.

'We shall soon see that one of his earliest productions was more serious than what comes from the generality of unfledged poets.

'Young perhaps ascribed the good fortune of Addison to the Poem to his Majesty, presented, with a copy of verses, to Somers, and hoped that he also might soar to wealth and honors on wings of the same kind. His first poetical flight was when Queen Anne called up to the House of Lords the sons of the Earls of Northampton and Aylesbury, and added in one day ten others to the number of peers. In order to reconcile the people to one at least of the new Lords, he published in 1712 An Epistle to the Right Honourable George Lord Lansdowne. In this composition the poet pours out his panegyrick with the extravagance of a young man, who thinks his present stock of wealth will never be exhausted.

'The poem seems intended also to reconcile the publick to the late peace. This is endeavoured to be done by shewing that men are slain in war, and that in peace "harvests wave, and commerce swells her sail." If this be humanity, is it politicks? Another purpose of this epistle appears to have been to prepare the publick for the reception of some tragedy of his own. His Lordship's patronage, he says, will not let him "repent his passion for the stage"; and the particular praise bestowed on Othello and Oroonoko looks as if some such character as Zanga was even then in contemplation. The affectionate mention of the death of his friend Harrison of New College, at the close of this poem, is an instance of Young's art, which displayed itself so wonderfully some time afterwards in the Night Thoughts, of making the publick a party in his private sorrow.

'Should justice call upon you to censure this poem, it ought at least to be remembered that he did not insert it into his works, and that in the letter to Curll, as we have seen, he advises its omission. The booksellers, in the late Body of English Poetry, should have distinguished what was deliberately rejected by the respective authors1. This I shall be careful to do with regard to Young. "I think," says he, "the following pieces in four volumes to be the most excuseable of all that I have written, and I wish less apology was needful for these. As there is no recalling what is got abroad, the pieces here republished I have revised and corrected, and rendered them as pardonable as it was in my power to do."

'Shall the gates of repentance be shut only against literary sinners?

'When Addison published Cato in 1713 Young had the honour of prefixing to it a recommendatory copy of verses. This is one of the pieces which the author of the Night Thoughts did not republish.

'On the appearance of his Poem on the Last Day, Addison did not return Young's compliment; but The Englishman of October 29, 1713, which was probably written by Addison, speaks handsomely of this poem. The Last Day was published soon after the peace. The vice-chancellor's imprimatur, for it was first printed at Oxford, is dated May the 19th, 1713. From the Exordium Young appears to have spent some time on the composition of it. While other bards "with Britain's hero set their souls on fire," he draws, he says, a deeper scene. Marlborough had been considered by Britain as her hero; but, when The Last Day was published, female cabal had blasted for a time the laurels of Blenheim. This serious poem was finished by Young as early as 1710, before he was thirty; for part of it is printed in The Tatler. It was inscribed to the Queen, in a dedication which, for some reason, he did not admit into his works. It tells her that his only title to the great honour he now does himself is the obligation he formerly received from her royal indulgence.

'Of this obligation nothing is now known, unless he alluded to her being his godmother. He is said, indeed, to have been engaged at a settled stipend as a writer for the court. In Swift's Rhapsody on poetry are these lines, speaking of the court: "Whence Gay was banish'd in disgrace, Where Pope will never shew his face, Where Y— — must torture his invention To flatter knaves, or lose his pension." 'That Y— — means Young is clear from four other lines in the same poem: "Attend, ye Popes and Youngs and Gays, And tune your harps and strew your bays; Your panegyricks here provide; You cannot err on flattery's side."

'Yet who shall say with certainty that Young was a pensioner? In all modern periods of this country have not the writers on one side been regularly called Hirelings, and on the other Patriots?

'Of the dedication the complexion is clearly political. It speaks in the highest terms of the late peace: it gives her Majesty praise indeed for her victories, but says that the author is more pleased to see her rise from this lower world, soaring above the clouds, passing the first and second heavens, and leaving the fixed stars behind her; nor will he lose her there, but keep her still in view through the boundless spaces on the other side of Creation, in her journey towards eternal bliss, till he behold the heaven of heavens open, and angels receiving and conveying her still onward from the stretch of his imagination, which tires in her pursuit, and falls back again to earth.

'The Queen was soon called away from this lower world to a place where human praise or human flattery even less general than this are of little consequence. If Young thought the dedication contained only the praise of truth, he should not have omitted it in his works. Was he conscious of the exaggeration of party? Then he should not have written it. The poem itself is not without a glance to politicks, notwithstanding the subject. The cry that the church was in danger had not yet subsided. The Last Day, written by a layman, was much approved by the ministry and their friends.

'Before the Queen's death The Force of Religion, or Vanquished Love was sent into the world. This poem is founded on the execution of Lady Jane Gray and her husband Lord Guildford in 1554—a story chosen for the subject of a tragedy by Edmund Smith, and wrought into a tragedy by Rowe. The dedication of it to the countess of Salisbury does not appear in his own edition. He hopes it may be some excuse for his presumption that the story could not have been read without thoughts of the Countess of Salisbury, though it had been dedicated to another. "To behold," he proceeds, "a person only virtuous stirs in us a prudent regret; to behold a person only amiable to the sight warms us with a religious indignation; but to turn our eyes on a Countess of Salisbury gives us pleasure and improvement: it works a sort of miracle, occasions the bias of our nature to fall off from sin, and makes our very senses and affections converts to our religion, and promoters of our duty." His flattery was as ready for the other sex as for ours, and was at least as well adapted.

'August the 27th, 1714, Pope writes to his friend Jervas that he is just arrived from Oxford; that every one is much concerned for the Queen's death, but that no panegyricks are ready yet for the King. Nothing like friendship had yet taken place between Pope and Young; for, soon after the event which Pope mentions, Young published a poem on the Queen's death and his Majesty's accession to the throne. It is inscribed to Addison, then secretary to the Lords Justices. Whatever was the obligation which he had formerly received from Anne, the poet appears to aim at something of the same sort from George. Of the poem the intention seems to have been to shew that he had the same extravagant strain of praise for a King as for a Queen. To discover at the very outset of a foreigner's reign that the Gods bless his new subjects in such a King, is something more than praise. Neither was this deemed one of his excusable pieces. We do not find it in his works.

'Young's father had been well acquainted with Lady Anne Wharton, the first wife of Thomas Wharton, Esq., afterwards Marquis of Wharton; a Lady celebrated for her poetical talents by Burnet and by Waller. To the Dean of Sarum's visitation sermon, already mentioned, were added some verses "by that excellent poetess Mrs. Anne Wharton," upon its being translated into English, at the instance of Waller, by Atwood. Wharton, after he became ennobled, did not drop the son of his old friend. In him, during the short time he lived, Young found a patron, and in his dissolute descendant a friend and a companion. The Marquis died in April, 1715. The beginning of the next year the young Marquis set out upon his travels, from which he returned in about a twelvemonth. The beginning of 1717 carried him to Ireland, where, says the Biographia, "on the score of his extraordinary qualities he had the honour done him of being admitted, though under age, to take his seat in the House of Lords."

'With this unhappy character it is not unlikely that Young went to Ireland. From his Letter to Richardson On Original Composition, it is clear he was, at some period of his life, in that country. "I remember," says he, in that Letter, speaking of Swift, "as I and others were taking with him an evening walk about a mile out of Dublin he stopt short; we passed on; but, perceiving he did not follow us, I went back, and found him fixed as a statue, and earnestly gazing upward at a noble elm, which in its uppermost branches was much withered and decayed. Pointing at it, he said, 'I shall be like that tree, I shall die at top.'"—Is it not probable that this visit to Ireland was paid when he had an opportunity of going thither with his avowed friend and patron?

'From The Englishman it appears that a tragedy by Young was in the theatre so early as 1713. Yet Busiris was not brought upon Drury-Lane Stage till 1719. It was inscribed to the Duke of Newcastle, "because the late instances he had received of his Grace's undeserved and uncommon favour in an affair of some consequence, foreign to the theatre, had taken from him the privilege of chusing a patron." The Dedication he afterwards suppressed.

'Busiris was followed in the year 1721 by The Revenge. Left at liberty now to chuse his patron he dedicated this famous tragedy to the Duke of Wharton. "Your Grace," says the Dedication, "has been pleased to make yourself accessary to the following scenes, not only by suggesting the most beautiful incident in them, but by making all possible provision for the success of the whole."

'That his Grace should have suggested the incident to which he alludes, whatever that incident be, is not unlikely. The last mental exertion of the superannuated young man, in his quarters at Lerida in Spain, was some scenes of a tragedy on the story of Mary Queen of Scots.

'Dryden dedicated Marriage la Mode to Wharton's infamous relation Rochester, whom he acknowledges not only as the defender of his poetry, but as the promoter of his fortune. Young concludes his address to Wharton thus: "My present fortune is his bounty and my future his care, which I will venture to say will be always remembered to his honour, since he, I know, intended his generosity as an encouragement to merit, though, through his very pardonable partiality to one who bears him so sincere a duty and respect, I happen to receive the benefit of it." That he ever had such a patron as Wharton, Young took all the pains in his power to conceal from the world, by excluding this dedication from his works. He should have remembered that he at the same time concealed his obligation to Wharton for "the most beautiful incident" in what is surely not his least beautiful composition. The passage just quoted is, in a poem afterwards addressed to Walpole, literally copied: "Be this thy partial smile from censure free! 'Twas meant for merit, though it fell on me."

'While Young, who, in his Love of Fame, complains grievously how often "dedications wash an thiop white," was painting an amiable Duke of Wharton in perishable prose, Pope was perhaps beginning to describe the "scorn and wonder of his days" in lasting verse.

'To the patronage of such a character, had Young studied men as much as Pope, he would have known how little to have trusted. Young, however, was certainly indebted to it for something material; and the Duke's regard for Young, added to his Lust of Praise, procured to All-souls College a donation which was not forgotten by the poet when he dedicated The Revenge.

Chancellor Hardwicke was to determine whether two annuities, granted by the Duke of Wharton to Young, were for legal considerations. One was dated the 24th of March, 1719, and accounted for his Grace's bounty in a style princely and commendable, if not legal—"considering that the publick good is advanced by the encouragement of learning and the polite arts, and being pleased therein with the attempts of Dr. Young, in consideration thereof, and of the love he bore him, etc." The other was dated the 10th of July, 1722.

Young, on his examination, swore that he quitted the Exeter family, and refused an annuity of 100l. which had been offered him for his life if he would continue tutor to Lord Burleigh upon the pressing solicitations of the Duke of Wharton, and his Grace's assurances of providing for him in a much more ample manner. It also appeared that the Duke had given him a bond for 600l. dated the 15th of March, 1721, in consideration of his taking several journeys and being at great expenses in order to be chosen member of the House of Commons at the Duke's desire, and in consideration of his not taking two livings of 200l. and 400l. in the gift of All-souls College, on his Grace's promises of serving and advancing him in the world.

'Of his adventures in the Exeter family I am unable to give any account. The attempt to get into Parliament was at Cirencester, where Young stood a contested election. His Grace discovered in him talents for oratory as well as for poetry. Nor was this judgment wrong. Young after he took orders became a very popular preacher, and was much followed for the grace and animation of his delivery. By his oratorical talents he was once in his life, according to the Biographia, deserted. As he was preaching in his turn at St. James's he plainly perceived it was out of his power to command the attention of his audience. This so affected the feelings of the preacher that he sat back in the pulpit, and burst into tears.—But we must pursue his poetical life.

'In 1719 he lamented the death of Addison in a Letter addressed to their common friend Tickell. For the secret history of the following lines, if they contain any, it is now vain to seek: "In joy once join'd, in sorrow, now, for years, Partner in grief, and brother of my tears, Tickell, accept this verse, thy mournful due."

'From your account of Tickell it appears that he and Young used to "communicate to each other whatever verses they wrote, even to the least things."

'In 1719 appeared a Paraphrase on Part of the Book of Job. Parker, to whom it is dedicated, had not long, by means of the seals, been qualified for a patron. Of this work the author's opinion may be known from his letter to Curll: "You seem, in the Collection you propose, to have omitted what I think may claim the first place in it; I mean A Translation from Part of Job, printed by Mr. Tonson." The Dedication, which was only suffered to appear in Tonson's edition, while it speaks with satisfaction of his present retirement, seems to make an unusual struggle to escape from retirement. But every one who sings in the dark does not sing from joy. It is addressed, in no common strain of flattery, to a Chancellor, of whom he clearly appears to have had no kind of knowledge.'

'Of his Satires it would not have been impossible to fix the dates without the assistance of first editions, which, as you had occasion to observe in your account of Dryden, are with difficulty found. We must then have referred to the poems to discover when they were written. For these internal notes of time we should not have referred in vain. The first Satire laments that "Guilt's chief foe in Addison is fled." The second, addressing himself, asks, "Is thy ambition sweating for a rhyme, Thou unambitious fool, at this late time? A fool at forty is a fool indeed." 'The Satires were originally published separately in folio under the title of The Universal Passion. These passages fix the appearance of the first to about 1725, the time at which it came out. As Young seldom suffered his pen to dry after he had once dipped it in poetry, we may conclude that he began his Satires soon after he had written the Paraphrase on Job. The last Satire was certainly finished in the beginning of the year 1726. In December, 1725, the King, in his passage from Helvoetsluys, escaped with great difficulty from a storm by landing at Rye; and the conclusion of the Satire turns the escape into a miracle, in such an encomiastick strain of compliment as poetry too often seeks to pay to royalty. 'From the sixth of these poems we learn, "Midst empire's charms, how Carolina's heart Glow'd with the love of virtue and of art"; since the grateful poet tells us in the next couplet, "Her favour is diffus'd to that degree, Excess of goodness! it has dawn'd on me." Her Majesty had stood godmother, and given her name, to a daughter of the lady whom Young married in 1731.

> 'The fifth Satire, On Women, was not published till 1727, and the sixth not till 1728.'

To these Poems, when, in 1728, he gathered them into one publication, he prefixed a Preface, in which he observes that "no man can converse much in the world but, at what he meets with, he must either be insensible or grieve, or be angry or smile. Now to smile at it and turn it into ridicule," adds he, "I think most eligible, as it hurts ourselves least and gives vice and folly the greatest offence.—Laughing at the misconduct of the world will, in a great measure, ease us of any more disagreeable passion about it. One passion is more effectually driven out by another than by reason, whatever some teach." So wrote, and so of course thought, the lively and witty Satirist at the grave age of almost fifty, who many years earlier in life wrote The Last Day. After all, Swift pronounced of these Satires that they should either have been more angry or more merry.

'Is it not somewhat singular that Young preserved without any palliation this Preface, so bluntly decisive in favour of laughing at the world, in the same collection of his works which contains the mournful, angry, gloomy Night Thoughts?

At the conclusion of the Preface he applies Plato's beautiful fable of the Birth of Love to modern poetry, with the addition "that Poetry, like Love, is a little subject to blindness, which makes her mistake her way to preferments and honours; and that she retains a dutiful admiration of her father's family; but divides her favours, and generally lives with her mother's relations." Poetry, it is true, did not lead Young to preferments or to honours; but was there not something like blindness in the flattery which he sometimes forced her, and her sister Prose, to utter? She was always, indeed, taught by him to entertain a most dutiful admiration of riches; but surely Young, though nearly related to Poetry, had no connexion with her whom Plato makes the mother of Love. That he could not well complain of being related to Poverty appears clearly from the frequent bounties which his gratitude records, and from the wealth which he left behind him. By The Universal Passion he acquired no vulgar fortune, more than three thousand pounds. A considerable sum had already been swallowed up in the South-Sea. For this loss he took the vengeance of an author. His Muse makes poetical use more than once of a South-Sea Dream.

'It is related by Mr. Spence, in his Manuscript Anecdotes, on the authority of Mr. Rawlinson, that Young, upon the publication of his Universal Passion, received from the Duke of Grafton two thousand pounds; and that, when one of his friends exclaimed, "Two thousand pounds for a poem!" he said it was the best bargain he ever made in his life, for the poem was worth four thousand.

'This story may be true, but it seems to have been raised from the two answers of Lord Burghley and Sir Philip Sidney in Spenser's Life.

'After inscribing his Satires, not without the hope of preferments and honours, to the Duke of Dorset, Mr. Dodington, Mr. Spencer Compton, Lady Elizabeth Germain, and Sir Robert Walpole, he returns to plain panegyrick. In 1726 he addressed a poem to Sir Robert Walpole, of which the title sufficiently explains the intention. If Young was a ready celebrator he did not endeavour, or did not choose, to be a lasting one. The Instalment is among the pieces he did not admit into the number of his excuseable writings. Yet it contains a couplet which pretends to pant after the power of bestowing immortality: "Oh! how I long, enkindled by the theme, In deep eternity to launch thy name!"

'The bounty of the former reign seems to have been continued, possibly increased, in this. Whatever it was, the poet thought he deserved it; for he was not ashamed to acknowledge what, without his acknowledgement, would now perhaps never have been known: "My breast, O Walpole, glows with grateful fire. The streams of royal bounty, turn'd by thee, Refresh the dry domains of poesy." If the purity of modern patriotism term Young a pensioner, it must at least be confessed he was a grateful one. 'The reign of the new monarch was ushered in by Young with Ocean, an Ode. The hint of it was taken from the royal speech, which recommended the increase and encouragement of the seamen; that they might be "invited, rather than compelled by force and violence, to enter into the service of their country"—a plan which humanity must lament that policy has not even yet been able, or willing, to carry into execution. Prefixed to the original publication were an Ode to the King, Pater Patriae, and an Essay on Lyrick Poetry. It is but justice to confess that he preserved neither of them, and that the ode itself, which in the first edition, and in the last, consists of seventy-three stanzas, in the author's own edition is reduced to forty-nine. Among the omitted passages is A Wish, that concluded the poem, which few would have suspected Young of forming; and of which few, after having formed it, would confess something like their shame by suppression.

'It stood originally so high in the author's opinion that he intitled the poem Ocean, an Ode. Concluding with a Wish. This wish consists of thirteen stanzas. The first runs thus: "O may I steal Along the vale Of humble life, secure from foes! My friend sincere, My judgement clear, And gentle business my repose!" The three last stanzas are not more remarkable for just rhymes; but altogether they will make rather a curious page in the life of Young. "Prophetick schemes, And golden dreams, May I, unsanguine, cast away! Have what I have, And live, not leave, Enamour'd of the present day! "My hours my own! My faults unknown! My chief revenue in content! Then leave one beam Of honest fame! And scorn the labour'd monument! "Unhurt my urn Till that great turn When mighty nature's self shall die, Time cease to glide, With human pride, Sunk in the ocean of eternity!"

It is whimsical that he, who was soon to bid adieu to rhyme, should fix upon a measure in which rhyme abounds even to satiety. Of this he said, in his Essay on Lyrick Poetry prefixed to the poem, "For the more harmony likewise I chose the frequent return of rhyme, which laid me under great difficulties. But difficulties overcome give grace and pleasure. Nor can I account for the pleasure of rhyme in general (of which the moderns are too fond) but from this truth." Yet the moderns surely deserve not much censure for their fondness of what, by his own confession, affords pleasure, and abounds in harmony.

'The next paragraph in his Essay did not occur to him when he talked of "that great turn" in the stanza just quoted. "But then the writer must take care that the difficulty is overcome. That is, he must make rhyme consistent with as perfect sense and expression as could be expected if he was perfectly free from that shackle."

'Another part of this Essay will convict the following stanza of, what every reader will discover in it, "involuntary burlesque." "The northern blast, The shatter'd mast, The syrt, the whirlpool, and the rock, The breaking spout, The stars gone out, The boiling streight, the monster's shock."

'But would the English poets fill quite so many volumes if all their productions were to be tried, like this, by an elaborate essay on each particular species of poetry of which they exhibit specimens?

'If Young be not a lyrick poet he is at least a critick in that sort of poetry, and, if his lyrick poetry can be proved bad, it was first proved so by his own criticism. This surely is candid.

'Milbourne was styled by Pope "the fairest of Criticks," only because he exhibited his own version of Virgil to be compared with Dryden's which he condemned, and with which every reader had it otherwise in his power to compare it. Young was surely not the most unfair of poets for prefixing to a lyrick composition an essay on Lyrick Poetry so just and impartial as to condemn himself.

'We shall soon come to a work, before which we find indeed no critical Essay; but which disdains to shrink from the touchstone of the severest critick, and which certainly, as I remember to have heard you say, if it contains some of the worst, contains also some of the best things in the language.

'Soon after the appearance of Ocean, when he was almost fifty, Young entered into orders. In April, 1728, not long after he put on the gown, he was appointed chaplain to George the Second.

'The tragedy of The Brothers, which was already in rehearsal, he immediately withdrew from the stage. The managers resigned it with some reluctance to the delicacy of the new clergyman. The Epilogue to The Brothers, the only appendage to any of his three plays which he added himself, is, I believe, the only one of the kind. He calls it an "historical" Epilogue. Finding that "Guilt's dreadful close his narrow scene denied," he, in a manner, continues the tragedy in the Epilogue, and relates how Rome revenged the shade of Demetrius, and punished Perseus "for this night's deed."

'Of Young's taking orders something is told by the biographer of Pope, which places the easiness and simplicity of the poet in a singular light. When he determined on the Church he did not address himself to Sherlock, to Atterbury, or to Hare for the best instructions in theology, but to Pope, who, in a youthful frolick, advised the diligent perusal of Thomas Aquinas. With this treasure Young retired from interruption to an obscure place in the suburbs. His poetical guide to godliness hearing nothing of him during half a year, and apprehending he, might have carried the jest too far, sought after him, and found him just in time to prevent what Ruffhead calls "an irretrievable derangement."

'That attachment to his favourite study which made him think a poet the surest guide in his new profession, left him little doubt whether poetry was the surest path to its honours and preferments. Not long indeed after he took orders he published in prose, 1728, A true Estimate of Human Life, dedicated, notwithstanding the Latin quotations with which it abounds, to the Queen, and a sermon preached before the House of Commons, 1729, on the martyrdom of King Charles, intituled An Apology for Princes, or the Reverence due to Government. But the Second Discourse, the counterpart of his Estimate, without which it cannot be called "a true estimate," though in 1728 it was announced as "soon to be published," never appeared, and his old friends the Muses were not forgotten. In 1730 he relapsed to poetry, and sent into the world Imperium Pelagi; a Naval Lyrick, written in Imitation of Pindar's Spirit, occasioned by His Majesty's Return from Hanover, September 1729, and the succeeding Peace. It is inscribed to the Duke of Chandos. In the Preface we are told that "the ode is the most spirited kind of Poetry, and that the Pindarick is the most spirited kind of ode." "This I speak," he adds with sufficient candour, "at my own very great peril. But truth has an eternal title to our confession, though we are sure to suffer by it." Behold again "the fairest of poets." Young's Imperium Pelagi as well as his tragedies was ridiculed in Fielding's Tom Thumb; but let us not forget that it was one of his pieces which the author of the Night Thoughts deliberately refused to own. 'Not long after this Pindarick attempt he published two Epistles to Pope, Concerning the Authors of the Age, 1730. Of these poems one occasion seems to have been an apprehension lest, from the liveliness of his satires, he should not be deemed sufficiently serious for promotion in the Church.

'In July, 1730, he was presented by his College to the rectory of Welwyn in Hertfordshire. In May, 1731, he married

Lady Elizabeth Lee, daughter of the Earl of Litchfield and widow of Colonel Lee. His connexion with this lady arose from his father's acquaintance, already mentioned, with Lady Anne Wharton, who was coheiress of Sir Henry Lee of Ditchley, in Oxfordshire. Poetry had lately been taught by Addison to aspire to the arms of nobility, though not with extraordinary happiness.

We may naturally conclude that Young now gave himself up in some measure to the comforts of his new connexion, and to the expectations of that preferment which he thought due to his poetical talents, or, at least, to the manner in which they had so frequently been exerted.

'The next production of his Muse was The Sea-piece, in two odes.

'Young enjoys the credit of what is called An Extempore Epigram on Voltaire, who, when he was in England, ridiculed, in the company of the jealous English poet, Milton's allegory of Sin and Death: "You are so witty, profligate, and thin, At once we think thee Milton, Death, and Sin." From the following passage in the poetical Dedication of his Sea-piece to Voltaire it seems that his extemporaneous reproof (if it must be extemporaneous) for what few will now affirm Voltaire to have deserved any reproof, was something longer than a distich, and something more gentle than the distich just quoted. "No stranger, Sir, though born in foreign climes; On Dorset downs, when Milton's page With Sin and Death provok'd thy rage, Thy rage provok'd, who sooth'd with gentle rhymes?" By "Dorset downs" he probably meant Mr. Dodington's seat. In Pitt's Poems is An Epistle to Dr. Edward Young, at Eastbury in Dorsetshire, on the Review at Sarum, 1722. "While with your Dodington retir'd you sit, Charm'd with his flowing Burgundy and wit," &c.

'Thomson, in his Autumn, addressing Mr. Dodington, calls his seat the seat of the Muses: "Where, in the secret bower and winding walk, For virtuous Young and thee they twine the bay." The praises Thomson bestows but a few lines before on Philips; the second "Who nobly durst, in rhymeunfetter'd verse, With British freedom sing the British song"; added to Thomson's example and success might perhaps induce Young, as we shall see presently, to write his great work without rhyme.

'In 1734 he published The foreign Address, or the best Argument for Peace: occasioned by the British Fleet and the Posture of Affairs. Written in the Charácter of a Sailor. It is not to be found in the author's four volumes.

'He now appears to have given up all hopes of overtaking Pindar, and perhaps at last resolved to turn his ambition to some original species of poetry. This poem concludes with a formal farewell to Ode, which few of Young's readers will regret: "My shell which Clio gave, which Kings applaud, Which Europe's bleeding Genius call'd abroad, Adieu!" In a species of poetry altogether his own he next tried his skill, and succeeded.

'Of the Night Thoughts, notwithstanding their author's professed retirement, all are inscribed to great or to growing names. He had not yet weaned himself from Earls and Dukes, from Speakers of the House of Commons, Lords Commissioners of the Treasury, and Chancellors of the Exchequer. In Night Eight the politician plainly betrays himself: "Think no post needful that demands a knave: When late our civil helm was shifting hands, So P— — thought; think better if you can." Yet it must be confessed that at the conclusion of Night Nine, weary perhaps of courting earthly patrons, he tells his soul, "Henceforth Thy patron he, whose diadem has dropt Yon gems of heaven; Eternity thy prize; And leave the racers of the world their own."

'The Fourth Night was addressed by "a much-indebted Muse" to the Honourable Mr. Yorke, now Lord Hardwicke, who meant to have laid the Muse under still greater obligations by the living of Shenfield in Essex, if it had become vacant.

'The First Night concludes with this passage: "Dark, though not blind, like thee, Meonides; Or Milton, thee. Ah! could I reach your strain; Or his who made Meonides our own! Man too he sung. Immortal man I sing. Oh! had he prest his theme, pursued the track Which opens out of darkness into day! Oh! had he mounted on his wing of fire, Soar'd, where I sink, and sung immortal man— How had it blest mankind, and rescued me!

'To the author of these lines was dedicated, in 1756, the first volume of an Essay on the Writings and Genius of Pope, which attempted, whether justly or not, to pluck from Pope his "Wing of Fire," and to reduce him to a rank at least one degree lower than the first class of English poets. If Young accepted and approved the dedication, he countenanced this attack upon the fame of him whom he invokes as his Muse.

'Part of "paper-sparing" Pope's third book of the Odyssey, deposited in the Museum, is written upon the back of a letter signed "E. Young," which is clearly the handwriting of our Young. The letter, dated only May the 2nd, seems obscure; but there can be little doubt that the friendship he requests was a literary one, and that he had the highest literary opinion of Pope. The request was a prologue, I am told.

"Dear Sir, May the 2nd. "Having been often from home I know not if you have done me the favour of calling on me. But, be that as it will, I much want that instance of your friendship I mentioned in my last; a friendship I am very sensible I can receive from no one but yourself. I should not urge this thing so much but for very particular reasons, nor can you be at a loss to conceive how a trifle of this nature may be of serious moment to me; and while I am in hopes of the great advantage of your advice about it, I shall not be so absurd as to make any further step without it. I know you are much engaged, and only hope to hear of you at your entire leisure. "I am, Sir, your most faithful, "and obedient servant, "E. YOUNG." Nay, even after Pope's death he says in Night Seven: "Pope, who could'st make immortals, art thou dead?" Either the Essay then was dedicated to a patron who disapproved its doctrine, which I have been told by the author was not the case; or Young, in his old age, bartered for a dedication an opinion entertained of his friend through all that part of life when he must have been best able to form opinions.

'From this account of Young two or three short passages, which stand almost together in Night Four, should not be excluded. They afford a picture, by his own hand, from the study of which my readers may choose to form their own opinion of the features of his mind and the complexion of his life. "Ah me! the dire effect Of loitering here, of death defrauded long; Of old so gracious (and let that suffice), My very master knows me not. I've been so long remember'd, I'm forgot. When in his courtiers' ears I pour my plaint, They drink it as the Nectar of the Great; And squeeze my hand, and beg me come to-morrow. Twice-told the period spent on stubborn Troy, Court-favour, yet untaken, I besiege. If this song lives, Posterity shall know One, though in Britain born, with courtiers bred, Who thought ev'n gold might come a day too late; Nor on his subtle death-bed plann'd his scheme For future vacancies in church or state." Deduct from the writer's age "twice-told the period spent on stubborn Troy," and you will still leave him more than forty when he sate down to the miserable siege of Court favour. He has before told us "A fool at forty is a fool indeed." After all, the siege seems to have been raised only in consequence of what the General thought his "death-bed." 'By these extraordinary poems, written after he was sixty, of which I have been led to say so much, I hope, by the wish of doing justice to the living and the dead, it was the desire of Young to be principally known. He entitled the four volumes which he published himself, The Works of the Author of the Night Thoughts. While it is remembered that from these he excluded many of his writings, let it not be forgotten that the rejected pieces contained nothing prejudicial to the cause of virtue or of religion. Were every thing that Young ever wrote to be published he would only appear perhaps in a less respectable light as a poet, and more despicable as a dedicator: he would not pass for a worse christian, or for a worse man. This enviable praise is due to Young. Can it be claimed by every writer? His dedications, after all, he had, perhaps, no right to suppress. They all, I believe, speak, not a little to the credit of his gratitude, of favours received; and I know not whether the author, who has once solemnly printed an acknowledgement of a favour, should not always print it.

In September, 1764, he added a kind of codicil, wherein he made it his dying intreaty to his housekeeper, to whom he left 1,000l., "that all his manuscripts might be destroyed as soon as he was dead, which would greatly oblige her deceased friend."

'It may teach mankind the uncertainty of worldly friendships to know that Young, either by surviving those he loved, or by outliving their affections, could only recollect the names of two friends, his housekeeper and a hatter, to mention in his will; and it may serve to repress that testamentary pride, which too often seeks for sounding names and titles, to be informed that the author of the Night Thoughts did not blush to leave a legacy to his "friend Henry Stevens, a hatter at the Temple-gate." Of these two remaining friends, one went before Young. But, at eighty-four "where," as he asks in The Centaur, "is that world into which we were born?"

'The same humility which marked a hatter and a housekeeper for the friends of the author of the Night Thoughts had before bestowed the same title on his footman, in an epitaph in his churchyard upon James Barker, dated 1749, which I am glad to find in the late collection of his works.

Young and his housekeeper were ridiculed, with more illnature than wit, in a kind of novel published by Kidgell in 1755, called The Card, under the names of Dr. Elwes and Mrs. Fusby.

'In April, 1765, at an age to which few attain, a period was put to the life of Young.

'He had performed no duty for the last three or four years of his life, but he retained his intellects to the last.

'Much is told in the Biographia, which I know not to have been true, of the manner of his burial; of the master and children of a charity-school, which he founded in his parish, who neglected to attend their benefactor's corpse; and of a bell which was not caused to toll so often as upon those occasions bells usually toll. Had that humanity, which is here lavished upon things of little consequence either to the living or to the dead, been shewn in its proper place to the living, I should have had less to say about Lorenzo. They who lament that these misfortunes happened to Young forget the praise he bestows upon Socrates, in the Preface to Night Seven, for resenting his friend's request about his funeral.

'During some part of his life Young was abroad, but I have not been able to learn any particulars. (137)'In his seventh Satire he says "When, after battle, I the field have seen Spread o'er with ghastly shapes which once were men." (138)'And it is known that from this or from some other "field" he once wandered into the enemy's camp, with a classick in his hand, which he was reading intently; and had some difficulty to prove that he was only an absent poet and not a spy.

'Again, Young was a poet; and again, with reverence be it spoken, poets by profession do not always make the best clergymen. If the author of the Night Thoughts composed many sermons he did not oblige the publick with many.

'Besides, in the latter part of life, Young was fond of holding himself out for a man retired from the world. But he seemed to have forgotten that the same verse which contains "oblitus meorum," contains also "obliviscendus et illis." The brittle chain of worldly friendship and patronage is broken as effectually, when one goes beyond the length of it, as when the other does. To the vessel which is sailing from the shore it only appears that the shore also recedes; in life it is truly thus. He who retires from the world will find himself in reality deserted as fast, if not faster, by the world. The publick is not to be treated as the coxcomb treats his mistress; to be threatened with desertion, in order to increase fondness.

'Young seems to have been taken at his word. Notwithstanding his frequent complaints of being neglected, no hand was reached out to pull him from that retirement of which he declared himself enamoured. Alexander assigned no palace for the residence of Diogenes, who boasted his surly satisfaction with his tub. 'Of the domestick manners and petty habits of the author of the Night Thoughts I hoped to have given you an account from the best authority: but who shall dare to say, to-morrow I will be wise or virtuous, or to-morrow I will do a particular thing? Upon enquiring for his housekeeper I learned that she was buried two days before I reached the town of her abode.

'In a letter from Tscharner, a noble foreigner, to Count Haller, Tscharner says he has lately spent four days with Young at Welwyn, where the author tastes all the ease and pleasure mankind can desire. "Every thing about him shews the man, each individual being placed by rule. All is neat without art. He is very pleasant in conversation, and extremely polite."

'This, and more, may possibly be true; but Tscharner's was a first visit, a visit of curiosity and admiration, and a visit which the author expected.

'Of Edward Young an anecdote which wanders among readers is not true, that he was Fielding's Parson Adams. The original of that famous painting was William Young. He too was a clergyman. He supported an uncomfortable existence by translating for the booksellers from Greek, and, if he was not his own friend, was at least no man's enemy. Yet the facility with which this report has gained belief in the world argues, were it not sufficiently known, that the author of the Night Thoughts bore some resemblance to Adams. 'The attention Young bestowed upon the perusal of books is not unworthy imitation. When any passage pleased him, he appears to have folded down the leaf. On these passages he bestowed a second reading. But the labours of man are too frequently vain. Before he returned a second time to much of what he had once approved he died. Many of his books, which I have seen, are by those notes of approbation so swelled beyond their real bulk, that they will not shut. "What though we wade in wealth, or soar in fame! Earth's highest station ends in, Here he lies! And dust to dust concludes her noblest song!" The author of these lines is not without his hic jacet.

'By the good sense of his son it contains none of that praise which no marble can make the bad or the foolish merit, which without the direction of a stone or a turf will find its way sooner or later to the deserving. M. S. Optimi parentis EDWARDI YOUNG, LL.D. Hujus Ecclesiae rect. Et Elizabethae faem. praenob. Conjugis ejus amantissimae Pio et gratissimo animo Hoc marmor posuit F. Y. Filius superstes.

'Is it not strange that the author of the Night Thoughts has inscribed no monument to the memory of his lamented wife? Yet what marble will endure as long as the poems?

'Such, my good friend, is the account I have been able to collect of Young. That it may be long before any thing like what I have just transcribed be necessary for you, is the sincere wish of,

'Dear Sir,
'Your greatly obliged Friend,
'HERBERT CROFT, Jun.
'Lincoln's Inn, Sept. 1780.'

'P.S. This account of Young was seen by you in manuscript you know, Sir; and, though I could not prevail on you to make any alterations, you insisted on striking out one passage only because it said that if I did not wish you to live long for your sake, I did for the sake of myself and of the world. But this postscript you will not see before it is printed; and I will say here, in spite of you, how I feel myself honoured and bettered by your friendship, and that, if I do credit to the church, after which I always longed and for which I am now going to give in exchange the bar, though not at so late a period of life as Young took orders, it will be owing in no small measure to my having had the happiness of calling the author of The Rambler my friend. 'H. C. 'Oxford, Sept. 1782.'

Of Young's poems it is difficult to give any general character, for he has no uniformity of manner: one of his pieces has no great resemblance to another. He began to write early and continued long, and at different times had different modes of poetical excellence in view. His numbers are sometimes smooth and sometimes rugged; his style is sometimes concatenated and sometimes abrupt, sometimes diffusive and sometimes concise. His plan seems to have started in his mind at the present moment, and his thoughts appear the effects of chance, sometimes adverse and sometimes lucky, with very little operation of judgement.

The Universal Passion is indeed a very great performance. It is said to be a series of Epigrams; but if it be it is what the author intended: his endeavour was at the production of striking distichs and pointed sentences; and his distichs have the weight of solid sentiment, and his points the sharpness of resistless truth. His characters are often selected with discernment and drawn with nicety; his illustrations are often happy and his reflections often just. His species of satire is between those of Horace and of Juvenal: he has the gaiety of Horace without his laxity of numbers, and the morality of Juvenal with greater variation of images. He plays, indeed, only on the surface of life; he never penetrates the recesses of the mind, and therefore the whole power of his poetry is exhausted by a single perusal: his conceits please only when they surprise. To translate he never condescended, unless his Paraphrase on Job1 may be considered as a version, in which he has not, I think, been unsuccessful; he indeed favoured himself by chusing those parts which most easily admit the ornaments of English poetry.

He had least success in his lyrick attempts, in which he seems to have been under some malignant influence: he is always labouring to be great, and at last is only turgid.

In his Night Thoughts he has exhibited a very wide display of original poetry, variegated with deep reflections and striking allusions, a wilderness of thought in which the fertility of fancy scatters flowers of every hue and of every odour. This is one of the few poems in which blank verse could not be changed for rhyme but with disadvantage. The wild diffusion of the sentiments and the digressive sallies of imagination would have been compressed and restrained by confinement to rhyme. The excellence of this work is not exactness, but copiousness; particular lines are not to be regarded: the power is in the whole, and in the whole there is a magnificence like that ascribed to Chinese Plantation, the magnificence of vast extent and endless diversity.

His last poem was the Resignation, in which he made, as he was accustomed, an experiment of a new mode of writing, and succeeded better than in his Ocean or his Merchant. It was very falsely represented as a proof of decaying faculties. There is Young in every stanza, such as he often was in his highest vigour

JOHN GAY (1685-1732)

Gay had a fresh individual talent for verse which operated naturally and freely within the limits set by current poetical forms. Born and educated at Barnstaple, north Devon, he was left an orphan and apprenticed to a mercer in London, but a small inheritance evidently gave him a chance to become a literary free-lance. Never a struggling hack writer, he was not servile, but came to depend on friendly patrons, and his life is to be written largely in terms of his relations with contemporary noblemen, politicians, and authors. By 1712 he was a friend of Pope's, and though not deeply involved in politics he drifted away from the Whigs and was drawn into the famous Scriblerus Club. The spirit of Scriblerus no doubt stimulated Gay's interest in burlesque and in literary impromptus and *jeux d'esprit*.

By the end of Anne's reign he had published *Wine* (I708) —an insipid imitation of John Philips' *Cyder—Rural Sports* (I713), another georgic exercise; *The Fan* (I713, dated 1714) in imitation of *The Rape of the Lock*, and best of all *The Shepherd's Week* (I714), a delightful series of burlesque pastorals following Virgil *Eclogues* and marked by keen and playful observation of the details of country life. All these poems follow leads given by contemporary literature; *The Shepherd's Week* develops from the interest in the pastoral form stimulated by the rivalry between Pope *Pastorals* and those of Ambrose, and ridicule of Philips is probably one of Gay's motives, though it cannot be shown that Pope incited him to the project.

Despite the imitative and conventional nature of much of Gay's work. he was a careful writer, and resisted the temptation which overcame many secondary poets of the time to turn out reams of mechanical verse. He rapidly extended his work in burlesque: *The What D'ye Call It* (I715) is a successful take-off of the high flown absurdities of tragedy, in the tradition of *The Rehearsal; Trivia,* or, *The Art of Walking the Streets of London* (1716) is the greatest of burlesque georgics, and also, as Gay's biographer Professor Irving says, "the greatest of all poems on London life." The abundant details are vivid and objective; the use of the literary formula is occasionally stiff and mechanical. The immediate model was furnished by Swift citypieces in the *Tatler, A Description of the Morning and A Description of a City Shower.* Parallel is Gay's development of the "town eclogue," an application of the pastoral form to city life; he published examples of this kind of work in 1720. He also collaborated with Arbuthnot and Pope in the farce *Three Hours after Marriage* (I717), which created a disturbance in town not so much because of its absurdity as because of the activities of Pope's enemies. A more attractive memorial of his friendship with Pope is the delightful set of verses, *Mr. Pope's Welcome from Greece,* celebrating the completion of the translation of the *Iliad.*

The Whig magnates in power did little to help Gay, and his friends put through a highly successful subscription for his *Poems* (I720). This brought a thousand pounds which he soon lost in South Sea stock. He was on good terms with the dissident-Whig leader Pulteney, Lord Burlington, the Duke and Duchess of Queensberry, and the family of the Prince of Wales. For the little prince William Augustus he began to write the *Fables* (I, 1727; II, 1738) which became one of the most widely read books of the century. Meanwhile his estrangement from Walpole and the Whigs became complete. This political background largely explains the origin of *The Beggar's Opera.* In this brilliant piece Gay exploits the familiar parallel between high and low life, between the man in great place and the criminal. His hero-highwayman Macheath was usually taken for Walpole. Swift's suggestion of a "Newgate pastoral" as far back as 1716 may have counted for something, but since 1724 the current interest in famous criminals like Jonathan Wild, Jack Sheppard, and "Blueskin" had brought forth various Newgate pieces on the stage. Gay's turn for burlesque reaches its height in the brilliant take-off of Italian opera. His talent for song writing had already appeared in the familiar pieces *Sweet William's Farewell* and *'Twas when the seas were roaring,* and now in the arias of *The Beggar's Opera* it produced a series of cynical little lyrics acceptable alike to the man on the street and the sophisticated. Produced at Lincoln's Inn Fields in January 1728 with Lavinia Fenton as Polly, Tom Walker as Macheath, and Hippisley as Peachum, *The Beggar's Opera* took the town by storm and had an unprecedented run. It established a type of ballad-opera, with the prose dialogue of comedy frequently interspersed with ballad airs, and many imitations appeared on the London stage, though Gay's success was never repeated. Here Hogarthian realism and lyric lightness combine to unique effect; clear of serious didactic purpose. The sequel *Polly* was denied production by the censorship of the Lord Chamberlain, but its publication brought Gay a thousand pounds. During the last years of his life he lived most of the time with his devoted friends, the Duke and Duchess of Queensberry. Although Gay and his loyal friends used to complain that he was too naïve to make his way in the world, we need not take these complaints too seriously. He reminds us in some respects of Goldsmith. Though he lacked the solidity and power of his greater contemporaries, his use of accepted literary forms has an ingenuity and charm that were freely enjoyed and amply rewarded.

Allan Ramsay (1685-1758) Alexander Pope (1688-1744) Lady Mary Wortley Montagu (1689-1762) Philip Dormer Stanhope, Fourth Earl of Chesterfield (1694-1773)

ALLAN RAMSAY (1685-1758)

Allan Ramsay was born in the remote Lanarkshire village of Leadhills in 1685. Around 1704 he moved to Edinburgh and became an apprentice wigmaker. Completing his apprenticeship in 1709, Ramsay became a Burgess the following year and opened a shop in the Grassmarket.

During this period Scotland was in a sad state of decline. Politically weakened by the Act of Union (1707) she was also in danger of cultural domination by England. Ramsay, a strong nationalist, became increasingly involved in Edinburgh intellectual and literary circles from 1710 on. In 1712 he co-founded the Easy Club a society with strong Jacobite leanings which met to discuss literature and politics. Many of Ramsay's early poems received their first public airing when read aloud to club members. Although sympathetic to the cause, Ramsay had no involvement in either the 1715 or 1745 Jacobite uprisings.

By 1720 Ramsay's interest in literature was such that he abandoned wigmaking and became a bookseller. In 1725 he moved to premises in the High Street where he opened what is generally regarded as Britain's first circulating library.

By this time he had become a successful poet, publishing his first collection of verse in 1721 and second in 1728. Ramsay wrote in both Scots and English but with markedly more success in the former. His English poems owe too obvious a debt to Alexander Pope, whereas his verse in Scots did much to initiate the eighteenth century revival of Scottish vernacular poetry - later continued by Fergusson and Burns.

Ramsay also deserves credit for his rediscovery of an earlier Scottish tradition. As the editor of *The Evergreen* (1724) he anthologised the work of long neglected poets including Dunbar and Henryson. *The Tea table miscellany* (5 volumes 1724-37) resurrected many traditional songs and ballads. He has, with some justice, been criticised for bowdlerising and altering the texts of these poems and songs but he performed a vital service in rescuing Scotland's forgotten literary legacy.

In 1736 Ramsay opened the New Theatre in Carruber's Close. Unfortunately, it soon fell foul of the 1737 Licensing Act and was closed, losing him a lot of money. Thereafter he retired to his house on the Castlehill until his death in 1758.

Ramsay frequently spent time at the home of his friends the Forbes of Newhall. Newhall House has been identified as the setting of his greatest triumph, the pastoral comedy *The Gentle shepherd* (1725). It concerns rustic life and courtship amongst the Pentland Hills. A huge popular success, it also received extravagant praise from, amongst others, Fergusson, Burns and James Boswell who spoke of its real picture of manners "and beautiful rural imagery":

Gae far'er up *the burn to Habbie's How,*
Where a'the sweets o spring and summer grow:

There 'tween twa birks, out ower a little lin,
The water fa's and maks a singin'din;
A pool breast-deep, beneath as clear as glass,
Kisses, wi' easy whirls, the bord'ring grass.

ALEXANDER POPE (1688-1744)

In the Revolution year 1688 was born the poet who was destined to perfect the formal style developed in the late seventeenth century and to dominate English verse for two generations. Alexander Pope was of Catholic parentage and therefore could not get his education at public school and university. Moreover, he was a sickly and deformed boy, and was denied a normal physical and social life. He was for the most part privately educated in his parents' country house at Binfield, on the edge of Windsor Forest. He read widely if not exactly, with the imitativeness and docility often found in bookish and precocious youth. From his study of Latin and English poetry and the neo-classical principles transmitted through Dryden and the French critics he developed a literary code and program which would pass as orthodox in any London coffee house or coterie of wits. He accepted what had become the official neo-classical view of the-history of English poetry—that modern English verse began with Waller's smooth couplets and reached its greatest glory in Dryden; yet it should be remembered that he knew and appreciated in his own way Shakespeare and Milton, to a less degree Chaucer and Spenser, and that he responded to the picturesque and the romantic. He was a sensitive young poet, not a mere rationalist or formalist. As to style, however, he accepted the advice which the minor poet and critic Walsh gave him: "He used to encourage me much, and used to tell me that there was one way left of excelling; for though we had several great poets, we never had any one great poet that was correct; and he desired me to make that my study and aim." The correctness here recommended perhaps meant a rigorous choice of words and nice adjustment of meter to get what Pope calls "sense" and "sweetness."

ILIAD TRANSLATION

Meanwhile he was trying work in various kinds—the Messiah (a Virgilian paraphrase of Isaiah first published in the *Spectator* in 1712), the artificial *Ode for Music on, St. Cecilia's Day*, and the passionate though rhetorical poems, *An Elegy to the Memory of an Unfortunate Lady and Eloisa to Abelard.* The collected edition of 1717 contains all his important work up to that time and shows a comparatively wide and experimental range of subject and style.

By his translation of the *Iliad* (proposed 1713, published 1715- 1720) Pope established his position as the foremost professional writer of the day, and attained financial security at a time when it was almost a unique thing for an author to be independent both of the caprices of patronage and of the booksellers. In the translation of the *Odyssey*, carried out with the partly unacknowledged aid of two minor versifiers Broome and Fenton, he did task-work of a somewhat less distinguished kind. The Homer as a whole became a sort of poetic model for the age, a treasury of spirited verse and elegant diction. Another project of this period was his edition of Shakespeare (I725). In 1718 he moved to his villa at Twickenham, on the Thames just out side London and opposite Richmond. Here he enjoyed a gentlemanly rural retirement, entertained his friends, nursed his grudges against his enemies, and busied himself with his gardening and his grotto. His gardening was in the picturesque and irregular English style.

AN ESSAY ON CRITICISM

Perhaps begun in 1704 and considerably revised before publication in 1711, the Essay sums up Pope's early literary studies and at the same time establishes his final position. He works here in the tradition of the Renaissance verse-essays on poetry, such as Vida De Arte Poetica and Boileau Art Poétique, which go back to Horace's Epistle to the Pisos or Ars Poetica. Preceding Pope in English were the Essay on Poetry (I682) by John Sheffield, Earl of Mulgrave, later Duke of Buckingham, the Essay on Translated Verse (I684) by

Roscommon, and Lansdowne Essay upon Unnatural Flights in Poetry (I701). In all these works principles of poetry taken as agreed upon by men of intelligence and taste are neatly and briefly set forth without formal argument. Pope is giving advice to the critic rather than the poet, but this makes little difference, for according to Pope the poet consciously uses the same standards which the critic will apply. These standards are said to be given or discovered in the order found in nature, which is also the order of reason. John Dennis put it thus: "As Nature is order and rule and harmony in the visible world, so Reason is the very same throughout the invisible creation." The great ancients, such as Homer, followed or imitated this order, and then the great critics, Aristotle, Horace, Quintilian, Longinus, described this order as found in the works of the poets, and so formulated the Rules, which are "Nature still, but Nature methodized." The theory is thus a series of identities—Nature-Reason-the Classicsthe Rules. The whole sequence is thought of as congenial to man's mind, or, as it is sometimes put, Pope's Nature is identified with the permanent or universal elements in human nature. The Rules are right not simply because the Ancients presented them; the Ancients presented them because they are right. In practice, however, the best way to get at the Rules is to study and imitate the Ancients. The poet at work is not exactly in the position of a philosopher dealing directly with Reason and Nature; he learns as every one else learns, by imitation; he is brought up in a tradition which reverences ancient authors, and he writes for a public which accepts that tradition. One great error of criticism is to become peremptory in formulating rules without regard to the practice of great writers, and thus to become dull and mechanical (ll. 104-117). In theory the critics whom Pope largely followed, Boileau and Dryden, handed on a moderate and liberal creed which reconciled free imitation of classical models with the imitation of Nature essential to all poetry. But in practice the example of the Ancients often came to have the weight usually attached to legal or religious authority. When Pope praises the unlicensed beauties not covered by the Rules, he hastens to add the warning:

But tho' the ancients thus their rules invade,
(As Kings dispense with laws themselves have made)
Moderns, beware! or if you must offend
Against the precept, ne'er transgress its end;
Let it be seldom, and compell'd by need;
And have at least their precedent to plead.
(ll. 161-166)

Because of the primacy of the Ancients, the later history of literature is a history of decline.

THE RAPE OF THE LOCK

(Original version in two cantos in Lintot's Miscellany. 1712; revised and enlarged version in five cantos, 1714.)

Robert Lord Petre had cut off a lock of Miss Arabella Fermor's hair, and this trifling episode had caused ill-will between their kinsfolk. Both families were prominent in Roman Catholic circles, and a common friend John Caryll asked Pope to help matters by turning the whole affair into a joke. Accordingly Pope wrote the first version of *The Rape of the Lock* in the summer or autumn of 1711. In the revised and final version Pope more than doubled the length of the poem by adding the machinery of the sylphs, which he took from a contemporary Rosicrucian romance in French. To the original episode, the tempest in a teapot, Pope applies the mock-heroic method; that is, he treats trifling matters in an elaborate and elevated style full of echoes from classical epic: the supernatural machinery, the set speeches, the description of the card-game (ombre) as a battle, the final combat between beaux and belles, the journey to the Cave of Spleen, all connect with traditional epic devices. In general method Pope follows Boileau *Lutrin,* which deals with the quarrels of the priests of the Sainte Chapelle, and Garth *Dispensary,* which deals with the quarrels of physicians. But Pope's subject, the contemporary world of fashion, entailed certain differences in method. The earlier burlesques often dealt with the low and ugly, and used the mock-heroic style chiefly to give a heavy caricature. Pope's theme is trivial rather than low; his mock-heroic elevation enlarges and illustrates it without distorting it; though he takes some specific hints for his satire of fashionable life from Garth, he avoids the ponderousness that usually appears in the employment of epic devices for humorous effect, and attains playful brilliance and elegance. His style is related to the graceful treatment of feminine fashions and ways in the *Tatler* and the *Spectator*, and it suggests some comparisons with the playful devices which Swift later used in the voyage to Lilliput. There are some touches of the grotesque, as in the caricature of Sir Plume and the details of the Cave of Spleen, but throughout there is a systematic use of idealized and heightened decoration, as in the description of the toilet table, the progress of the heroine Belinda up the Thames, and the party at Hampton Court. The mocking overstatements and elaborate style in the hands of a less skilful artist would be clumsy exaggeration, but here form an essential part of the decorative pattern, and are kept in place by Pope's systematic use of the device of anticlimax. This artificial society is not rejected or denounced; it is accepted as a fascinating spectacle, yet there is a didactic note—vanity, folly, spite are censured, and good sense and good humor are recommended. Such control of cynicism and satire, except for a few lines in which the underlying theme of sex is too grossly expressed, shows the great change in manners as we pass from Restoration comedy to Pope and Addison. For all these reasons, *The Rape of the Lock* has been Pope's most popular poem, not only in its day of publication but in later periods which looked back on the eighteenth century as a kind of costume piece.

THE DUNCIAD

(Books I-III, 1728; *Dunciad Variorum*, with satirical notes and much introductory and appended matter, 1729; *New Dunciad* (Book iv), 1742; complete edition in four books, 1743.)

Pope developed from about 1725 to 1727, with the help and advice of Swift, a comprehensive satire in which he might take revenge on his literary enemies and deride the whole tribe of dull and mercenary scribblers. Behind the whole project, along with personal animus, was the contempt felt by the inner circle of great writers for what they took to be the cheapening of authorship in an age of journalism, pamphleteering, and hackwork. A specific purpose of the *Dunciad* of 1728 and 1729 was to attack pedantry in the person of Lewis Theobald, whose *Shakespeare Restored* (I726) had effectively attacked Pope's work as an editor of Shakespeare, and who was continuing his campaign in the newspapers. The notes in the variorum edition serve this purpose. This is an extension of a device used in *A Tale of a Tub* and in earlier skits on pedantry by the Scriblerus Club. The plan of the poem is mock-epic, though it does not have the skillfully unified structure of *The Rape of the Lock*. In Book I the Goddess of Dulness chooses Theobald for her own—Cibber was substituted later. The basic scheme here is from Mac Flecknoe. Elaborating the idea of a contest among the dunces for supremacy, Book II burlesques the account of the funeral games for Anchises in *Æneid V*; the dunces run races, dive in filth, and so forth. In Book III the hero has an epic vision of the Progress of Dulness (the original title of the piece) from the most remote past to the final triumph of Chaos and Night. The tone throughout is often broad and jocular rather than malicious and bitter. The *New Dunciad* of 1742, written with the advice of Warburton, gives a sweeping view of defective education and of the follies of pedantry, antiquarianism, scientific virtuosity, and free thought. The book is less personal than the first three, and relatively grave, decent, and elegant. The general scheme is that of a court reception at which the Goddess of Dulness bestows honors or favors upon groups of her followers and subjects; Professor Sherburn has suggested that Pope may have taken this device from Fielding's popular farces of the 1730's. When Cibber is substituted for Theobald in the version of 1743 we see that the term dunce is made to cover a good deal; a dunce may be pedantic, as Pope said Theobald was, or "lively," like Cibber, but always wrong-headed. Against all varieties of folly and error the true wit must break a lance; it follows, as Pope said, that "the life of a wit is a warfare upon earth."

AN ESSAY ON MAN

The four epistles that make up the *Essay* were published anonymously from February 1733 to January 1734. The work strikes the moral or didactic note which is prominent in Pope's work after the *Dunciad*. It is his most ambitious philosophic effort, and indeed the most familiar and frequently quoted piece of popular philosophy in the eighteenth century. "Essay" does not seem to mean here something merely tentative, but a fairly systematic treatise. Although Pope talks much about man's weakness and blindness, and his presumption in aspiring to understand the whole, the poet nevertheless undertakes to set forth a coherent scheme of the universe, and thus to "vindicate the ways of God to man." An ancient conception, widely popularized and generally accepted in Pope's day, was that God in his overflowing goodness must create the best of all possible worlds, that is, a world in which all possible forms of being, low and high, simple and complex, are actually realized: the universe is thus an unbroken chain, scale, or continuum, and everything must be just what it is and where it is in order that the great scheme may be realized. The history of this idea is fully told in Lovejoy's classic study *The Great Chain of Being* (1936), and to the exposition of such a scheme of things Pope devotes a large part of the first epistle. He has been much censured for this hasty leap into metaphysics. Bolingbroke was his philosophic guide; it is uncertain how definite Bolingbroke's actual contributions to the *Essay* were, but it seems that they were probably made orally rather than in writing. In any case both men were rather beyond their depth and showed no original philosophic power. We should not underestimate, however, the power of general ideas, particularly the vision of the chain of being, to touch the poet's imagination and to inspire brilliant aphoristic verse.

The one thing needful is to know one's place in the chain—"Order is Heaven's first law." This means acceptance of and resignation to the world order, avoidance of the cardinal sin and error of Pride. But obviously man falls short here. In Epistle II Pope finds that human nature does not fit easily into the perfect scheme expounded in Epistle I. Man's reason is at war with his passions ("modes of selflove"), and competing passions themselves may be, usually are, overmastered by the ruling passion. Now a thoroughgoing optimism might argue that since partial evil becomes universal good, the passions, like everything else, work for good. It is also possible to view the spectacle of contending passions as a dramatic or aesthetic pattern. But Pope easily slips back into his rôle of satirist, and emphasizes the irrational element in man and man's responsibility for keeping that element under control. "Whatever is, is right," and yet sin, error, and folly keep preachers and satirists busy. Popular philosophy is often a matter of basic images or metaphors; for the image of the perfect and static chain in Epistle I Pope here substitutes the image of strong conflicting forces which it is man's duty to keep in equilibrium. The conflict of reason and passion in the *Essay on Man* is exactly parallel to the conflict of wit and judgment in the *Essay on Criticism*.

In the account of the development of human society in Epistle III, Pope again expounds a divinely ordered scheme, in which the operations of the lower animals determined by God-given instinct, and the relations between men in the state of nature by God-given benevolence. The familiar primitivistic idea of the Golden Age appears here. The basic conception is that of divine design, or what Pope's contemporaries called physico-theology. Of course the whole scheme of the chain of being might be thought of in terms of design, but the arguments of contemporary physico-theology concerned themselves not so much with metaphysics as with the evidences of design which appeared in the new findings of science. Man should not be encouraged to think of himself as the center of the universe, but nothing is more salutary than to observe how exquisitely all things have been planned by the Creator. As we contemplate this grand scheme, it appears that even the conflicts and stresses of human nature are divinely arranged, for "true self-love and social are the same." In Epistle IV Pope considers the good life, the way to happiness, and thus shows how the *Essay* connects with the *Moral Essays* and *Satires* to follow. The general connection between the system of the *Essay* and contemporary satire is seen in *Spectator* No. 404:

> The Creator of the universe has appointed everything to a certain use and purpose, and determined it to a settled course and sphere of action, from which if it in the least deviates, it becomes unfit to answer those ends for which it was designed. . . . The civil economy is formed in a chain as well as the natural; and in either case the breach but of one link puts the whole in some disorder. . . . Most of the absurdity and ridicule we meet with in the world is generally owing to the impertinent affectation of excelling in characters men are not fit for, and for which Nature never designed them.

The *Essay* deals with natural, not revealed, religion. It is not Christian but deistic, though most of the ideas it expresses were the common property of freethinkers and orthodox in Pope's day. The system is largely that of Shaftesbury, who was definitely hostile to Christianity. When we come across ideas which can be labeled deistic, it is often hard to tell whether they are thought of as coexisting with and supporting orthodox Christianity, or as constituting a natural religion sufficient in itself. Pope would never say that he was setting forth the ideas of the *Essay*, in opposition to the Roman Catholic faith which he nominally professed. His *Universal Prayer*, published in 1738, was also taken as deistic, his orthodoxy was seriously attacked, and he was very grateful to his new friend and champion Bishop Warburton for undertaking to demonstrate in opposition to his critic Crousaz that the *Essay on Man* was really the utterance of a Christian.

LADY MARY WORTLEY MONTAGU(1689-1762)

Lady Mary Wortley Montagu, one must imagine, was a lady of far more masculine understanding and knowledge than most of the classical ladies of whose attainments Johnson thought highly. As a descriptive topographer, she was a keen observer, not superior to the love of gossip, with a quick eye for the telling features of a story or a situation and an easy, effective style. Her manner is one of conscious superiority. She belonged to the great whig aristocracy which ruled England. Her father, Evelyn Pierrepont, was connected with the Evelyns of Wootton, and married Mary Feilding, daughter of the earl of Denbigh, from one of whose brothers Henry Fielding the novelist descended. Mary was born in May, 1689; a year later, her father became earl of Kingston and, at the whig triumph of 1715, duke of Kingston; she was brought up, carelessly enough, in a library. One of her girl friends was Anne Wortley Montagu, a granddaughter of the first earl of Sandwich (Pepys's chief), whose father had, on marrying an heiress, taken the name Wortley. Anne's favourite brother Edward, a most unromantic young man, was strongly attracted by Lady Mary's lucidity of both mind and visage. A number of letters between them are extant. The young pair were, unmistakably, in love; but Kingston was inexorable on the subject of settlements and tried to coerce his daughter into another match; whereupon, she eloped with Edward Wortley (August, 1712). With the whigs' advent to power, the period of narrow means came to an end, and Edward, a relative of Halifax, became M.P. for Westminster and, in 1716, was appointed ambassador to the Porte. In 1717, the couple journeyed to Constantinople, by way of Vienna and Belgrade. Her most vivid letters were written during this period and remain an imperishable monument of her husband's otherwise undistinguished embassy; for it was upon his successors that devolved the important task of concluding the peace of Passarowitz. It must not be supposed that we have the letters in their original form. Moy Thomas came upon a list of letters written by the ambassadress, with notes of their contents. The published letters correspond but imperfectly to the *précis,* and only two are indexed as copied at length. Of those remaining to us, some that had been copied were reproduced with small alteration; the majority were reconstructed from the diary in which she was accustomed to note the events and thoughts of every day, and from which she had presumably drawn freely for the original correspondence; others, less finished in form, for the most part, have been found and incorporated since. The substance of many letters hitherto unknown was given as late as 1907 by "George Paston" in her *Lady Mary Wortley Montagu and her Times.*

PHILIP DORMER STANHOPE, FOURTH EARL OF CHESTERFIELD (1694-1773)

Philip Dormer Stanhope, 4th Earl of Chesterfield (22 September 1694 - 24 March 1773) was a British statesman and man of letters.

A Whig, Lord Stanhope, as he was known until his father's death in 1726, was born in London, and educated at Cambridge and then went on the Grand Tour of the continent. The death of Anne and the accession of George I opened up a career for him and brought him back to England, His relative James Stanhope, the king's favorite minister, procured for him the place of gentleman of the bedchamber to the Prince of Wales. In 1715 he entered the House of Commons as Lord Stanhope of Shelford and member for St Germans, and when the impeachment of the Duke of Ormonde, came before the House, he used the occasion (5 August 1715) to put to proof his old rhetorical studies.

His maiden speech was youthfully fluent and dogmatic; but on its conclusion the orator was reminded with many compliments, by an honorable member, that he wanted six weeks of his majority, and consequently that he was amenable to a fine of 500 for speaking in the House. Lord Stanhope quitted the Commons with a low bow and started for the continent. From Paris he rendered the government important service by gathering and transmitting information respecting the Jacobite plot; and in 1716 he returned to England, resumed his seat, and took frequent part in the debates. In that year came the quarrel between the king and the heir apparent. Stanhope, whose politic instinct obliged him to worship the rising rather than the setting sun, remained faithful to the prince, though he was too cautious to break entirely with the king's party. He was on friendly terms with the prince's mistress, Henrietta Howard, afterwards Countess of Suffolk. He maintained a correspondence with this lady which won for him the hatred of the Princess of Wales. In 1723 a vote for the government got him the place of captain of the Gentlemen Pensioners. In January 1725, on the revival of the Bath, the red riband was offered to him, but was declined.

In 1726 his father died, and Lord Stanhope became Earl of Chesterfield. He took his seat in the Upper House, and his oratory, never effective in the Commons by reason of its want of force and excess of finish, at once became a power. In 1728 Chesterfield was sent to The Hague as ambassador. In this place his tact and temper, his dexterity and discrimination, enabled him to do good service, and he was rewarded with Walpole's friendship, a Garter and the place of Lord Steward. In 1732 there was born to him, by a certain Mlle du Bouchet, the son, Philip Stanhope, for whose advice and instruction were afterwards written the famous Letters. He negotiated the second Treaty of Vienna in 1731, and in the next year, being somewhat broken in health and fortune, he resigned his embassy and returned to England.

A few months' rest enabled him to resume his seat in the Lords, of which he was one of the acknowledged leaders. He supported the ministry, but his allegiance was not the blind fealty Walpole exacted of his followers. The Excise Bill, the great premier's favorite measure, was vehemently opposed by him in the Lords, and by his three brothers in the Commons. Walpole bent before the storm and abandoned the measure; but Chesterfield was summarily dismissed from his stewardship. For the next two years he led the opposition in the Upper House, leaving no stone unturned to effect Walpole's downfall. In 1741 he signed the protest for Walpole's dismissal and went abroad on account of his health.

He visited Voltaire at Brussels and spent some time in Paris, where he associated with the younger Crebillon, Fontenelle and Montesquieu. In 1742 Walpole fell, and Carteret was his real, though not his nominal successor.

Although Walpole's administration had been overthrown largely by Chesterfield's efforts the new ministry did not count Chesterfield either in its ranks or among its supporters. He remained in opposition, distinguishing himself by the courtly bitterness of his attacks on George II, who learned to hate him violently.

In 1743 a new journal, *Old England; or, the Constitutional Journal* appeared. For this paper Chesterfield wrote under the name of "Jeffrey Broadbottom." A number of pamphlets, in some of which Chesterfield had the help of Edmund Waller, followed. His energetic campaign against George II and his government won the gratitude of the Dowager Duchess of Marlborough, who left him 20,000 as a mark of her appreciation. In 1744 the king was compelled to abandon Carteret, and the coalition or "Broad Bottom" party, led by Chesterfield and Pitt, came into office in coalition with the Pelhams. In the troublous state of European politics the earl's conduct and experience were more useful abroad than at home, and he was sent to the Hague as ambassador a second time. The object of his mission was to persuade the Dutch to join in the War of the Austrian Succession and to arrange the details of their assistance. The success of his mission was complete; and on his return a few weeks afterwards he received the Lord-Lieutenancy of Ireland, a place he had long coveted.

Short as it was, Chesterfield's Irish administration was of great service to his country, and is unquestionably that part of his political life which does him most honor. To have conceived and carried out a policy which, with certain reservations, Burke himself might have originated and owned, is indeed no small title to regard. The Earl showed himself finely capable in practice as in theory, vigorous and tolerant, a man to be feared and a leader to be followed; he took the government entirely into his own hands, repressed the jobbery traditional to the office, established schools and manufactures, and at once conciliated and kept in check the Orange and Roman Catholic factions. In 1746, however, he had to exchange the lord-lieutenancy for the place of

Secretary of State. With a curious respect for those theories his familiarity with the secret social history of France had caused him to entertain, he hoped and attempted to retain a hold over the king through the influence of Lady Yarmouth, though the futility of such means had already been demonstrated to him by his relations with Queen Caroline's "ma bonne Howard," The influence of Newcastle and Sandwich, however, was too strong for him; he was thwarted and over-reached; and in 1748 he resigned the seals, and returned to cards and his books with the admirable composure which was one of his most striking characteristics. He declined any knowledge of the *Apology for a late Resignation,* in a *Letter from an English Gentleman to his Friend at The Hague,* which ran through four editions in 1748, but there is little doubt that he was, at least in part, the author.

The dukedom offered him by George II, whose ill-will his fine tact had overcome, was refused. He continued for some years to attend the Upper House, and to take part in its proceedings. In 1751, seconded by Lord Macclesfield, president of the Royal Society, and Bradley, the eminent mathematician, he distinguished himself greatly in the debates on the calendar, and succeeded in making the new style a fact. Deafness, however, was gradually affecting him, and he withdrew little by little from society and the practice of politics. In 1755 occurred the famous dispute with Johnson over the dedication to the English Dictionary. In 1747 Johnson sent Chesterfield, who was then Secretary of State, a prospectus of his *Dictionary,* which was acknowledged by a subscription of 10 pounds. Chesterfield apparently took no further interest in the enterprise, and the book was about to appear, when he wrote two papers in the *World* in praise of it. It was said that Johnson was kept waiting in the anteroom when he called while Gibber was admitted. In any case the doctor had expected more help from a professed patron of literature, and wrote the earl the famous letter in defence of men of letters. Chesterfield's "respectable Hottentot," now identified with George, Lord Lyttelton, was long supposed, though on slender grounds, to be a portrait of Johnson.

During the twenty years of life that followed this episode, Chesterfield wrote and read a great deal, but went little into society.

His famous jest (which even Johnson allowed to have merit), "Tyrawley and I have been dead these two years, but we don't choose to have it known," is the best description possible of his humour and condition during the latter part of this period of decline. To the deafness was added blindness, but his memory and his fine manners only left him with life; his last words ("Give Dayrolles a chair") prove that he had neither forgotten his friend nor the way to receive him. He died on the 24 March 1773.

Chesterfield was selfish, calculating and contemptuous; he was not naturally generous, and he practiced dissimulation till it became part of his nature. In spite of his brilliant talents and of the admirable training he received, his life, on the whole, cannot be pronounced a success. His anxiety and the pains he took to become an orator have been already noticed, and Horace Walpole, who had heard all the great orators, preferred a speech of Chesterfield's to any other; yet the earl's eloquence is not to be compared with that of Pitt. Samuel Johnson, who was not perhaps the best judge in the world, pronounced his manners to have been exquisitely elegant; yet as a courtier he was utterly worsted by Robert Walpole, whose manners were anything but refined, and even by Newcastle. He desired to be known as a protector of letters and literary men; and his want of heart or head over the *Dictionary* dedication, though explained and excused by Croker, none the less inspired the famous change in a famous line "Toil, envy, want, the patron, and the jail." His published writings have had with posterity a very indifferent success; his literary reputation rests on a volume of letters never designed to appear in print. The son for whom he worked so hard and thought so deeply failed especially where his father had most desired he should succeed.

As a politician and statesman, Chesterfield's fame rests on his short but brilliant administration of Ireland. As an author he was a clever essayist and epigrammatist. But he stands or fails by the *Letters to his Son,* first published by Stanhope's widow in 1774, and the *Letters to his Godson* (1890). The Letters are brilliantly written, full of elegant wisdom, of keen wit, of admirable portrait-painting, of exquisite observation and deduction.

Among the quotations attributed to him are:

"The world is a country which nobody ever yet knew by description; one must travel through it one's self to be acquainted with it."

"An able man shows his spirit by gentle words and resolute actions."

"I recommend you to take care of the minutes, for the hours will take care of themselves."

James Thomson (1700-1748)
Henry Fielding (1707-1754)
Samuel Johnson (1709-1784)
Laurence Sterne (1713-1768)

JAMES THOMSON (1700-1748)

Thomson is the greatest of modern poets born in Scotland before Burns, and, except for Pope, the most celebrated British poet of the first half of the eighteenth century—in the long run, indeed, his popularity was greater than Pope's. He was born at Ednam, Roxburghshire, but spent his boyhood at Southdean, in the valley of the Jed, a tributary of the Tweed. The local color and the history of this famous region were later immortalized by Scott. Thomson's earliest memories were of the Border landscape and of simple country life, and this background counted for much in his work, though he makes little direct use of the specific Scottish scene. His father, who died in 1716, was a Presbyterian clergyman, and Thomson was originally intended for the ministry when he entered the University of Edinburgh. His work as a student of arts and divinity gave much of the literary and philosophical background for his poetry. The Presbyterian faith was being softened and liberalized in Scottish university circles. The Bible, Milton, and Virgil set literary themes, and Locke and Shaftesbury gave a framework of ideas. Science too was studied, especially), in the popular form of physico-theology, the use of new scientific detail to demonstrate the work of God in the creation. Such a union of religious, scientific, and literary motives had been made by Richard Blackmore, especially, in his *Creation* and *Paraphrase of Job*, mediocre work which is nevertheless historically important. All this may sound more formidable than it actually was; Thomson wrote juvenile verse in an undergraduate club at Edinburgh without being fully conscious of the forces at work upon him.

In 1725 he went to London, and soon decided to become a poet, not a preacher. His first important poem, *Winter*?, was published in the spring of 1726; *Summer* followed in 1727, *Spring* in 1728, and *Autumn* and the concluding *Hymn* with the collected *Seasons* published by subscription in 1730. Thomson worked rapidly in these years, publishing also *A Poem Sacred to the Memory of Sir Isaac Newton* (I727) and *Britannia* (I729). His tragedy *Sophonisba* was successfully produced at Drury Lane in 1730, though in general his dramas have added nothing to his after-fame. At the end of 1730 he went abroad as tutor to Charles Talbot, son of the Solicitor General, and traveled in France and Italy. His next literary project was the long and overambitious poem *Liberty* (I735-36), elaborately setting forth the familiar view that political liberty was attained in ancient Greece and Rome, lost in the Middle Ages and again in the degenerate Italian culture of modern times, preserved and renewed in the northern Germanic tradition most completely exemplified in Great Britain. The poem disappointed admirers of *The Seasons*. Its ideas are characteristic of the Whig opposition. As early as *Britannia* Thomson had been dissatisfied with the peace policy of Walpole and had paid tribute to the Prince of Wales, about whom the opposition was beginning to center. This allegiance is expressed in the dedications of *Liberty*, the dramas Agamemnon (I738) and Edward and Eleonora (prohibited under the terms of the new Licensing Act but published in 1739), and the masque *Alfred* (I740), in which he collaborated with David Mallet. This piece is famous for the song *Rule Britannia*: Thomson's authorship seems certain, though it has been questioned.

The Seasons (I744, final version 1746). In 1748 he published his most charming poem, *The Castle of Indolence*. This piece, the most successful Spenserian imitation of the eighteenth century, began as "little more than a few detached stanzas in the way of raillery on himself, and on some of his friends, who would reproach him with indolence, while he thought them at least as indolent as himself." The poem is nominally on the side of progress, and in Canto II the Knight of Arts and Industry breaks the spell cast by the wizard Indolence, but the best stanzas are those that present the delights of reverie, relaxation, and the refined pleasures of the senses. The less serious side of Thomson's personality, the playfulness characteristic of one side of eighteenth-century art, and the example of Spenser's rich verse combine to form one of the most pleasing poems of the age. Thomson died at the age of forty-eight, and William Collins wrote a poem to his memory.

THE SEASONS

Thomson, it is often said, "returned to nature" in the artificial age of Pope. His fine descriptions of landscape and atmospheric effect and his genre pictures have always given pleasure. But contemporaries thought of *The Seasons* as not merely descriptive but didactic and reflective. They accepted in Thomson the conception of the poet as a seer, like Virgil and Milton, a virtuoso and patriot, like Shaftesbury and Addison; his mind was open alike to the inspiration of literary models, the new findings of science, and the ideals of patriotism and philanthropy. It is in this spirit that Thomson writes in the Preface to the second edition of Winter: "I know no subject more elevating, more amusing, more ready to awake the poetical enthusiasm, the philosophical reflection, and the moral sentiment, than the works of Nature." Such, he goes on to say, are the themes of the greatest poets, Virgil, Milton, and the author of Job. *Winter* was originally a short meditative-descriptive poem somewhat on the plan of *Il Penseroso*. The success of this piece encouraged him not only to extend it but to proceed to describe "the various appearance of Nature . . . in the other Seasons," as he says in the Preface to the second edition. This led to the full development of the long descriptive-didactic poem, with a loose structure which admits easy transitions and digressions. The influence of the georgic form and of Miltonic style is always marked. Thomson's interest in science and in natural religion was evidently at its height in the years 1726-30. The lines on Newton express the same interest. The scheme of a universe ordered by divine Harmony and Reason, expounded in Thomson's day not only by Shaftesbury but by more orthodox authorities, is filled up to some extent with scientific detail. This practice may be called Newtonian, but in a poet like Thomson it has no scientific rigor, and can easily be combined with the benevolism of Shaftesbury and Hutcheson. Ethical, philanthropic, and patriotic themes appear frequently. The later version shows elaborate additions drawn from the literature of geography and travel, particularly the descriptions of the Far North in *Winter* and of the *Tropics in Summer*. Set topographical descriptions of English scenes, such as Lyttelton's Hagley and the view from Richmond Hill, are also added. The common opinion that these additions are inferior is hardly justified; Thomson is uneven, but he shows no marked decline of poetic power. It is true, however, that his greatest success is in exact and delicate notation of sense effects in a setting planned on a fairly large scale, and for this combination the scenes inspired by English and Scottish landscapes are of course the best.

Thomson's diction is often a handicap; his Miltonic phrases and Latinized vocabulary exemplify to a far greater degree than Pope the poetic diction which Wordsworth was to attack. His opinions show inconsistencies which need not trouble us much. In the spirit of Whig panegyric he is a believer in progress, and yet, like many others, he is at times fascinated by the ideal of the Golden Age, by the virtues of simple Laplanders and Indians, and uses such themes in a polemic against luxury and sophistication. His religious views are deistic. His quiet substittution of the God of Nature for the God of Revelation is characteristic of the time. There can be no doubt that he was a Shaftesburian freethinker, not, like most of the Newtonians, an orthodox Christian. But the average reader of *The Seasons* troubled himself as little about Thomson's theology as about Milton's; the poem was read for pleasure and for edification in countless families and schools in Great Britain and America for over a century after the poet's death.

HENRY FIELDING (1707-1754)

British writer, playwright and journalist, founder of the English Realistic school in literature with Samuel Richardson. Fielding's career as a dramatist has been shadowed by his career as a novelist. His aim as a novelist was to write comic epic poems in prose - he once described himself as "great, tattered bard."

"When I'm not thanked at all, I'm thanked enough;
I've done my duty, and I've done no more."
(from *Tom Thumb the Great*, 1730)

Henry Fielding was born at Sharpham Park, Somerset. He was by birth a gentleman, close allied to the aristocracy. His father was a nephew of the 3th Earl of Denbigha, and mother was from a prominent family of lawyers. Fielding grew up on his parents farm at East Stour, Dotset. His mother died when Fielding was eleven, and when his father remarried, Henry was sent to Eton. He studied at Eton College (1719-1724), where he learned to love ancient Greek and Roman literature.

Encouraged by his cousin, Lady Mary Wortley Montagu, Fielding started his career as a writer in London. In 1728 he wrote two plays, of which *Love In Several Masques* was successfully performed at Drury Lane. In the same year he went to the University of Leiden in the Netherlands, enlarging his knowledge of classical literature. After returning to England, he devoted himself to writing for the stage. Fielding also became a manager of the Little Theatre in the Haymarket. In 1730 he had four plays produced, among them *Tom Thumb,* which is his most famous and popular drama. According to a story, it made Swift laugh for the second time in his life. In 1736 Fielding took over the management of the New Theatre, writing for it among others the satirical comedy *Pasquin.* For several years Fielding's life was happy and prosperous.

However, Fielding's sharp burlesques satirizing the government gained the attention of the prime minister Sir Robert Walpole and Fielding's career in theater was ended by Theatrical Licensing Act - directed primarily at him. In search for an alternative career he became editor of the magazine *Champion,* an opposition journal. After studies of law Fielding was called in 1740 to the bar. Because of increasing illness - he suffered from gout and asthma - Fielding was unable to pursue his legal career with any consistency.

Between the years 1729 and 1737 Fielding wrote 25 plays but he acclaimed critical notice with his novels. The best known are *The History Of Tom Jones, A Foundling* (1749), in which the tangled comedies of coincidence are offset by the neat, architectonic structure of the story, and *The History Of The Adventures Of Joseph Andrews* (1742), a parody of Richardson's *Pamela* (1740). Although Fielding wrote in *Tom Jones* "That monstrous animal, a husband and wife", he married in 1734 Charlotte Cradock, who became his model for Sophia Western in *Tom Jones* and for the heroine of *Amelia,* the author's last novel. It was written according to Fielding "to promote the cause of virtue and to expose some of the most glaring evils, as well public as private, which at present infect the country..." In the story an army officer is imprisoned. His virtuous wife resists all temptations and stays faithful to him. With Charlotte Fielding enjoyed ten years of happiness until her death in 1744. Fielding's improvidence led to long periods of considerable poverty, but he was greatly assisted at various periods of his life by his friend R. Allen, who was the model for Allworthy in *Tom Jones*.

> "What is commonly called love, namely the desire of satisfying a voracious appetite with a certain quantity of delicate white human flesh." (from *Tom Jones*)

In 1747 Fielding caused some scandal by marrying his wife's maid and friend Mary Daniel - he was condemned by every snob in England. Actually she was about to bear his child, and Fielding wished to save her from disgrace. After Walpole had been replaced by another prime minister, Fielding came to the defense of the Establishment. As a reward for his governmental journalism he was made justice of the peace for the City of Westminster in 1748 and for the county of Middlesex in 1749. Together with his half brother Sir John Fielding, he established a new tradition of justice and suppression of crime in London, organizing a detective force that later developed into Scotland Yard. Fielding's writings became more socially orientated - he opposed among others public hangings. From the court in Bow Street he continued his struggle against corruption and and saw successfully implemented a plan for breaking up the criminal gangs who were then flourishing in London.

When the author's health was failing and he was forced to use crutches, he went with his wife and one of his daughters to Portugal to recuperate. Fielding died on October 8, 1754 in Lisbon. His travel book, *The Journal Of A Voyage To Lisbon,* appeared posthumously in 1755.

The History of Tom Jones, A Foundling was enthusiastically revived by the general public, if not by Richardson, Dr. Johnson and other literary figures. Coleridge declared that the plot of *Tom Jones* was one of the three perfect plots in all literature, the others were Ben Jonson's *Alchemist* and Sophocles's *Oedipus Rex.* In its 'Preface' Fielding stated: "The excellence of the entertainment consists less in the subject than in the author's skill in well dressing it up... we shall represent human nature at first to keep appetite of our reader, in that more plain and simple manner in which it is found in the country, and shall hereafter hash and ragout it with all the high French and Italian seasoning of affectation and vice which courts and cities afford." - Much of the action unfolds against the backdrop of the 1745 Jacobite rebellion. The introductory chapters that preface each of the novel's 18 books cultivate the reader in a way that was then unprecedented in English fiction. The kindly, prosperous Mr Allworthy finds a baby boy on his bed. He adopts the child, naming it Tom Jones. Allworthy suspects that Jenny Jones, a maid-servant to the wife of the schoolmaster Partridge, is the mother. Jenny leaves with Partridge the neighborhood. Allworthy's sister Bridget marries Captain Blifil, they have a son. Tom and the young and mean-spirited Blifil are raised together. Years later a rivalry over the attention of Sophia Western arises between them. Because of an affair with the gamekeeper's daughter Molly Seagrim, and because of Blifil's treachery, Tom is expelled from the house. He experiences adventures in the picaresque section of the novel, drifts into an affair with Lady Ballaston, nearly kills his opponent in a duel, and is imprisoned. Meanwhile Sophia flees to London to escape the marriage with Blifil. Jenny Jones turns up to reveal that Bridget is the mother of Tom, and Blifil's cruelties to Tom over the years are exposed - Blifil knew the truth of Tom's birth. Tom marries Sophia, who forgives him for his infidelities, and Tom becomes the heir of Allworthy. Ford Madox Ford's comment on the work was: "Obviously, marital bliss is possible to the wives of the worst of rakes and to the rakes themselves. But to convince us that that is the lot of one or other of his characters the writer must take much more trouble... and write much better."

SAMUEL JOHNSON (1709-1784)

Samuel Johnson was born in Lichfeld as the son of a bookseller. His childhood was marred by ill health: a tubercular infection affected both his sight and hearing and his face was scarred by scrofula. Johnson was educated at Pembroke College, Oxford. His father died in 1731 and left the family in poverty. Johnson's studies were cut short and he returned to Lichfield, affected by depression which haunted him for his life. He worked as a teacher at the grammar school in Market Bosworth and published his first essays in the *Birmingham Journal*. In 1735 he married Mrs Elisabeth Porter, a widow 20 years his senior. They started a school at Edial, near Lichfeld, but the school did not prosper. Johnson's lack of degree and convulsive mannerisms hindered his success as a teacher. Two years later they moved to London where Johnson worked for Edward Cave, the founder of *The Gentleman's Magazine*.

Samuel Johnson was the subject and James Boswell the author of the greatest biography in the language and one of the most interesting books in the world. The reader who has fallen under the spell of Boswell will inevitably think of Johnson's life and personality as greater than the sum of his literary work. This judgment is correct, yet it should be our purpose to find the true Johnson both in the life and the works. And this, as we shall see, involves a just estimate of Boswell also. If we say that Boswell merely reported Johnson, we underestimate Boswell's skill and art. If we say that Johnson lives in Boswell's work, we should understand that Johnson is much more than a fascinating, humorous, and eccentric character in a book.

The Johnson we know in Reynolds familiar portraits and in the pages of Boswell is a veteran man of letters who has won his place in the world but who keeps to the last the dogged resolution, intellectual honesty, and masculine power that carried him all the way. He had always followed his early bent and his inherited loyalties. His father Michael Johnson was a bookseller in the cathedral town of Lichfield, Staffordshire. When he became a glutton of books, and like his father he was always a Tory and a High Churchman. He entered Pembroke College, Oxford, but was in residence only a little more than a year, and left at the end of 1729 because he did not have enough money to carry him through. In later years he always looked on Oxford with pride and affection.

He spent the next few years in the neighborhood of Lichfield and Birmingham, teaching school and tutoring, and doing for a Birmingham bookseller his first piece of hackwork a translation of Lobo *Voyage to Abyssinia* (I735). He then married a widow, Mrs. Elizabeth Porter, some twenty years older than he was, and in 1736 tried to start a school at Edial, near Lichfield. The next year, in company with one of his pupils, David Garrick, he came up to London bringing his unfinished tragedy *Irene*. He attracted attention almost immediately by his impressive though academic satire *London* (I738). But he made his way by resolute routine work, not by the leisurely production of finished masterpieces. With his own career in mind, he names the ills that assail the aspirant to literary fame-"Toil, envy, want, the garret [later 'the patron'], and the jail" (*The Vanity of Human Wishes*). A more moderate statement would be that he spent his early years in London in the garret, the bookshop, and the tavern. He was soon doing miscellaneous work for Edward Cave, the publisher of the *Gentleman's Magazine*, of which Johnson might be considered in the early 40's as the editor. In 1744 he published his *Life of Richard Savage*, a remarkable account of a disreputable literary adventurer who had been one of his earliest London associates. In 1747 he issued the plan for his *Dictionary*, for which he had already contracted with Dodsley and other booksellers and which took most of his time and energy for eight years. Thus he continued to live the life of a hack-writer, though he was no longer desperately poor. During this period he was living in the house in Gough Square, north of Fleet Street, now a Johnsonian shrine, though badly damaged by German bombs. The *Dictionary* (I755) established his reputation as an authority on language and literature. The age sought a norm in language as in other fields, and welcomed one who undertook to regularize English usage. The basis for the work was a wide and discriminating reading of English writers of the seventeenth and eighteenth centuries; the definitions are for the most part clear and sound, and the illustrative quotations are of rich and varied interest. The famous humorous definitions, as for oats, lexicographer, Whig, etc., should not cause us to overlook the real importance of the *Dictionary.* Meanwhile Johnson had published his second great Juvenalian satire, *The Vanity of HumanWishes* Wishes (I749), and in the same year Garrick had produced his tragedy Irene with indifferent success. His *Rambler* (I750-52) was one of the most important of essay-periodicals; though Johnson does not have the varied appeal and the light touch of Addison and Steele at their best, he sets forth impressive moralizings in his heavy balanced style. The height of his moralistic work is reached in the famous tale of *Rasselas* (I759), written in the month of his mother's death. A new series of periodical essays in somewhat lighter vein, the *Idlcr,* appeared in the *Universal Chronicle,* 1758-60.

In 1762 the Tory government of George III gave Johnson a pension of £300, and thus enabled him to live and talk at leisure. A long delayed project was the edition of Shakespeare which he brought out at last in 1765. But he no longer felt it necessary to take on big jobs. He met Boswell in 1763, the famous Club was founded in 1764, and in the next year began his famous friendship with the Thrales. Thus the immortal circle dominated by Johnson and recorded by Boswell was formed within this decade. Burke and Goldsmith and Garrick are in the foreground, and the vivacious Mrs. Thrale is the principal feminine figure; we know the group like old friends, and yet the scene is endlessly varied by new visitors and new topics of conversation. The characteristic situation is the gathering of a group about Johnson in coffee house or chambers or at the Thrale's villa at Streatham, and the fluctuating but always vigorous reactions of Johnson himself give dramatic quality to the most trivial episode. The spirit of these meetings is well expressed in Johnson's own words: "As soon as I enter the door of a tavern, I experience an oblivion of care, and a freedom from solicitude. . . . I dogmatize and am contradicted, and in this conflict of opinions and sentiments I find delight."

His pamphlets on the American crisis (I770-75) are of merely historical interest, and his *Journey to the Western*

Islandsof Scotland of Scotland (I775) is overshadowed by Boswell's account of the same journey, *The Journal of a Tour to the Hebrides* (I785); but the preface and notes to his Shakespeare, and above all his *Lives of the English Poets* (I781) show the full weight of his personality and intelligence applied to literary criticism.

RASSELAS

Rasselas is a philosophic tale with a nominally oriental setting, though the geographical color is confined to a few details drawn from Lobo *Abyssinia* and perhaps from Baratti *Travels* (English translation 1670), and Lockman translation of *Travels of the Jesuits* (I743). The plan of the story seems to have been developed from two papers in the *Rambler* (Nos. 204, 205) which describe a vain quest for pleasure by "*Seged, Lord of Ethiopia.*" In *Rasselas*, Johnson begins by describing the confinement of the Abyssinian princes in the Happy Valley, whence the hero escapes, suffering from the boredom of pleasure and security, and goes to see the world in the company of the sage Imlac, while he ponders "the choice of life" or "the pursuit of happiness." Rasselas is warned by one example after another that romantic reverie, romantic love, the flights of the imagination, the daring speculations of philosophy, the great discoveries of science—all do harm to man by giving him an inaccurate estimate of what life has to offer and encouraging false hopes. The demands of real life are best met not by seeking actual perfection, but by calculating what may be the lesser evil. Man has to act, not merely to speculate and hope; but even in choosing among good things one excludes the other, and further limits on happiness are imposed by incalculable fatalities. The attack is partly directed against the optimism of the eighteenth century, or more generally against all simple formulas which profess to lead man to happiness, against all glib generalizations about the goodness of nature and the satisfactions of solitude, of learning, or of social life. To be sure, man should make the most of what order and reason he can find, but it is folly to stake one's hopes on a facile discovery of divine order in the world we see. Johnson is interested in ethics, not in physico-theology, and he warns the sensible man out of the area occupied in common by deism and liberal Christianity. *Rasselas* has often been compared with Voltaire *Candide*; the two works were published only a few weeks apart. Voltaire's work is also an attack on optimism, but is more exclusively concerned than Johnson with an attack on philosophical optimism, the Leibnizian conception of the best of all possible worlds, and is of course more purely satirical.

Johnson teaches that life is to be accepted on these terms with Christian resignation. "Happiness is to be placed only in virtue, which is always to be obtained," he had said in the Life of Savage. His praise of resolution and patience approaches Christian Stoicism, though he repeatedly says that the ideal Stoic indifference is impracticable (*Rambler* No. 32). *Rasselas* is a formal statement of the ethical position to be found in Johnson's satires and essays, and to be assumed as underlying his innumerable pungent comments in Boswell and the *Lives of the Poets*. Paraphrased and reported, his views seem commonplace to the last degree, but as he utters them they gain significance. The style is pompous and polysyllabic at times, but at its best simple and forceful, and the thought is always clear. Johnson does not try to be ingratiating or picturesque; *Rasselas* strikes us as hardly a work of imaginative fiction at all, but Johnson's claim would be that he is true to the general human situation which is his theme. As he said at the end of the *Rambler* (No. 208), "In the pictures of life I have never been so studious of novelty or surprise, as to depart wholly from all resemblance."

THE LIVES OF THE ENGLISH POETS

This is the last and the most important of Johnson's large-scale literary tasks. In opposition to an Edinburgh publisher, a syndicate of London booksellers undertook to bring out a collected edition of the English poets, and Johnson hastily agreed to write introductory notices for the series. But the accounts of the individual poets grew on his hands; he put into the work the fruits of a lifetime of reading and of his long familiarity with the London literary scene. His opinions are at times prejudiced and erroneous, but they are seldom perfunctory or languid. They do not represent mere eighteenth-century convention, but convention as experienced and interpreted anew by Samuel Johnson. His unsympathetic treatment of Milton and Gray is notorious. His estimates of Dryden and Pope and his praise of Addison are from the eighteenth-century point of view definitive. Other lives make famous contributions to criticism, e.g., the description of metaphysical poetry in the life of Cowley, the account of Collins's romanticism, and the argument that the mysteries of the Christian religion are not suitable for poetry. Johnson did not trouble himself, like Boswell, to unearth new biographical material; he used what was at hand, and inserted at full length his earlier life of Savage; but the *Lives* abound in shrewd comment on the personalities of the poets, and on the actual operations of literary ambitions and rivalries, and the unique quality of the work is due to the combination and fusion of biography and criticism.

LAURENCE STERNE (1713-1768)

Laurence Sterne (1713-1768) English author, b. Ireland. Educated at Cambridge, he entered the Anglican church and was given the living of Sutton-in-the-Forest, Yorkshire, in 1738, where he remained until 1759. He came to London the following year and was a great social success. Unhappily married, he was involved with various women during his lifetime, most notably Mrs. Eliza Draper, for whom he wrote the *Journal to Eliza* (1767). He led a somewhat dissolute life and much of the time was plagued by ill health, dying finally of tuberculosis. In 1760 the first volume of his masterpiece *Tristram Shandy* appeared. Although it was denounced on moral and literary grounds by Dr. Johnson, Horace Walpole, and others, the book was a popular success and eight subsequent volumes followed (1761–67). As a result of his travels to the Continent (1762–66) he wrote, but left unfinished, *A Sentimental Journey* (1768). He also published in his lifetime several volumes of sermons. One of the most entertaining and original literary works in English, *Tristram Shandy* is, in a sense, a parody of a novel. It is a hodgepodge of character sketches, blank pages, dramatic action, transposed chapters, and various digressions. Sterne constantly obtrudes himself into the novel and is by turns witty, satiric, sentimental, knowledgeable, and obscene. Beneath this apparent chaos, however, is a structure based on the association of ideas. In *Tristram Shandy* Sterne enlarged the scope of the novel from the mere recording of external incidents to the depiction of a complex of internal impressions, thoughts, and feelings.

Laurence Sterne's masterpiece, Tristram Shandy, is seldom read any more outside of graduate seminars. This is a sad fate for the author whom Nietszche deemed "the most liberated spirit of all time," and whose style, in its day, was considered "the most rapid, the most happy, the most idiomatic of any that is to be found.... The pure essence of English conversational style." The novel was wildly popular for years after its appearance. As the enthusiastic James Boswell rhymed, "Who has not Tristram Shandy read?/ Is any mortal so ill-bred?"

The book's initial success was due in no small part to its heavy flirtation with obscenity. Such smut was considered bad enough, by certain critics, when the book was published anonymously; when it became known that its author was an Anglican minister, it caused an outright scandal. One correspondent in a popular magazine of the day voiced a widespread objection: "It were greatly to be wished he had been more sparing in the use of indecent expressions. Indecent! Nay, even downright gross and obscene expressions are frequently to be met with throughout the book." This revulsion was shared by Samuel Richardson, at that time the torchbearer of high decorum in fiction: "One extenuating circumstance attends [Sterne's] works, that they are too gross to be inflaming.... His own character as a clergyman seems much impeached by printing such gross and vulgar tales, as no decent mind can endure without extreme disgust!"

All this notwithstanding, Sterne was always able to evade the charge of outright obscenity by the skillful use of insinuation and double-entendre: if the reader is dirty-minded enough to draw certain conclusions, the author implies, he has no one but himself to blame. For instance:

La Fosseuse's voice was naturally soft and low, yet 'twas an articulate voice: and even, letter of the word whiskers fell distinctly upon the queen of Navarre's ear – Whiskers! cried the queen, laying a greater stress upon the word, and as if she had still distrusted her ears – Whiskers; replied La Fosseuse, repeating the word a third time – There is not a cavalier, madam, of his age in Navarre, continued the maid of honour, pressing the page's interest upon the queen, that has so gallant a pair – Of what? cried Margaret, smiling – Of whiskers, said La Fosseuse, with infinite modesty.

This is a peculiarly English species of humor that has survived more on stage and television than in fiction:

Those who were out of sympathy with this style of humor accused Sterne of inserting it merely to attract the vulgar and the prurient. To give him credit, it seems in fact to have sprung to life perfectly spontaneously. Had not his fellow-clerics Rabelais and Swift used obscenity whenever their message required it? "A Very Able Critick & One of My Colour too [i.e. another priest]—who has Read Over tristram—Made Answer Upon My saying I Would consider the colour of my Coat, as I corrected it—That the very. Idea in My head would render My Book not worth a groat —still I promise to be Cautious—but I deny I have gone as farr as Swift—He keeps a due distance from Rabelais—& I keep a due distance from him—Swift has said a hundred things I durst Not Say," he insisted, adding mischievously, "—Unless I was Dean of St. Patricks."

Tristram Shandy was published in 1759, when Sterne was forty-six. His sort of dirty joke, or to put it more nicely, Rabelaisian humor, was already going out of style at the time of his death eight years later. Well aware of the changing

Zeitgeist, he wrote his travel book, A Sentimental Journey Through France and Italy (of which he completed only the first volume), in accordance with the new vogue for pathos and sensibility. Published only three weeks before his death, it was nearly as popular as its predecessor and was instrumental in changing public perceptions of its mercurial author.

Already in 1762 John Langhorne in The Monthly Review was opining that Sterne's "excellence lay not so much in the humorous as in the pathetic" – a judgment that seems scarcely credible today. The 1782 publication of a tremendously popular anthology, The Beauties of Sterne, completed the author's transformation into a proto-Romantic. The editors of this volume isolated the pathetic and sentimental portions of Tristram Shandy, A Sentimental Journey, and Sterne's published sermons from their frequently ironic contexts.

The Victorians rejected Sterne's bawdy side even more emphatically than their Romantic fathers had. Dickens was highly unusual, for his era, in his enthusiasm for Sterne's humor; Thackeray – hardly the most puritanical man of his age – was more typical in his impatient dismissal: "Some of that dreary double entendre may be attributed to freer times and manners than ours, but not all. The foul satyr's eyes leer out of the leaves constantly."

Tristram Shandy has a hero who is not even born until well into the third volume: its preface appears in volume III, its dedication in volume IX; it contains chapters that consist only of one or two lines, or of blank pages. Its storyline, if it can be said to have one, is no more than a series of increasingly absurd digressions, and at one point the author even inserts a graphic representation of the meandering, self-consuming narrative. "Non enim excursus hic ejus, sed opus ipsum est," he quotes in the seventh volume, gently chiding any reader who might still, at that late date, be hoping for the traditional sequence of protasis, epitasis, catastasis, catastrophe, and peripeteia.

Sterne may have been a free spirit, but he was born into constrained circumstances from which he never really escaped: his story, written with sympathy and elegance but without much wit or spark by Ian Campbell Ross, makes for rather sad reading. Sterne was by all accounts an extremely amusing man—Boswell, who was intimately acquainted with some of the most entertaining people of all time, pronounced him "the best companion I ever knew"—but Ross seems incapable of bringing this side of his subject to life. His intelligence, yes; his aberrant and self-destructive behavior, his dissatisfaction, his lust, but the wild spirits that made him so popular—and, to many, so unpopular—simply do not come across.

Sterne was born in 1713, the year of the Treaty of Utrecht that ended the War of the Spanish Succession in which his father, Roger Sterne, had served, first as a private and then as an ensign. The Sternes had achieved a position of some prominence in seventeenth-century Yorkshire—the novelist's great-grandfather, a supporter of the Stuarts during the Civil War, had been rewarded with the Archbishopric of York by Charles II—but Roger Sterne, the younger son of a younger son, had to make his own way in life, a task for which he was singularly ill-equipped. The novelist would later describe him in a family memoir:

> *My Father was a little Smart Man—active to the last Degree in all Exercises—most patient of Fatigue and Disappointments of wch it pleased God to give him in full Measure—He was in his Temper some what Rapid & Hasty —but of a kindly sweet Disposition—void of all Designe; & so innocent in his own Intentions, That he suspected no one, So that you might have cheated him ten times in a Day—if nine had not been sufficient.*

Roger's good-heartedness, along with his military experiences—he fought in Flanders, at the sieges of Douai and Bethune—have suggested him as an inspiration for Tristram Shandy's good-hearted Uncle Toby.With the Treaty of Utrecht, Roger Sterne, like countless other army officers, was reduced to half-pay. The family was in fairly desperate straits; the novelist's earliest memories are of moving about from one army barracks to another, in England and abroad. In 1723 or 1724, Roger Sterne took his son from Ireland back to England to leave him at Hipperholme School near Halifax, under the care of his brother, Richard Sterne, who accepted responsibility for this unknown nephew with an ill grace. Roger Sterne never saw his son again: he was to die, in Jamaica, in 1731.

There were very few avenues open to a well-educated but penurious young man at that time, and Laurence Sterne seems never to have questioned the decision that he go into the church. It was a field for which, with his intelligence and his sympathetic, imaginative character, he was at least superficially suited, and to the extent that he could rely on any family influence at all it was in that world, for another uncle, Jaques Sterne, was archdeacon of Cleveland and precentor of York Minster. "Jaques Sterne," comments Ross, "might serve as a model of one kind of eighteenth-century clergyman: clever, intensely ambitious, and decidedly world"—a sort of precursor of Trollope's Archdeacon Grantly.

Sterne was sent to Jesus College, Cambridge to prepare for taking orders. He received a scholarship established by his ancestor, the archbishop of York, for the benefit of poor scholars. He was ordained deacon in 1737 and, benefiting from his uncle's influence, was licensed to a curacy in Huntingdonshire.

Sterne must have been well aware of the precariousness of his position and the uncomfortable degree to which his future depended on his imperious uncle's goodwill. "If, in entering the Church, Sterne was apparently avoiding the frustrations of the military, career his father had followed with so little success," Ross points out, "then he was entering an organization whose rigidly hierarchical structure was essentially no different from that of the eighteenth-century arm)," and he quotes Joseph Addison, who remarked that the clergy, like the military, were divided into "Generals, Field-Officers, and Subalterns." Sterne, while clearly more intelligent than his father, turned out not to be much more provident; on top of which, he showed a marked aversion for the hard exercise involved in paying court and currying favor. Despite his natural advantages, his ecclesiastical career turned out to be hardly more profitable than his father's military one had been.

Sterne was ordained priest in 1738 and obtained the living of Sutton-on-the-Forest, some eight miles north of York. Soon afterward he met his future wife, Elizabeth Lumley. Elizabeth, who came from a family as financially straitened as his own, was not much of a catch from a worldly point of view, or from any other point of view for that matter. By the time they married in 1741 she was ill with consumption, as was Sterne himself; she also seems to have been no beauty. A cousin of Elizabeth's summed up the couple's chances rather brutally: "What hopes our relation may have of settling the affections of a light and fickle man I know not, but I imagine she will set about it not by means of beauty but of the arm of flesh."

It is interesting to discover that even at this early age Sterne was considered "light and fickle"; his reputation did not improve with the passing years. The Sternes' marriage, which resulted in several pregnancies but produced only one surviving child, Lydia, was to prove uncomfortable and unhappy almost from the beginning: on the Sunday following the wedding, in fact, Sterne is known to have preached on the text "We have toiled all the night and taken nothing." As the years went on Sterne affected (when not in the pulpit) to disapprove of marriage in general. Samuel Johnson's confidante Hester Thrale recalled him abusing the institution; when one of his audience dissented, saying that "Jesus Christ once honored a wedding with his presence," Sterne supposedly replied, "but between You & I Sir ... that was not the best thing he ever did."

In 1741 Sterne became a prebendary in York Minster. To be a prebendary, as one contemporary described it, was "a pretty easy way of dawdling away one's time; praying, walking, visiting;—& as little study as your heart would wish." But Sterne had other responsibilities: Jaques Sterne was cashing in his chips. He was a political powerbroker dedicated to promoting Whig interests in Yorkshire, and in exchange for his exertions on his nephew's behalf he expected the young man to put his talent for writing to work in the Whig cause.

Sterne's career as a political journalist provided him with more stress than pleasure or excitement. While he was a sincere supporter of the Whig political program, sometimes even an ardent one (as he proved by writing some disturbingly anti-Catholic polemics after the Battle of Culloden in 1745), he was in truth not much of a political animal, and eighteenth-century electioneering was violent, corrupt, and unscrupulous--even more so than it is today. He made more enemies than friends during his years of bondage to the Whigs, and eventually abandoned his uncle's cause and, in effect, his own hopes for high office in the church. From then on he was on his own; the solitary, battle for preferment was not to be an easy one.

In 1744 Sterne acquired a second living, that of the parish of Stillington which adjoined Sutton-on-the-Forest, and for the next two decades did duty in both parishes, as well as frequent substitute preaching at York Minster for a bit of extra cash. He and Elizabeth also took up farming, which they continued hopefully for years despite their predictable lack of success: "They kept a Dairy Farm at Sutton," remembered one friend, "had seven milch cows, but they always sold their Butter cheaper than their Neighbors, as they had not the least idea of oeconomy, so that they were always behindhand and in arrears with Fortune."

Sterne was not entirely unsuited to his priestly calling: he was notably compassionate to his flock, and performed numerous acts of private charity in the parish; he was also a gifted preacher. A servant of his claimed that "the audience were quite delighted with him, & he never preached at Sutton but the congregation were in tears." Yet he was an odd clergyman: not only was he an indiscreetly unfaithful husband, but he also appears to have been skeptical almost, on occasion, to the point of agnosticism, and he kept company with a famously irreligious social set.

In 1759 Sterne ill-advisedly re-entered the political fray when he penned a pamphlet called A Political Romance, or The History of a Good Warm Watch-Coat, somewhat in the manner of Swift's Tale of a Tub, in support of the dean of York Minster in a struggle against the archbishop. Sterne, predictably, had backed the wrong horse, and all five-hundred copies of a Political Romance were removed from the printers and burned. (A few copies in fact survive, although Sterne himself was not aware of their existence.) It was Sterne's last effort to win favor in the church. Soon he had declared his independence and embarked upon the first volumes of Tristram Shandy.

"Now you desire of knowing the reason of my turning author? why truly I am tired of employing my brains for other people's advantage.—'Tis a foolish sacrifice I made for some years to a foolish person." His friends preached caution: "Get Your Preferment first Lory!" said one—"& then Write & Welcome," but Sterne was fed up with patience and diplomacy. "But suppose preferment is long acoming," he objected, "(& for aught I know I may not be preferr'd till the Resurrection of the Just)."

During this time Sterne was as reckless in his personal life as he was in his career. Elizabeth had suffered a severe nervous breakdown, by most accounts the result of her husband's frequent infidelities, and for a time she was so deranged as to imagine herself the Queen of Bohemia. Apparently Sterne dallied with a number of ladies, but had one particular girlfriend: Catherine Fourmantel, a singer who had created something of a stir at the York Assembly Rooms. "Perhaps because of the unhappy months he had spent during his wife's illness, Sterne threw himself With abandon into this new relationship," Ross writes. "Sterne did not even scruple to sign his full name to compromising billets-doux suggests that his affection for Catherine Fourmantel was fully reciprocated."

The affair with Fourmantel coincided with his completion of the first two volumes of Tristram Shandy. Sterne initially offered it to the publisher Robert Dodsley, saying that he thought the book worth fifty pounds; Dodsley disagreed and made a counter offer of twenty. Sterne then decided to stake his own money on it instead, and borrowed enough cash to produce "a lean Edition, in 2 small Vols."

That Sterne had a great deal of confidence in his novel was evident from his willingness to take financial risks he could scarcely afford. His campaign of self-promotion was equally audacious: he wrote out a letter praising the book and induced Catherine Fourmantel to send it to David Garrick as though it were her own. As a special inducement Sterne added, in the person of Fourmantel, that "the Graver People however say, tis not fit for young Ladies to read his Book. so perhaps you'l think it not fit for a young Lady to recommend it however the Nobility, & great Folks stand up mightily for it. & say tis a good Book tho' a little tawdry in places."

No such puffery, as it turned out, was needed. Not everyone knew quite what to make of this odd novel; an anonymous reviewer in The Critical Review, for one, simply abandoned the attempt to provide a coherent review. "This is a humorous performance," he wrote, "of which we are unable to convey any distinct ideas to our readers." But sales were brisk, surpassing even Sterne's most sanguine hopes, and he achieved the sort of overnight literary celebrity that comes along only once every two or three decades. Perhaps Boswell described Sterne's rise to fame better than anyone:

In 1760 Sterne acquired a new living, at Coxwold on the edge of the moors north of York. There he lived, performing his parochial duties and working on the next volumes of Tristram Shandy. "I shall write as long as I live, 'tis, in fact, my hobby-horse," he decided. It seems clear that Sterne had no particular plan for his magnum opus; he simply put out new installments every year or two, and though some critics, most notably Wayne Booth, have attempted to demonstrate that Tristram Shandy was carefully constructed and that it ends, with volume IX, just as Sterne had always planned it to end, such arguments are exceedingly unconvincing. In fact the novel ends at the moment when Sterne's always-frail health finally gave out, and also at the time when his audience began to tire of the novel's discursive, absurdist style. Even enthusiasts wearied of the fun by the later installments: as Sir Horace Mann remarked, "Nonsense pushed too far becomes insupportable."

Among Sterne's many fans was Thomas Jefferson, who once declared surprisingly that "The writings of Sterne ... form the best course of morality that ever was written." Jefferson was rather an original moralist in his own right, and Sterne, too, was occasionally accused of paying mere lip service to the tenets of his creed—with some justice, it must be admitted. "Tristram pleads his cause well," the scapegrace John Wilkes remarked upon reading Sterne's collected sermons, "tho' he does not believe one word of it."

Was Jefferson right to represent Tristram Shandy as containing in itself a moral system? It is easy for modern readers to appreciate Sterne's spectacular stylistic genius, or his remarkable way with bawdy and innuendo; to appreciate or even to understand the moral underpinnings of his writing one must imaginatively enter the intellectual world of an eighteenth-century free-thinker who had little choice but to work within a traditional Christian system not only of values but of beliefs.

Ross somewhat ponderously describes Tristram Shandy as dealing in essence with the old unanswerable: "If an all-powerful, ever-present God exists, and is the 'best of beings,' why does He allow accident, mere chance, so often to intervene in human life?" It is hard, though, to find much evidence of such tortured and pointless thought in either Tristram Shandy or A Sentimental Journey; instead, over and over again, the author hints that both enthusiasm and doctrine are irrelevant if not dangerous (Tristram Shandy's heated debates between the Nosarians and the Antinosarians are a brilliant parody of Reformation polemic), and that true religion lies only in goodness, tolerance, generosity—whether they be of the Protestant variety, as with Tristram Shandy's Uncle Toby, Corporal Trim, and Yorick, or even the Catholic type, as with Father Lorenzo in A Sentimental Journey.

Sterne had only contempt for the human race's exalted opinion of its own place in the universe. Man—"with powers which dart him from earth to heaven in a moment—that great, that most excellent, and most noble creature of the world—the miracle of nature, as Zoroaster in his book called him—the *Shekinah* of the divine presence, as Chrysostom—the image of God, as Moses—the ray of divinity, as Plato—the marvel of marvels, as Aristotle." None of his characters is anything but earthbound. And he significantly makes Tristram's father, who personifies pure intellect detached from judgment and sense, recoil from the new scientific notion that the seat of the soul is in the cerebellum. "The very idea of so noble, so refined, so immaterial, and so exalted a being as the Anima, or even the Animus, taking up her residence, and sitting dabbling, like a tadpole, all day long, both summer and winter, in a puddle,— or in a liquid of any kind, how thick or thin soever, he would say, shock'd his imagination"—whereas the cannier Tristram knows very well that "the soul and body are joint-sharers in every thing they get."

In fact, if Laurence Sterne had lived two centuries later and had had other means of getting his living, it is doubtful whether he would have been any sort of Christian at all—though he would undoubtedly have retained his active, ironical interest in moral questions and human perversity in general. But while a moral system is easier to read into Tristram Shandy than any other sort of system, it is finally impossible—and completely undesirable—to impose any interpretation on the book. To do so is instantly to turn oneself into Tristram's pedantic father—although many, God knows, have tried.

This sort of theorizing immediately self-destructs—or deconstructs, if you will—in Sterne's anarchic laughter, and both explicator and reader end up none the wiser. Tristram Shandy resists interpretation in the most resolute way, and for that reason its survival more as an academic object than as a popular "fun read" is sad and pointless.

Horace Walpole (1717-1797)
Richard Hurd (1720-1808)
William Collins (1721-1759)
Mark Akenside (1721-1770)

HORACE WALPOLE (1717-1797)

Horace Walpole was born in London, 24 September 1717, the third surviving son of Sir Robert Walpole and his wife Catherine. Given the contrast between his effete vivacity and his father's robust forcefulness, there has always been a rumour that he was in fact the product of an adulterous liaison of his mother's, but he also bore a strong resemblance to one of his father's illegitimate children. Walpole lived primarily with his mother, who was in effect separated from his father. He was educated at Eton from 1727 to 1734, where he met the future poet Thomas Gray, and King's College, Cambridge, from 1735 to 1738. At Cambridge he studied mathematics, music and anatomy, but left, as was common practice among gentlemen, without taking a degree. He learned to paint. His mother, to whom he was devoted, died in 1737 and his father promptly married his mistress, Maria Skerrett. In 1739 Walpole began a grand antiquarian and social tour of France and Italy, in the company of Gray, with whom he quarreled at Reggio. At Florence he met Lady Mary Wortley Montagu, about whose appearance and amorous adventures he wrote somewhat cattily. The theory that Walpole was an active homosexual has recently been advanced by Timothy Mowl in *Horace Walpole: The Great Outsider* (1996), which contends that Walpole first fell in love with Henry Fiennes-Clinton, ninth Earl of Lincoln, at Eton and pursued sexual adventures with him at Cambridge and in Italy, incurring the jealousy of Gray, another recently-outed writer. Walpole never married (though the Earl of Lincoln did), and clearly preferred the company of women who were unmarriageable, most because of their slightly scandalous past. Many contemporaries regarded him as "effeminate", and, when it was necessary for the government to vilify him in 1764, he was openly accused of being a "hermaphrodite"; but much of Mowl's argument is highly tendentious, and his attempts to map the question of sexuality onto Walpole's literary work are not very convincing.

Walpole's father secured his election as Member of Parliament for a sequence of boroughs, places which he held until 1768. His father also found him lucrative sinecures in the Exchequer and Custom House which ensured a very comfortable income for life. Sir Robert Walpole resigned from office in 1742 and died in March 1745; Walpole was in attendance throughout the final illness. His filial piety found expression in *Aedes Walpolianae* (1747), a catalogue of his father's important collection of paintings and somewhat opinionated discussion of the main schools of European art represented in it. In 1747 Walpole settled at Strawberry Hill, an estate of some forty acres at Twickenham, near where Pope had lived, and set about remodeling it with Gothic details drawn from a wide variety of architectural sources. This was in marked contrast to the prevailing geometric classicism of the age, including his father's house at Houghton. He was helped by two friends, the amateur architect John Chute and the artist Richard Bentley. Extending the house along its axis, Walpole built himself a library, an armoury, a gallery, a "star chamber", a "tribune" (a sort of shrine), a china closet, bedrooms in several colours, and an oratory. There were towers, battlements, and stained glass rescued from demolished buildings. The house is often cited as a major stimulant to the Gothic Revival and the kind of effect Walpole was aiming for can be understood from an excited letter of June 1753: "The armoury bespeaks the ancient chivalry of the lords of the castle and I have filled Mr Bentley's Gothic lanthorn with painted glass which casts a most venerable gloom on the stairs that was ever seen since the days of Abelard". Whiggish and anti-Catholic as his political sympathies always were, in aesthetic and literary terms Walpole preferred the psychological stimulus of a gothic church. Walpole also decorated the interiors in an uninhibited fashion filling the house with a very miscellaneous art collection: paintings, sculpture, china, armour, vases. Much of the architectural detail is actually very superficial: the fan vaulting in the gallery, a copy from Westminster Abbey, was made of papier mache. The house was much visited by the aristocracy and gentry after 1763, when Walpole began issuing tickets.

Walpole was reconciled with Gray in 1745, and in 1753 he arranged the publication of a luxury edition of six poems by Gray, with illustrations by Bentley. Subsequently he published two Pindaric odes by Gray to inaugurate his private press at Strawberry Hill (1757). Among the important works printed on this press was *The Life of Edward Lord Herbert of Cherbury* (1764), an early example of autobiography. The press ran until 1789, printing many of his own works, some antiquarian material, much aristocratic ephemera, and closing with a poem by Hannah More. Walpole's own writing continued with the aristocratic *Catalogue of Royal and Noble Authors of England* (1758) and *Anecdotes of Painting in England* , based on notes left by the engraver George Vertue, and *A Catalogue of Engravers* (1762-1771).

Walpole observed rather than participated in politics, though he did use his influence to delay the execution of Admiral Byng in 1757, afterwards publishing a caustic political pamphlet, "A Letter from Xo Ho" describing political events of the day as they might be seen by a Chinese visitor. Some interventions in the struggle for power of the early 1760s brought two violent denunciations upon him from government writers in 1764. Late in that year Walpole published under an elaborately deceptive title page the story for which he is best known, and which virtually invented a new literary genre, *The Castle of Otranto*, the first true gothic novel. This set forth all the main components of literary gothic, including an encounter with a ghost:

Pushing open the door gently, he saw a person kneeling before the altar. As he approached nearer, it seemed not a woman, but one in a long woollen weed, whose back was turned towards him. The person seemed absorbed in prayer. And then the figure, turning slowly round, discovered to Frederic the fleshless jaws and empty sockets of a skeleton, wrapt in a hermit's cowl. Angels of grace, protect me! cried Frederic recoiling. Deserve their protection, said the spectre.

Set in a castle in a remote and wild Italian landscape, the tale of a moody tyrant's attempts to escape an ancestral curse, and of the subjection of innocence to the menace of sexual violence, has been linked to Walpole's situation in a number of ways: as a literary response to his architectural endeavours, as a punishment-dream for unresolved hatred towards his father, and as an attempt to pose as vigorously masculine in response to the public suggestion of homosexuality. The book was a huge success, spawning many imitations and the story was adapted for the stage in 1781. Over 150 editions of *Otranto* have been published, many with illustrations which emphasise the gloomier aspects of the story.

Soon after *Otranto* Walpole decamped to France to nurse his gout and enjoy a busy social schedule. Here he formed a close attachment to the blind Madame Du Deffand, a witty, intelligent woman with a splendidly chequered past. She was twenty-one years his senior, but pursued him with some ardour; 400 of her letters to him survive, with almost none of his replies. On Christmas Day 1766, he began a gothic tragedy to match or even outdo his gothic novel and perhaps establish some sort of literary control over his complicated relationship with her. *The Mysterious Mother*, which he completed in 1768, concerns the adultery of a mother with her son and its catastrophic consequences. The portrait of the mother in question is, however, surprisingly sympathetic. Walpole was very attached to the play, which he had printed on his press for private circulation, but did not formally publish. He ceased to sit in parliament in 1768, having informally ended his political career with a second political satire, "An Account of the Giants lately discovered" (1766). His next work examined political manoeuvring in a medieval context: *Historic Doubts on the Life and Reign of Richard III* (1768) attempted to cast doubt on the received accounts of Richard's extreme villainy and to view the arbitrary exercise of power in the context of his period. This involved him later in protracted controversy with a number of antiquaries. The year after this he was approached by Thomas Chatterton with the offer of some of his (fabricated) medieval material for a new edition of the *Anecdotes of Painting*. Walpole smelt a rat soon afterwards, and was later blamed, probably unjustly, for the young poet's apparent suicide in London in 1770.

By 1774 Walpole considered his house complete enough to issue *A Description of the Villa of Mr Horace Walpole*, which he continued revising until a definitive version in 1784, with engravings of the house from pictures by Paul Sandby, floor plans, and inventories of the contents. He produced a few other literary works: a short essay, "On Modern Gardening" (1780), based on his practice at Strawberry Hill, and some sportive, psychedelic "Hieroglyphic Tales", of which six copies were printed at the Strawberry Hill press in 1785. But after 1770 his main energies as a writer went into the great series of letters describing the literary, theatrical, political and artistic events of the day to his friends. Among his numerous correspondents were William Cole, a High-Church parson, Walpole's contemporary at Eton and King's, with whom he conversed about literary and antiquarian matters; Gray, the poet; William Mason, Gray's biographer, himself a poet; Hannah More, the poet and reformer; Voltaire; and Sir Horace

Mann, a British diplomat at Florence, with whom he corresponded about foreign affairs. Walpole gathered in his library collections of poems published in the reign of George III, and a similar collection of plays, with a design to form a sort of national historic collection. He also compiled two series of *Memoirs* of the political life of the nation.

He enhanced his collections through auctions, sales and exhibitions, producing a number of catalogues of his own collections, as well as those of others. He also kept miscellany notebooks about his reading and other studies from time to time. At Little Strawberry Hill, a modest house on his estate, he installed Kitty Clive, a retired comic character actress with whom Walpole played cards, took tea, and conversed. She occupied the house until her death in 1785. From 1791 until his death, it was then inhabited by Mary and Agnes Berry, and their father, whom he had met in 1787. Mary in particular became a close companion. In 1791 Walpole succeeded to the title of fourth Earl of Orford, but never took his seat in the House of Lords. Walpole kept writing alert and lively letters to within a month of his death, which took place, after increasingly acute attacks of gout, on 2 March 1797, at his London house in Berkeley Square.

The task of preparing a posthumous edition of Walpole's writings was nominally assigned to Mary Berry's father, but it was she who actually edited the five-volume *Works* of 1798, suppressing some passages out of prudery or sensitivity to the living. Walpole's *Memoirs* of the reigns of George II and George III were left in a chest which was not to be opened until 1818, when the majority of the figures mentioned in them were dead. Again there was some editorial suppression, but the two journals were regarded as major sources of political history throughout the nineteenth century.

Despite Byron's high opinion of Walpole, his reputation as a literary writer plummeted in the Romantic period. The gothic novel took itself to greater extremes, which made *Otranto* look tame, or silly; his letters were regarded as gossipy and malicious; and Walpole's lightness of touch and sense of humour made him appear insufficiently serious. In an article in the *Edinburgh Review* (1833), Macaulay damned him as unhealthy, disorganized, artificial, capricious, fastidious, and inconsistent. However, his reputation rose significantly during the twentieth century. His letters have come to be valued not only as a ready source of commentary on the period, but for their personal content. The Yale Edition of Walpole's correspondence in 48 volumes (completed in 1983) made available properly annotated texts of his huge output of letters, and the general editor, W. S. Lewis, whose very large personal collection of Walpoliana is now part of the library at Yale, was responsible for many exhibitions and books on Walpole's life and work. His roles as politician, connoisseur, and dramatist have been re-evaluated. The ongoing popularity of the gothic novel as a subject of study has ensured the continuing presence of *Otranto* as a key text. *The Mysterious Mother* and *Hieroglyphic Tales* have proved more accessible in an age more interested in and less troubled by their psychological range; they have both been edited recently. Walpole's historical *Memoirs* have also been re-edited in full, giving historians the chance to evaluate them more fairly.

RICHARD HURD (1720-1808)

Richard Hurd (January 13, 1720 - May 28, 1808) was an English divine and writer, the bishop of Worcester.

he was born at Congreve, in the parish of Penkridge, Staffordshire, where his father was a farmer. He was educated at the grammar school of Brewood and at Emmanuel College, Cambridge. He took his B.A. degree in 1739, and in 1742 he proceeded M.A. and became a fellow of his college. In the same year he was ordained deacon, and given charge of the parish of Reymerston, Norfolk, but he returned to Cambridge early in 1743. He was ordained priest in 1744. In 1748 he published some *Remarks on an Enquiry into the Rejection of Christian Miracles by the Heathens* (1746), by William Weston, a fellow of St John's College, Cambridge.

He prepared editions, which won the praise of Edward Gibbon, of the *Ars poetica* and *Epistola ad Pisones* (1749), and the *Epistola ad Augustum* (1751) of Horace. A compliment in the preface to the edition of 1749 was the starting-point of a lasting friendship with William Warburton, through whose influence he was appointed one of the preachers at Whitehall in 1750. In 1765 he was appointed preacher at Lincoln's Inn, and in 1767 he became archdeacon of Gloucester.

In 1768 he proceeded D.D. at Cambridge, and delivered at Lincoln's Inn the first Warburton lectures, which were published later (1772) as *An Introduction to the Study of the Prophecies concerning the Christian Church.* He became bishop of Lichfield and Coventry in 1774, and two years later was selected to be tutor to the prince of Wales and the duke of York. In 1781 he was translated to the see of Worcester. He lived chiefly at Hartlebury Castle, where he built a fine library, to which he transferred Alexander Pope's and Warburton's books, purchased on the latter's death.

He was extremely popular at court, and in 1783, on the death of Archbishop Cornwallis, the king pressed him to accept the primacy, but Hurd, who was known, says Madame d'Arblay, as "The Beauty of Holiness," declined it as a charge not suited to his temper and talents, and much too heavy for him to sustain. He died, unmarried, on the 28th of May 1808.

Hurd's *Letters on Chivalry and Romance* (1762) retain a certain interest for their importance in the history of the romantic movement, which they did something to stimulate. They were written in continuation of a dialogue on the age of Queen Elizabeth included in his *Moral and Political Dialogues* (1759) Two later dialogues *On the Uses of Foreign Travel* were printed in 1763. Hurd wrote two acrimonious defences of Warburton *On the Delicacy of Friendship* (1755), in answer to Dr J Jortin and a Leüer (1764) to Dr Thomas Leland, who had criticized Warburton's Doctrine of Grace. He edited the *Works of Willian Warburton,* the *Select Works* (1772) of Abraham Cowley, and left materials for an edition (6 vols., 1811) of Addison. His own works appeared in a collected edition in 8 vols. 1811.

WILLIAM COLLINS (1721-1759)

Biographically, William Collins is an elusive figure. We know the bare facts of his life, but these lead to many more questions than answers. He was born on Christmas Day 1721 in Chichester, West Sussex, to fairly elderly parents. His father, William Collins, was a hatter by trade, who had twice been Mayor of Chichester. From 1725 to 1733 Collins was probably educated at the Prebendal School in the town. At the end of his time there, two crucial events occurred: on 30 September 1733 his father died. Around five months later Collins was admitted as a Scholar to Winchester School in Hampshire, where his contemporaries included Joseph Warton, who became a fellow poet, and remained Collins's close friend throughout his life. Indeed a feature of Collins's biography is the significance of circles of male friends – it is in their letters to each other that we can piece together a commentary on Collins's movements and activities throughout his life. Collins almost never speaks for himself in his biography; only two letters exist in his own hand. We rely for the rest of our information on friends and acquaintances like Warton, Samuel Johnson, and the naturalist Gilbert White.

At Winchester, Collins began to write poetry. In 1739 his first poems – "To Miss Aurelia C____r" and "Sonnet" – are published pseudonymously in the *Gentleman's Magazine*. Upon leaving the school his uncle informed him that he was "too indolent even for the Army" and advised him to enter the church. Instead he went to university. In 1740, after being placed first on the list of Scholars for New College Oxford only for no place to become available, he began at Queen's College Oxford. In 1742 Collins's published his first major collection of poems (his first, but one of few), *Persian Eclogues.* These are conventional in certain respects (the rhyming couplets echoing Pope), but Collins keeps up a pretence that the poetry is translated from a Persian original. Though they are about as Persian as he is (he himself later admitted that they could equally have been called *Irish Eclogues*), the conceit signals that he wishes to depart from the "strong and nervous" conventions of Augustan poetry, as he puts it in the Preface, and approximate the "rich and figurative" style of the Middle East instead. This suggests Collins's importance as a poet: while never treated as more than a "minor" figure in literary history, he nevertheless represents a vital stage in the movement from neo-classicism to romanticism in the course of the eighteenth century. Around the end of 1743 or the beginning of 1744 Collins published an *Epistle* (originally called *Verses*) *to Sir Thomas Hanmer,* the editor of a new edition of Shakespeare. Though the form is again reminiscent of Pope, the sentiments continue with his broadside against the current state of English literature, as the piece becomes an essay in verse arguing that English drama had developed little since Shakespeare.

Had things turned out differently, Collins might have become a major poet. He certainly had the talent for innovation. What he seemed to lack was application. Like his contemporary Thomas Gray, Collins' bibliography boasts an impressive list of works never completed. All his life — he is still promising to finish it in his last years — he planned to write *The History of the Revival of Learning*. For almost as long, he intended to produce a *Clarendon Review*. He began but did not finish a translation of Aristotle's *Poetics,* and was commissioned to write entries for the *Biographia Britannica* but these (as we might expect of one whose own life is so shadowy) never appeared. In 1750 Collins' *An Epistle to the Editor of Fairfax his Translation of Tasso's Jerusalem* was advertised, but was never published. After graduating from Oxford in 1743 he lived in London, mainly in Soho, eking out a living from subscriptions to his forthcoming poetry and from the generosity of friends. Mulso tells Gilbert White in 1744 that Collins is living as e"ntirely an author." In that year he applies for a curacy in the parish of Birdham, near Chichester, but is dissuaded from taking it by John Hardham, under-treasurer of Drury Lane Theatre. Actors and writers (including Dr Johnson and David Garrick) made up the circle of which Collins was a part, and much of his time in London seemed to be spent enjoying a vigorous social life in the coffee houses and theatres. In 1745 a letter by Gilbert White describes Collins "spending his time in all the dissipation of Ranelagh, Vauxhall, and the playhouses."

In 1746 (though it is dated 1747) Collins *Odes on Several Descriptive and Allegoric Subjects* – his major work, comprising just twelve poems – appears. The *Odes* were popular, but much less so than the similar collection his friend Warton had brought out a few weeks earlier (they had originally planned a joint-authored volume), no doubt because they are more obscure and difficult. In 1749, when his favourite uncle – and father-substitute – Colonel Martin died leaving him a £2000 inheritance, Collins seems to have used the money to buy back all the remaining copies of *Odes on Several Descriptive and Allegoric Subjects* and "resigned them to the flames". In fact he published only one more poem in his lifetime, his *Ode* on the death of the poet James Thompson (1749). But other poems were rumoured or published posthumously. In 1754 Collins showed Warton a version of his "Superstitions Ode" (written much earlier – 1749 or 1750) and what seemed to be a new Ode, *Bell of Arragon* and perhaps fragments of others, which Warton thought were promising but "too loose and imperfect for publication". In 1750 he presented the Scottish dramatist John Home with a manuscript of *Ode on the Popular Superstitions of the Highlands,* which was eventually published in 1788.

In the 1750s, Collins becomes more elusive still as a biographical subject. There are a series of glimpses of him in letters by his friends, most of which portray him in poor health, verging on madness. From 1751-4 he seems to have travelled in France and made a trip to Bath to recover from illness. He then moved back to London, to Islington. From 1754 his sister Anne appears to have taken control, bringing him back to Chichester from a madhouse in Chelsea to look after him. In 1756 some of his friends believe he is dead. On 12 June 1759 Collins dies and is buried in St. Andrew's Church, Chichester three days later.

Like so much about Collins, there is a mysterious vagueness surrounding his illness. Biographers and critics have debated whether his physical symptoms were rooted in his mental condition or vice versa. One put it down to melancholia brought on by "the stress of poverty and worry", perhaps to "his dissipation and intemperance". His condition is described in different ways by his contemporaries: Warton calls it "a disordered or debilitated understanding", John Ragsdale more dramatically as "a deplorable state of idiotism", Thomas as deplorable langour of body, and dejection of mind', James Hampton said as a" nervous disorder, which continued, with but short intervals, till his death . . . and with which disorder his head and intellects were at times affected". Dr Johnson's piece on Collins published in 1763 is the most interesting because of what it implies rather than states. It takes care to highlight his general high moral character and literary talent, but hints at severe weaknesses for indulgences which are left unclear. In a letter to Thomas Warton he says "I have a notion that by very great temperance or more properly abstinence he might yet recover".

The illness, whatever it was exactly, is important because it severely hampered Collins's poetic output. All his poetry was written before he was thirty; he was destined therefore to remain a poet of great potential rather than solid achievement. Nevertheless, as part of a group of poets in the mid-eighteenth-century (alongside Joseph and Thomas Warton, and Mark Akenside), whom Johnson described as being "eminently delighted with those flights of imagination which pass the bounds of nature", Collins became a major influence for poets who followed. As a master of the form of the ode in particular, Collins anticipates the great romantic odes by Keats and Shelley, addressing his odes to abstract entities, like "Fear" or "the Passions", rather than specific historical figures and demonstrating how these animate the poet. Collins's work thus exhibits a romantic self-consciousness about his art as well as an ambition to move poetry beyond imitating classical models. His close friend Joseph Warton produced a kind of manifesto for the new group which neatly encapsulates this aspect of Collins's work, setting against the poetry of "familiar life" (i.e. Pope), *true* poetry, which embodies a "creative and glowing imagination". Above all, Collins's value is as a poet of the sublime, one of the dominant concerns of romanticism: his work is preoccupied with how an overwhelmingly powerful but essentially unrepresentable force animates the human mind and poetry itself – just as his life was eventually determined by the force of an unspecified but debilitating condition.

MARK AKENSIDE (1721-1770)

Mark Akenside (November 9, 1721 - June 23, 1770), was an English poet and physician.

Akenside was born at Newcastle upon Tyne, the son of a butcher; he was slightly lame all his life from a wound he received as a child from his father's cleaver. All his relations were dissenters, and, after attending the free school of Newcastle, and a dissenting academy in the town, he was sent (1739) to Edinburgh to study theology with a view to becoming a minister, his expenses being paid from a special fund set aside by the dissenting community for the education of their pastors. He had already contributed *The Virtuoso, in imitation of Spenser's style and stanza* (1737) to the *Gentleman's Magazine*, and in 1738 *A British Philippic, occasioned by the Insults of the Spaniards, and the present Preparations for War* (also published separately).

After one winter as a theology student, he changed to medicine. He repaid the money that had been advanced for his theological studies, and became a deist. His politics, said Dr Johnson, were characterized by an "impetuous eagerness to subvert and confound, with very little care what shall be established," and he is caricatured in the republican doctor of Tobias Smollett's *Peregrine Pickle*. He was elected a member of the Medical Society of Edinburgh in 1740. His ambitions already lay outside his profession, and his gifts as a speaker made him hope one day to enter parliament. In 1740 he printed his "Ode on the Winter Solstice" in a small volume of poems. In 1741 he left Edinburgh for Newcastle and began to call himself surgeon, though it is doubtful whether he practised, and from the next year dates his life-long friendship with Jeremiah Dyson (1722-1776).

During a visit to Morpeth in 1738, he had the idea for his didactic poem, *The Pleasures of the Imagination*, which was well received, and was subsequently translated into more than one foreign language. He had already acquired a considerable literary reputation when he came to London about the end of 1743 and offered the work to Robert Dodsley for £120. Dodsley thought the price exorbitant, and only accepted the terms after submitting the manuscript to Alexander Pope, who assured him that this was "no everyday writer." The three books of this poem appeared in January 1744. His aim, Akenside tells us in the preface, was "not so much to give formal precepts, or enter into the way of direct argumentation, as, by exhibiting the most engaging prospects of nature, to enlarge and harmonize the imagination, and by that means insensibly dispose the minds of men to a similar taste and habit of thinking in religion, morals and civil life." His powers fell short of this ambition; his imagination was not brilliant enough to surmount the difficulties inherent in a poem dealing so largely with abstractions; but the work was well received. Thomas Gray wrote to Thomas Warton that it was "above the middling," but "often obscure and unintelligible and too much infected with the Hutchinson jargon."

William Warburton took offence at a note added by Akenside to the passage in the third book dealing with ridicule. Accordingly he attacked the author of the *Pleasures of the Imagination*—which was published anonymously—in a scathing preface to his *Remarks on Several Occasional Reflections, in answer to Dr Middleton* ... (1744). This was answered, nominally by Dyson, in *An Epistle to the Rev. Mr Warburton*, in which Akenside probably had a hand. It was in the press when he left England in 1744 to secure a medical degree at Leiden. In little more than a month he had completed the necessary dissertation, *De ortu et incremento foetus humani*, and received his diploma.

Returning to England he unsuccessfully attempted to establish a practice in Northampton. In 1744 he published his *Epistle to Curio,* attacking William Pulteney (afterwards Earl of Bath) for having abandoned his liberal principles to become a supporter of the government, and in the next year he produced a small volume of *Odes on Several Subjects,* in the preface to which he lays claim to correctness and a careful study of the best models. His friend Dyson had meanwhile left the bar, and had become, by purchase, clerk to the House of Commons. Akenside had come to London and was trying to make a practice at Hampstead. Dyson took a house there, and did all he could to further his friend's interest in the neighborhood. But Akenside's arrogance and pedantry frustrated these efforts, and Dyson then took a house for him in Bloomsbury Square, making him independent of his profession by an allowance stated to have been £300 a year, but probably greater, for it is asserted that this income enabled him to "keep a chariot," and to live "incomparably well." In 1746 he wrote his much-praised "Hymn to the Naiads," and he also became a contributor to Dodsley's *Museum, or Literary and Historical Register.* He was now twenty-five years old, and began to devote himself almost exclusively to his profession. He was an acute and learned physician. He was admitted M.D. at the University of Cambridge in 1753, fellow of the Royal College of Physicians in 1754, and fourth censor in 1755. In June 1755 he read the Gulstonian lectures before the College, in September 1756 the Croonian lectures, and in 1759 the Harveian oration. In January 1759 he was appointed assistant physician, and two months later principal physician to Christ's Hospital, but he was charged with harsh treatment of the poorer patients, and his unsympathetic character prevented the success to which his undeniable learning and ability entitled him. At the accession of George III both Dyson and Akenside changed their political opinions, and Akenside's conversion to Tory principles was rewarded by the appointment of physician to the queen. Dyson became secretary to the treasury, lord of the treasury, and in 1774 privy councillor and cofferer to the household.

Akenside died at his house in Burlington Street, where the last ten years of his life had been spent. His friendship with Dyson puts his character in the most amiable light. Writing to his friend so early as 1744, Akenside said that the intimacy had "the force of an additional conscience, of a new principle of religion," and there seems to have been no break in their affection. He left all his effects and his literary remains to Dyson, who issued an edition of his poems in 1772. This included the revised version of the *Pleasures of Imagination*, on which the author was engaged at his death. Akenside's verse was better when it was subjected to severer metrical rules. His odes are rarely lyrical in the strict sense, but they are dignified and often musical.

Tobias George Smollett (1721-1771) Christopher Smart (1722-1771) Thomas Warton (1728-1790) Edmund Burke (1729-1797)

TOBIAS GEORGE SMOLLETT (1721-1771)

Smollett was a less prolific novelist than Scott, and his books are not as readable as Stevenson's, but he was the first Scottish novelist and he has never been surpassed. Indeed, Smollett can be said to have prefigured the Scottish fiction of the nineties of the twentieth century - the fiction of Irvine Welsh and his contemporaries, descriptive of low life as it really is. It is unlikely that critics nowadays would malign an author for satire which made readers writhe, or for the grotesqueness of his imagery, but Smollett was upbraided for this, and, even, for his use of researchers in wide-ranging works of non-fiction. Smollett was an original whose worth has rarely been properly acknowledged, not least because his contemporaries, Fielding, Richardson and Sterne, were in the same class as he was, but also because he was an Anglo-Scot, whose countrymen have never identified with him in the same way as they identified, for example with the other exile Stevenson.

He was born in 1721 at Dalquhurn in Renton, Dumbartonshire, and educated at the University of Glasgow. His early life was strongly hinted at in his first successful comic novel, *Roderick Random* (1748); both his learned schoolmaster in Dumbarton, and his first employer in Glasgow are satirised in it. At fourteen he was apprenticed to a Glasgow doctor, and lived in a back attic in Gibson's Land in the merchant city of the Glasgow tobacco barons.

He became a surgeon's mate in the navy and, later, in 1744, began practice as a surgeon in the London of Johnson, Garrick and Handel. His first literary work was an historical play called *The Regicide* about James I which he conceived in Glasgow. It was refused by Garrick, who was never quite forgiven, and others.

He then turned to political satire, but it was his picaresque novels that made him famous. *Roderick Ransom* is a vigorous, coarse comedy about sailors' lives during the British expedition against Cartagena in the West Indies in the War of Jenkins' Ear of 1739-41 (one of the most farcical episodes in British history). It places Smollett in the first rank as a novelist of the sea. He met and married his beloved wife in the West Indies, and encountered Robert Graham of Gartmore, a lifelong friend, there. The expedition to Cartagena later landed him in gaol for libel, when Admiral Knowles published a pamphlet defending his competence in a disastrous raid on Rochefort, and Smollett drew attention to his defects in one of the finest pieces of sustained invective in the English language.

Smollett was his own worst enemy and succeeded in offending many people. Never quite well, he had a short temper and was free with plain insults, and, worse, bitter irony. He quarrelled with Rich, the manager of Covent Garden and, as a consequence, his masque *Alceste* to music by Handel was never performed. The composer is reported as saying "Dat Scot is ein tam fool; I could have made his vork immortal!". However, his friends included Dr Alexander Carlyle and Dr John Moore, his first biographer, both of whom found much to delight them in the irascible author.

Several other episodic novels, full of grotesque characters and broad satire, among them *The Adventures of Peregrine Pickle* (1751), a well-regarded satire on the Grand Tour, and *Ferdinand Count Fathom* (1753) came next and were so successful that Smollett abandoned his practice of surgery. As a doctor he was a great advocate of spas and one of the first to promote sea bathing. Indeed, he was an early tourist, and it is a matter for great regret that he did not write up his occasional visits to Scotland because what is often regarded as his finest work is *Travels in France and Italy* (1766), a witty and perceptive journal of a tour in search of good health late in life.

However, his last novel, *The Expedition of Humphry Clinker* (1771), written initially during the last two years of his life, told in a series of letters, is about the travels of a family through England and Scotland and deals with sex, politics and religion in resorts for gentlefolk. The Scottish passages are probably based on his long visit in 1766 when he saw his sister in Edinburgh, and his old friends in Edinburgh and Glasgow. They are particularly funny and display his real affection for his native land. There is a shrewd portrait, too, of "Doctor Smollett" in Chelsea, surrounded by minor authors and hangers-on.

Smollet's comic inventiveness influenced Sheridan, Dickens and Thackeray, and Scott paid tribute to his impact on him, pointing out Smollett's ability to make readers laugh out loud. Smollett's other books include a *Complete history of England* (1757-58), which was popular and financially successful, *The Present state of all nations*, a world geography, notable for its time, and *The History and adventures of an atom* (1769), a coarse satire on English public affairs.

Smollett played a part in Britain's first Scottish administration, that of the Earl of Bute. After editing the *Critical review* (1756-63), he produced *The Briton* (1762-63) a government propaganda sheet, which more than met its match in the opposition's *North Briton*, edited by Wilkes. He also translated the French picaresque romance *Gil Blas* by Le Sage and the Spanish classic *Don Quixote*. His poetry includes

The Tears of Scotland, a heartfelt lament for Culloden, and his *Ode to Leven Water*, celebrating the famous river, which flowed past his childhood home.

Smollett died an invalid near Leghorn in Italy in 1771. His monument in Renton, a fine Tuscan column with a Latin inscription partly by Johnson, is worth visiting as it is the focal point of a number of sites associated with him described mainly in *Humphry Clinker*. His sister's house at the head of St John Street in Edinburgh has a plaque. *Smollett's Scotland* by Louis Stott deals with these and other localities. The most recent biography is Louis Knapp's *Tobias Smollett* (1949). Smollett's principal novels are readily available in paperback.

Some of his works are

Advice: a Satire (1746); Reproof: a Satire (1747); The Adventures of Roderick Random (1748); The Regicide, or James I of Scotland (1749); The Adventures of Peregrine Pickle (1751); A Faithful Narrative of the Base and Inhuman Arts that were Lately Practised upon the Brain of Habbakkuk Wilding (1752); An Essay upon the External Use of Water (1752); The Adventures of Ferdinand, Count Fathom (1753); The Reprisal, or the Tars of Old England (1757); A Complete History of England from the Descent of Julius Caesar to the Treaty of Aix-la-Chapelle, 3 vols. (1757-58); The Adventures of Sir Launcelot Greaves (1762); A Continuation of the Complete History (1766); Travels through France and Italy (1766); The History and Adventures of an Atom (1769); The Expedition of Humphry Clinker (1771); Ode to Independence (1773).

CHRISTOPHER SMART (1722-1771)

Christopher Smart (April 11, 1722 – May 21, 1771) was an English poet. His works include *A Song to David* and *Jubilate Agno*, both of which were at least partly written during his confinement in an insane asylum.

EARLY LIFE

Smart was the son of Peter Smart, of an old north country family, was born at Shipbourne, Kent. His father was steward for the Kentish estates of William, Viscount Vane, younger son of Lord Barnard of Raby Castle, Durham.

Christopher Smart received his first schooling at Maidstone, and then at the grammar school of Durham. He spent part of his vacations at Raby Castle, and his gifts as a poet gained him the patronage of the Vane family. Henrietta, Duchess of Cleveland, allowed him a pension of 40 pounds yearly which was paid until her death in 1742. Thomas Gray, writing to his friend Thomas Wharton in 1747, warned him to keep silent about Smart's delinquencies lest they should come to the ears of Henry Vane (afterwards Earl of Darlington), and endanger his allowance. At Cambridge, where he was entered at Pembroke College in 1739, he spent much of his time in taverns, and got badly into debt, but in spite of his irregularities he became fellow of his college, praelector in philosophy and keeper of the common chest in 1745. In November 1747 he was compelled to remain in his rooms for fear of his creditors. At Cambridge he won the Seaton prize for a poem on one of the attributes of the Supreme Being in 1750 (he won the same prize in 1751, 1752, 1753 and 1755); and a farce entitled A Trip to Cambridge, or The Grateful Fair, performed in 1747 by the students of Pembroke, was from his pen. In 1750 he contributed to The Student,or,The Oxford and Cambridge Monthly Miscellany. During one of his visits to London he had made the acquaintance of John Newbery, the publisher, whose step-daughter, Anna Maria Carman, he married with the result of forfeiting his fellowship in 1753.

PROFESSIONAL LIFE

About 1752 he left Cambridge permanently, for London, though he kept his name on the college books, as he had to do in order to compete for the Seaton prize. He wrote in London under the pseudonyms of Mary Midnight and Pentweazle. He edited The Midwife, or the Old Womans Magazine (1751-1753), and had a hand in many other Grub Street productions. Some criticisms made by Sir John Hill (1716-1775) on his Poems on Several Occasions (1752) provoked Smart's satire of the Hilhiad (1753), noteworthy as providing the model for the Rohliad. In 1756 he finished a prose translation of Horace, which was widely used, but brought him little profit. He agreed in the same year to produce a weekly paper entitled The Universal Visitor, for which Samuel Johnson wrote some numbers.

ASYLUM CONFINEMENT

In 1751 Smart had shown symptoms of mental aberration, which developed into religious mania. Smart was wont to accost passers-by in Hyde Park and demand that they kneel down and pray for him, and between 1756 and 1758 he was in St. Luke's Hospital, an asylum. Dr Johnson visited him and thought that he ought to have been at large. He once stated, "I'd as lief pray with Kit Smart as anyone else." During his confinement he conceived the idea of the single poem that has made him famous, A Song to David, though the legend that Smart scratched his poems into the wainscoting of his cell with a key, and shaded in with charcoal, must be taken with a grain of salt. It shows no trace of morbid origin. After his release Smart produced other religious poems. His wife and children had gone to live with friends as he was unable to support them, and for some time before his death, he lived in the rules of Kings Bench, and was supported by small subscriptions raised by Dr Burney and other friends.

WORKS

Of all that he wrote, *A Song to David* is generally thought to be the most significant. Unlike anything else in 18th. century poetry in its simple forceful treatment and impressive directness of expression, as has been said, the poem on analysis is found to depend for its unique effect also upon a certain ingenuity of construction, and the novel way in which David's ideal qualities are enlarged upon. This will be more readily understood on reference to the following verse, the first twelve words of which become in turn the key-notes, so to speak, of the twelve succeeding verses: Great, valiant, pious, good, and clean, Sublime, contemplative, serene, Strong, constant, pleasant, wise!

Bright effluence of exceeding grace; Best man the swiftness, and the race, The peril, and the prize.

The last line is characteristic of another peculiarity in *A Song to David*, the effective use of alliteration to complete the initial energy of the stanza in many instances. But in the poem throughout is revealed a poetic quality which eludes critical analysis.

Another of Smart's poems penned during his confinement, his idiosyncratic *Jubilate Agno*, was published in 1939 and has become relatively well-known. The *Jubilate* praises the divine architecture of the natural world. Many modern critics posit that Smart meant the poem to serve as an alternative to the conventional Anglican liturgical text. One section of the poem, beginning with "For I Will Consider My Cat Jeoffrey", has been reprinted separately and is popular among cat-lovers. The modern English composer Benjamin Britten used the *Jubilate* as the basis for his festival cantata "Rejoice in the Lamb".

THOMAS WARTON (1728-1790)

Thomas Warton was the second son of the Rev. Thomas Warton, Vicar of Basingstoke, and master of the ancient grammar school in that town. At Basingstoke, in 1728, Thomas was born, and there he was brought up and educated mainly by his father, until at sixteen he was admitted to Trinity College, Oxford. His elder brother, Joseph, went to Winchester College, and subsequently became Headmaster.

Young Tom took early to poetry and at the age of nine sent to his sister 'the first production of my little Muse,' a translation from Martial

On Leander's Swimming Over The Hellespont To Hero

When bold Leander sought his distant Fair, (Nor could the sea a braver burthen bear) Thus to the swelling wave he spoke his woe, Drown me on my return – but spare me, as I go.

Old Thomas Warton, although he 'had the character of a very honest, ingenious, and good-natur'd man,' was not particularly wealthy. He had formerly (I718-1728) been Professor of Poetry at Oxford, where in 1719 he had very boldly preached 'a Jacobite sermon,' and had triumphed in the subsequent proceedings against him. The worst that came out of this incident was the enmity of Nicholas Amhurst, who attacked him here and there in print and called him 'squinting Tom of Maudlin.' His Jacobite leanings led him to write some verses addressed to ' James III,' Thomas Hearne tells us, and a satire on George I called *The Turnip Hoer,* occasioned by the King's suggestion that St. James's Park should be turned into a turnip field. These verses have not survived, and were apparently never printed.

The Poetry Professor was not much inclined to profess his own poetry – after his death his papers were found to include enough original verse to fill a fair-size volume, but his sons had never seen or heard a line of it. The old man died in 1746 leaving no money and a quantity of debts. It was in order to discharge these that Joseph Warton proceeded to print his father's poems by subscription, and about the same time he wrote to his brother at Oxford: 'Do not doubt of being able to get some money this winter; if ever I have a groat, you may depend upon having twopence.' The brothers were always firm friends, and indeed were very similar in temperament, and in the course their lives took.

Old Thomas Warton's book is so rare, and his fame so small, that I am tempted to leave young Thomas at Oxford awaiting twopence while I copy a few of his father's verses; for although it cannot have influenced the brothers much, since they were writing verse long before they ever saw it, this work of their father's is the product of a mind remarkably similar to those of his sons.

Astrophil To His Son, Aged Seven Months

O Thou! with whom I fondly share My faithful Stella's Love, and Care, To thee 'tis giv'n to tumble o'er Thy absent Sire's poetic Store, (With eager hands these Lines to seize And tear, or lose era, as you please,) Thou too from Pedantry art free, And I can safely sing to thee.

What tho' thy Age no Skill can boast, In one small Round of Follies lost; Yet ev'n thy Joys, and Tears, and Strife, Act all the World in little Life. Alike Man aims at all he can, And Imitation teaches Man: – But then has Man his Play-things too? – Yes sure – Amusements all allow, And are more serious Fools – than thou. We differ, only in th' Intent As idle, but less innocent.

Also in these *Poems on Several Occasions* we find one of the earliest (perhaps the very earliest) of the 18th century imitations of Spenser, several Odes which anticipate the manner of Gray, a line or two which may have given a hint to Johnson – 'All human Race, from *China* to *Peru,* Pleasure, howe'er disguised by Art, pursue,' – and some *Verses Written After Seeing Windsor Castle* which recall one of Joseph's stories of his brother as a child.

The two brothers went with their father to see Windsor Castle, and old Tom was much concerned to notice an apparent lack of interest in young Tom. ' Thomas goes on,' he said sadly to Jospeh, 'and takes no notice of anything he has seen!' But Joseph 'in maturer years made this reflection: "I believe my brother was more struck with what he saw, and took more notice of every object, than either of us."' His great interest in ancient architecture in later years came at a time when such studies were very unusual; he would go off during vacations scrambling over the ruins of old castles, and measuring abbeys, and exploring cathedrals, with indefatigable interest. Some of the earliest written appreciation of Gothic in English appears in his *Observations on The Faerie Queene* (1754; but the 'gothic essay' was added in the 2nd edition, 1762.)

In 1747 Warton took his B.A., and in the same year he entered into Holy Orders. He became a Tutor in his college, though perhaps not a very efficient one; Lord Eldon wrote years later: 'Poor Tom Warton! He was a Tutor at Trinity; at the beginning of every term he used to send to his pupils to know whether they would *wish* to attend lectures that term." This willingness to fulfill obligations without undue inconvenience to himself no doubt also explains why he is said to have had only two sermons for all occasions – one by his father, and one out of a book.

His academic career proceeded smoothly; he was M.A. in 1750, Fellow of his College in 1751, B.D. in 1767. In 1757 he succeeded Mr. Hawkins of Pembroke College as Professor of Poetry, an office which, like his father before him, he held for the usual ten years. In 1785 – a little before succeeding to the Laureateship – Warton was elected Camden Professor of History at Oxford. Thus his career had been progressively successful in the academic world.

The new Laureate had not made the composition of poetry his primary concern in authorship, but in one way or another it had been his main study; his observations on Spenser *Faerie Queene* (I754) had been followed by editions of the Greek Anthology (I766) and of Theocritus (I770) and in the year of the Laureateship by his edition of Milton *Minor Poems,* as truly a landmark in Miltonic criticism as the *Observations* were in Spenserian. Then there was the great *History of English Poetry,* the three volumes of which appeared 1774-1781. This gigantic undertaking was never completed and the existing work breaks off in Elizabeth's reign before the appearance of the greater part of English poetry. This book led Warton into the most serious of his literary scrapes – a far worse affair than any satire occasioned by the Laureateship.

Joseph Kitson, an able scholar but a most unamiable man, very quickly put out a volume of critical emendation and comment, expressed in terms of violent contempt and abuse. His *Observations on the three first volumes of the History of English Poetry: In a familiar letter to the author* (I782) lists one hundred and sixteen errors, some of considerable magnitude. Maliciously, he ordered the *Observations* to be printed 'in the size of Mr. Warton's History,' as 'extremely proper to be bound up with that celebrated work, to which they will be found a very useful appendix.' And in private letters he exulted over his victory: 'I have at last put my libel upon

Warton into the hands of a bookseller,' and, later, 'What say you to my scurrilous libel against Warton?

Warton himself said little, but the public condemned the pamphlet for its violence; such a work as Warton's, undertaken by one man, with no previous comparable history for guidance, must certainly contain errors. If temperately conveyed, criticisms would have been welcomed by any candid historian; as it was, Warton's credit was not particularly undermined and in later years Ritson is said to have repented of his illiberal tone.

Even these massive labours did not represent the end of Warton's prose works; he published biographies of Ralph Bathurst (I761) and Sir Thomas Pope (I772), various specimens of local history, some critical essays, and a number of trifles, including several lively essays in Johnson *Idler*.

His poetry at the time of the Laureateship made a respectable collection, as might be expected from one whose Muse commenced operations at the age of nine. His first published poem had been an *Ode to a Fountain*, included in his brothers' *Odes on Various Subjects* (I746), and his first independent work the characteristically titled *Pleasures of Melancholy* (I747), which shows the young poet to have read much in Milton when most young men were reading Pope. Two years later *The Triumph of Isis* provided a modest triumph for its author.

Mason had recently published his *Isis, an Elegy*, a poem containing various strictures on the university, particularly for its alleged Jacobite sympathies during the '45 rebellion. Warton's reply 'excelled more in manly expostulation and dignity, than the poem that produced it did in neatness and elegance.' It was a gentlemanly contention on both sides and neither poet at first printed his poem in his collected works, until at last – nearly thirty years later – Mason said he hoped *The Triumph of Isis* was not to be allowed to remain out of print on his account, and Warton then put it into his next collection.

This performance, by a young man of twenty-one, was very favourably received, and the learned Dr. King is reported to have left five guineas at the bookseller's 'if they would be of any service to the young man, that had written the poem.' Thus Warton did rather better financially by his first success than Whitehead had done.

At Oxford in his younger days Warton was not at all the studious small boy who sat in a cold chamber studying; he studied, true enough, but he also enjoyed to the full the pleasures of being young in a fine city. This gay life is reflected in those early poems which he included in *The Oxford Sausage*, an anthology which he put forth in 1764. Another light-hearted enterprise was the celebrated *A Companion to the Guide and a Guide to the Companion* (I760), which is an Oxford guide-with-a-difference; most guide-books content themselves with notes on colleges and antiquities; this one does not overlook the taverns and other places of resort popular with those who have examined tombs enough to be going on with. Finally in 1777 and 1791 Warton published collected editions of his poetry.

It is a pity Dr. Johnson did not live to see Warton's Laureate odes, for his opinion of them beside his remarks on those of Cibber and Whitehead would have been interesting. Johnson knew Warton well, and respected and esteemed him, although he once remarked that Tom Warton was the only man of genius he knew that was without a heart. The Doctor also wrote a little parody of Warton's later manner:

'Hermit hoar, in solemn cell, Wearing out life's evening gray; Smite thy bosom, sage, and tell, What is bliss? and which the way?

Boswell."But why smite his bosom, Sir?"

Johnson."Why, to show he was in earnest," (smiling.) – He at an after period added the following stanza:

Thus I spoke; and speaking sigh'd; – Scarce repress'd the starting tear; -When the smiling sage reply'd – Come, my lad, and drink some beer.'

Boswell adds, 'I cannot help thinking the first stanza very good solemn poetry, as also the three first lines of the second. Its last line is an excellent burlesque surprise on gloomy sentimental inquirers. . . .

When Warton was appointed, Mason himself was still alive, and he may have remembered the excuse made to him formerly when he was passed over, that 'being in orders, he was thought, merely on that account, less eligible for the office than a layman.' Warton, 'being in orders,' was nevertheless found eligible.

His Birthday Ode for 1785 duly appeared and met with little favour. George III was not used to this sort of thing:

. . . To Kings like these, her genuine theme, The Muse a blameless homage pays; To GEORGE, of Kings like these supreme, She wishes honoured length of days, Nor prostitutes the tribute of her lays.

'Tis his to bid neglected genius glow, And teach the regal bounty how to flow . . .

It almost appeared that, after six weeks in office, the new Laureate was looking for an advance of salary. Richard Mant remarks that this first Ode was perhaps the poet's worst production. At all events, it was a godsend to the satirists, who as usual were waiting to have a word with the new Laureate.

Within a few weeks (for in the eighteenth century a book could be produced remarkably quickly) appeared *Probationary Odes for The Laureateship,* with a preliminary discourse by 'Sir John Hawkins, Knt.' This was Dr. Johnson's 'unclubbable man,' but his presence was part of the joke; he never wrote anything in his life so lively as the preliminary discourse. The *Probationary Odes* were the work of the authors of *The Rolliad* – French Laurence, George Ellis, Lord John Townshend, Joseph Richardson, Richard Tickell and others – and follow the tradition of the various 'sessions of the Poets' but with a new twist: each of the alleged candidates presents his own 'probationary ode' -and pretty bad they are, though mighty amusing. The worst is usually thought to be the one assigned to Thomas Warton (which happens to be his own genuine Birthday Ode).

Tom Warton seems to have been a good fellow; some of the stories told about him effectively discredit Johnson's remark that he had no heart — and indeed his long friendship with the Doctor was only now and then mildly clouded, and who shall say that the fault lay with Tom? It was partly his influence that obtained for Johnson his M.A. at Oxford (a degree with which Johnson desired to grace the title page of his *Dictionary,* then about to be published) and in a number of other ways Sam had no reason to complain of Tom. He greatly enjoyed Warton's hospitality at Oxford, except perhaps on one occasion. The Professor of Poetry and the learned Lexicographer took a walk together into the surrounding meads and after a lengthy perambulation turned homewards: when the visitor found himself unable to keep up with Warton's swinging pace. So, perforce, from far in the rear he was obliged to cry out to him to stop, but even in this crisis he had the presence of mind to employ the Latin tongue.

Warton's fondness for a pot of ale was well known — indeed, he had written a popular poem called *A Panegyre on Oxford Ale* — and if he could sup this delicacy in the company of a group of bargees in a canal-side tavern his pleasure was complete. Like Johnson, he had no love for clean linen, either on himself or on others. But he did have a great love for martial music. Hartley Coleridge records (but admits the story to be open to doubt) that on one occasion when Warton was not to be found anywhere a military band with fife and drum was despatched to play along the streets; and sure enough, from a low tavern to see the fun, appeared the Professor of Poetry.

In speech he 'gobbled like a turkey,' Johnson (that refined elocutionist) tells us. And the authors of the *Probationary Odes* give us a glimpse of his appearance: a little, thick, squat, red-faced man . . . in a very odd dress' who unexpectedly confronts the King on the chapel stairs. He is about to be thrown out when 'by a certain hasty spasmodic mumbling, together with two or three prompt quotations from Virgil, the person was discovered to be none other than the Rev. Mr. *Thomas Warton* himself. . . .' Needless to say, the chapel concerned was not the Rev. Mr. Warton's. Although he held a couple of livings he seldom ventured anywhere near them.

Warton died on May 21st, 1790, as the result of a stroke. He was sincerely mourned by the whole university, and at their own request the Vice-Chancellor, the Heads of Houses, and the Proctors attended the funeral. More thoughtful than some of his predecessors, the late laureate left his Birthday Ode all ready for use on June 4th. Ironically enough, it is all about the blessings of good health.

EDMUND BURKE (1729-1797)

Born in Dublin, Ireland, Burke was the son of a Protestant solicitor and a Catholic mother, whose maiden name was Nagle. Burke was raised in his father's faith and would remain throughout his life a practicing Anglican. He received his early education at a Quaker school in Ballitore and in 1744 he proceeded to Trinity College, Dublin. In 1747, he set up a Debating Club, known as Edmund Burke's Club, which in 1770 merged with the Historical Club to form the College Historical Society. The minutes of the meetings of Burke's club remain in the collection of the Historical Society. He graduated in 1748. Burke's father wished him to study for the law, and with this object he went to London in 1750 and entered the Middle Temple, but soon thereafter he gave up his legal studies in order to travel in Continental Europe.

Burke was the greatest genius ever produced by the Anglo-Irish culture which has so largely enriched British life and letters. As an undergraduate he read the classics, enjoyed the theater, and wrote an Addisonian essay-periodical *The Reformer* (I748). He does not seem to have been acquainted at this time with his fellow-student Oliver Goldsmith. Early publications showed his originality and speculative power: his *Vindication of Natural Society* (I756) is a reductio ad absurdum of Bolingbroke's attack on revealed religion. Just as Bolingbroke had used the corruption of the Church to support his argument for natural religion, so Burke ironically adduces social wrongs and injustices to support an argument for merely "natural" society. Rousseau was soon to use such an argument in good earnest, but Burke here announces his lifelong opposition to fine spun political theorizing. *A Philosophical Enquiry into the Origin of our Ideas of the Sublime and Beautiful* (I757) is a pioneer study in the psychological basis of aesthetic enjoyment; Burke's doctrine that "a mode of terror or pain is always the cause of the sublime" indicates the growing preference for the "Gothic" and the wild. The range of Burke's interests is shown by his numerous contributions of reviews and summaries of current events to Dodsley *Annual Register* for more than thirty years from 1758. In 1764 Burke, with Johnson and Reynolds, had a main hand in forming the famous Club, and he is thereafter one of the principal figures in Johnson's circle, though Boswell does not record his conversation so fully as we could wish.

Burke began his career in politics as secretary to William Gerard Hamilton, chief secretary for Ireland, but the two parted company when Hamilton wanted to monopolize his services. He then became a lieutenant of Lord Rockingham, the leader of one of the Whig factions, all in opposition to George III and all at odds with one another. Thus Burke could not get on with the elder Pitt, and stayed outside his last administration (I766-68). A series of unwise measures by George III's ministers was making it certain that the Empire would lose America. Yet while America was being lost India was being won. Throughout all these events Burke remained the commentator and parliamentary critic; he was never the administrator. His comment was magnificently eloquent and philosophical, going to the roots of political theory. Most of his important pieces were in the form of orations, but called for sustained attention and close reading. He did not indulge in mere personal abuse, like Junius, though he used invective more and more as time went on. His central principle, clearly formulated in *Thoughts on the Cause of the Present Discontents*

(I770) and constantly restated and reapplied, was that politics is an art, not a science, that it deals with men and nations in actuality, never with bloodless abstractions, pure theories or principles. This put him in opposition alike to parliamentary legalists and French *philosophes*. Until the end of the North ministry (I782) it led him to recommend practical, moderate, and conciliatory policies. He deplored the long feud between the government and Wilkes; he tried to relieve Irish Catholics of the oppressive Penal Laws; he supported the repeal of the Stamp Act, though with the passage of the Declaratory Act (declaration of the right to tax). In two of his most famous speeches, *On American Taxation* (April 19, 1774), and *On Conciliation with America* (March 22, 1775), he developed his magnificent view of an America fired with the English love of liberty in comparison with which the claim of an abstract right to tax sinks into insignificance. Here Burke is positive, constructive, and profound; his view of an empire based on Anglo-Saxon traditions of liberty, though it did not alter and probably could not have altered the course of events in the eighteenth century, still bears on the problems of the twentieth. In the practical politics of the day Burke did not stand supreme; when his party came into office in 1782 he was not taken into the Cabinet; he went along with the unfortunate Fox-North coalition of 1783, and his opposition to the younger Pitt, as to the elder, was partisan. But he always centered on the great issues of the Empire—England's relations with America and Ireland, and in the last twelve years of his life England's relations with India and France. If we substitute Russia for France, one revolution for another, we see how up to date much of this is.

Burke's concern with India came to a climax in the great prosecution of Warren Hastings. As governor general of India, Hastings had built up British power, but he had played a corrupt financial and political game, and his political opponents, especially Sir Philip Francis and Edmund Burke, tried to make him the scapegoat for all the abuses connected with the régime of the East India Company. The impeachment of Hastings, a long drawn out process which ran from 1788 to his acquittal in 1795, was a last great field day for eighteenth-century oratory. From 1785, with the Speech on the *Nabob of Arcot's Debts*, Burke rose to heights of eloquence on the subject, but his zeal and indignation carried him beyond the facts. His fine style was becoming somewhat strained and exaggerated.

Lastly, the French Revolution called forth all his heavy artillery. His *Reflections on the French Revolution* (1790) fuses moral and religious feeling, political philosophy, literary power, and personal feeling in such a way as to form the great classic of British conservatism. Burke was now with his old foes, the Tories, against the "New Whigs," the pro-French wing led by his former friend and ally Charles James Fox. Burke had interpreted the Revolution of 1688 and the American Revolution as just assertions of rights guaranteed by the British constitution; he opposed the French Revolution because, he thought, it broke the framework of tradition altogether. Against the philosophical radicals and the Foxite Whigs Burke "proclaimed the sacred continuity of the social fabric." Externally the established order is protected by all the accumulated sanctions of society, church, and state; internally it should be protected against mere theory or speculation by the instincts, emotions, habits, and prejudices of man. For the divine right of kings is substituted the divine right of established institutions. Burke's final conception of the state leaves scope only for the most gradual change, development, or adjustment to new conditions. As Lord Acton says, "The authority of history devoured all the rest of his principles." Thus Burke was a traditionalist, like his friends Johnson and Reynolds, but he looked toward the past with an imaginative ardor which had the color of Scott's romantic Toryism, the heightened sense of the national past which came in the romantic period. England recoiled against the Revolution, but Burke was not happy. He proudly defended himself against the impudent Duke of Bedford in his finely written *Letter to a Noble Lord* (1796), and continued to the last his campaign against revolutionary France in his *Letters on the Proposals for Peace with the Regicide Directory of France* (I-II, 1796; III, 1797).

HIS FAMOUS QUOTATIONS

- "Parliament is not a congress of ambassadors from different and hostile interests; which interests each must maintain, as an agent and advocate, against other agents and advocates; but parliament is a deliberative assembly of one nation, with one interest, that of the whole; where, not local purposes, not local prejudices ought to guide, but the general good, resulting from the general reason of the whole. You choose a member indeed; but when you have chosen him, he is not a member of Bristol, but he is a member of parliament. *(Speech to the electors of Bristol, 3 November 1774)*
- "Young man, there is America - which at this day serves for little more than to amuse you with stories of savage men, and uncouth manners; yet shall, before you taste of death, show itself equal to the whole of that commerce which now attracts the envy of the world." (*Speech on Concilliation with America, 22 March 1775*)
- "The use of force alone is but temporary. It may subdue for a moment; but it does not remove the necessity of subduing again: and a nation is not governed which is perpetually to be conquered.".
- "All protestantism, even the most cold and passive, is a sort of dissent. But the religion most prevalent in our northern colonies is a refinement on the principle of resistance: it is the dissidence of dissent, and the protestantism of the Protestant religion.".
- "I do not know the method of drawing up an indictment against an whole people.".
- "A state without the means of change is without the means of its conservation."
- "They defend their errors as if they were defending their inheritance."
- "Custom reconciles us to everything."

- [*On whether America should belong to Britain*] "If we have equity, wisdom, and justice, it will belong to this country; if we have it not, it will not belong to this country."
- "It is now sixteen or seventeen years since I saw the Dauphiness, at Versailles; and surely never lighted on this orb, which she hardly seemed to touch, a more delightful vision. I saw her just above the horizon, decorating and cheering the elevated sphere she just began to move in, - glittering like the morning star, full of life, and splendour, and joy... . Little did I dream that I should have lived to see disasters fallen upon her in a nation of galant men, in a nation of men of honour, and of cavaliers. I thought ten thousand swords must have leaped from their scabbards to avenge even a look that threatened her with insult. But the age of chivalry is gone. That of sophisters, economists, and calculators, has succeeded; and the glory of Europe is extinguished for ever." (Reflections on the Revolution in France)
- "In my course I have known, and, according to my measure, have co-operated with great men; and I have never yet seen any plan which has not been mended by the observations of those who were much inferior in understanding to the person who took the lead in the business."
- "Make the Revolution a parent of settlement, and not a nursery of future revolutions."
- "Neither the few nor the many have a right to act merely by their will, in any matter connected with duty, trust, engagement, or obligation."
- "Nobody made a greater mistake than he who did nothing because he could do only a little."
- "When bad men combine, the good must associate: else they will fall one by one, an unpitied sacrifice in a contemptible struggle."

- "Jacobinism is the revolt of the enterprising talents of a country against its property."
- "The true danger is when liberty is nibbled away, for expedients, and by parts."
- "Your representative owes you, not his industry only, but his judgment; and he betrays, instead of serving you, if he sacrifices it to your opinion."
- "The only thing necessary for evil to triumph is for good men to do nothing."
- "When bad men combine, the good must associate; else they will fall one by one, an unpitied sacrifice in a contemptible struggle."

Thomas Percy (1729-1811)
Charles Churchill (1731-1764)
William Cowper (1731-1800)
James Beattie (1735-1803)

THOMAS PERCY(1729-1811)

Thomas Percy, clergyman, scholar, poet, was born on 24 April 1729, the son of Arthur Lowe Piercy and his wife Jane Nott. His father was a wealthy wholesale grocer and tobacconist, and later a chamberlain and bailiff of Bridgnorth, Shropshire. The young Percy (he changed the spelling of his name in 1756) exhibited an early interest in tales of chivalry, but also had a precocious literary taste and by the age of 17 had compiled a library of 265 books. He attended Newport School, from where he won an Exhibition to Christ Church, Oxford in 1746. He was awarded his BA in 1750, and three years later was ordained and awarded his MA. He received the living of Easton Maudit in Northamptonshire, which he took up in 1756 when he was also appointed rector of Wilby.

By then Percy had made the acquaintance of the poet William Shenstone, and also acquired from his friend Humphrey Pitt a "folio manuscript" of songs and ballads compiled in the mid-seventeenth century.. This would form the basis of his anthology *Reliques of Ancient English Poetry*.He was able to use the Earl of Sussex's library and had as a neighbour the Anglo-Saxonist Edward Lye. Percy was helping his friend James Grainger on an edition of Tibullus, published in 1758, but also attended local dances and described his lifestyle at this time to his cousin William Cleiveland, "When I am in a studious fit, I can bury myself in books without fear of Interruption: When in a gay Mood, I can gallant it among the Ladies."

From 1758 Percy began corresponding with Shenstone on the subject of the ballads in the folio manuscript. Shenstone was overseeing Robert Dodsley's influential anthology *A Collection of Poems, by Several Hands* (1748-58) through the press, and Percy was able to contribute two pieces including his song "O Nancy", which Robert Burns declared to be "perhaps, the most beautiful Ballad in the English language". The song is usually held to be a tribute to his fiancée, Anne Gutteridge, whom he met in about 1757 and married in 1759 (in fact, he had written it by 1755). They were married for 47 years before Anne's death in 1806, during which time they had five daughters and one son, though sadly three daughters died before they reached maturity, and Percy's son died while an undergraduate at Cambridge.

In the same year of his marriage, Percy began work on a series of books: a translation (from the Portugese) of a Chinese novel, *Hau Kiou Choaan* (published in 1761), a collection of cautionary tales about widows, *The Matrons* (1762), *Miscellaneous Pieces relating to the Chinese* (1762), *Five Pieces of Runic Poetry* (1763), a translation of *The Song of Solomon* which assigned each verse a speaker (1764), and his *Key to the New Testament* (1765). He also signed contracts with Jacob Tonson to edit the *Tatler, Spectator,* and *Guardian,* negotiated to translate Paul-Henri Mallet's *Introduction à l'histoire de Dannemarc* (1755-6), and worked on editions of Buckingham and Surrey. Other plans during the period included an account of the royal entertainments at Kenilworth, a collection of tracts on poetry, a series of the verse of different nations, a book of military instructions, and an edition of metrical romances. He also helped Grainger to edit his poem *The Sugar-Cane* (1764).

Percy's main literary activity during this time, however, was compiling and editing what was to become "Percy's *Reliques*" - a three volume anthology of popular songs and ballads inspired by his old folio manuscript. Grainger had introduced him to Samuel Johnson in 1756, who exhorted him to publish a version of the manuscript. Work started in earnest in 1761, and the book eventually appeared in 1765. During this period he built a network of fellow scholars and critics, among them Richard Farmer and Thomas Warton, bought and borrowed thousands of volumes, including David Garrick's collection of old plays, visited the Pepys Library at Magdalene College, Cambridge for two and a half weeks, and was frequently in London with Johnson.

On 25 June 1764, Johnson famously visited Percy at Easton Maudit, bringing with him the blind poet Anna Williams and his black servant Francis Barber. They stayed for almost eight weeks. Johnson proofread his edition of Shakespeare and Percy finalized the *Reliques*; both works were published the following year. They also collaborated: Percy contributed some notes to Johnson's edition, and Johnson wrote the dedication to the *Reliques* for Elizabeth, Countess of Northumberland - a patron who was to prove most valuable. Percy in fact claimed distant kinship with the Northumberland House of Percy, and it was one reason he had changed the spelling of his name. There were also several significant Northumbrian ballads in the *Reliques*.

By the time the *Reliques* was published in three volumes in 1765, Percy was a regular visitor to Northumberland House in Charing Cross, London. He agreed to write a history of the Percys, was appointed private tutor to the younger son, Algernon Percy, and spent the first of many summers at Alnwick Castle in Northumberland. He wrote an interestingly early picturesque description, *A Letter Describing the Ride to Hulne Abbey from Alnwick in Northumberland* (1765), and with

Algernon and John Brown, author of *A Dissertation on Poetry and Music* (1763), visited Scotland. Upon his return to London, the loyal Percy was given apartments in Northumberland House.

Further editions of the *Reliques* followed in 1767, 1775, 1794 and 1812. Bertram Davis says of the four essays in the 1767 edition (also published separately) that they formed "the most comprehensive and authoritative literary history that Percy's contemporaries could turn to until Thomas Warton published his *History of English Poetry* about a decade later". Percy was the first, for example, to investigate the alliteration of Middle English, consider the significance of metrical romances, and research the origins of English drama. He was now planning an improved and supplemented edition of *Don Quixote* as Tonson's death in 1767 had suspended the printing of five of Percy's projects. The *Tatler, Spectator,* and *Guardian* were passed over to John Calder in 1773 and published in 1786, 1788, and 1789 respectively, but the editions of Surrey and Buckingham languished in a warehouse.

Percy was elected to Johnson's "Club" in 1768. Boswell, describing Percy to Johnson on their Hebridean tour, said that anecdotes flowed from him "like one of the brooks here", and Johnson later declared that he is a man "out of whose company I never go without having learned something". Joseph Cradock called his conversation "lofty", Fanny Burney described him as "perfectly easy & unassuming, very communicative, & though not very entertaining, because too prolix, . . . intelligent & of good commerce", while Hannah More thought Percy "quite a sprightly modern, instead of a rusty antique, as I expected".

The family, meanwhile, found London apartments and Anne became a wet nurse to Edward, Duke of York, the son of Queen Charlotte and later father of Queen Victoria. Percy was appointed one of the King's Chaplains in Ordinary in 1769 and was made a Doctor of Divinity (Cambridge) in 1770. Shortly afterwards he lobbied with Beilby Porteus for a review of the Thirty-Nine Articles of the Church of England, a reform not implemented until 1865.

Percy's translation of Mallet, *Northern Antiquities*, was published in 1770, along with the *Northumberland Houshold Book*, an antiquarian record of accounts. In the following year appeared his 200-stanza Northumbrian ballad, *The Hermit of Warkworth*, which went through six editions in eleven years. It was a pioneering achievement to sustain a narrative across such length, but is now unfortunately better known as the object of Johnson's ridicule against the ballad form. Percy tried to avoid become embroiled in the Rowley Controversy over whether Thomas Chatterton had forged medieval verse, although he worked behind the scenes to prove the manuscripts were fakes; when one of the documents went missing, however, he was pilloried in the press. Percy's literary interest lay instead in a continuation of the *Reliques* - either a fourth volume, or another three volume anthology of ancient English and Scottish poems taken from the Maitland and Bannatyne manuscripts, the latter of which he borrowed for two years in 1773. A collection of translations from the Spanish, *Ancient Songs chiefly on Moorish Subjects*, reached proof stage in 1775-6 before it was abandoned, but he did write the Percy entry for Collins's *Peerage of England* (1779), commenced a biography of Oliver Goldsmith, and researched the history of the wolf, which again excited Johnson's mirth. It may be no coincidence that in 1778 he had a notorious row with Johnson, and with Percy's increasing clerical responsibilities and relocations, the two saw less and less of each other.

In 1778 Percy was made Dean of Carlisle and in 1782, Bishop of Dromore, Ireland. As he rose in the church, he distanced himself from his earlier literary endeavours, describing the *Reliques* as "the follies of my youth". Moreover, disaster had struck in 1780 when Northumberland House caught fire and gutted Percy's apartments, consuming many books and most of his collection of black-letter poems; he also lost his portrait by Joshua Reynolds (1773-4). Still, he wrote the entry on the poet John Cleveland for *Biographia Britannica* (1784) - Cleveland was the brother of Percy's great-grandfather - and in 1786 he was elected a Fellow of the Society of Antiquaries.

He found particularly distasteful the attacks on his scholarly integrity made by Joseph Ritson. Percy felt that it was indecorous for a bishop to be drawn into a literary squabble about editing ballads, and while he did entirely re-edit the *Reliques* for a fourth edition, partly in response to Ritson's criticisms, he published under the name of his nephew and namesake, Thomas Percy, Fellow of St John"s, Oxford. He wrote a little for the *Gentleman's Magazine,* negotiated for an edition of Goldsmith incorporating his memoir (published in 1801 and re-written by Samuel Rose), and aided Robert Anderson on his *Life of Johnson* (1815). The sheets for the long-suspended editions of Surrey and Buckingham were destroyed in Nichols's warehouse fire in 1808. Thomas Percy died peacefully at Dromore on 30 September 1811.

CHARLES CHURCHILL (1731-1764)

English poet and satirist, born in Vine Street, Westminster, in February 1731. His father, rector of Rainham, Essex, held the curacy and lectureship of St. John's, Westminster, from 1733, and the son was educated at Westminster School, where he became a good classical scholar, and formed a close and lasting intimacy with Robert Lloyd. Churchill was entered at Trinity College, Cambridge, in 1749, but never resided. He had been refused at Oxford, ostensibly on the unlikely ground of lack of classical knowledge, but more probably because of a hasty marriage which he had contracted within the rules of the Fleet in his eighteenth year. He and his wife lived in his father's house, and Churchill was afterwards sent to the north of England to prepare for holy orders. He became curate of South Cadbury, Somersetshire, and, on receiving priest's orders (1756), began to act as his father's curate at Rainham. Two years later the elder Churchill died, and the son was elected to succeed him in his curacy and lectureship. His emoluments amounted to less than £100 a year, and he increased his income by teaching in a girls' school. He fulfilled his various duties with decorum for a while, but his marriage proved unfortunate, and he spent much of his time in dissipation in the society of Robert Lloyd. He was separated from his wife in 1761, and would have been imprisoned for debt but for the timely help of Lloyd's father, who had been an usher and was now a master of Westminster School.

Churchill had already done some work for the booksellers, and his friend Lloyd had had some success with a didactic poem, "The Actor." His intimate knowledge of the theater was now turned to account in the *Rosciad,* which appeared in March 1761. This reckless and amusing satire described with the most disconcerting accuracy the faults of the various actors and actresses on the London stage. Its immediate popularity was no doubt argely due to its personal character, but its real vigor and raciness make it worth reading even now when the objects of Churchill's wit are many of them forgotten. The first impression was published anonymously, and in the *Critical Review,* conducted by Tobias Smollett, it was confidently asserted that the poem was the joint production of George Colman, Bonnell Thornton and Robert Lloyd. Churchill owned the authorship and immediately published an *Apology addressed to the Critical Reviewers,* which, after developing the subject that it is only the caste of authors that prey on their own kind, repeats the fierce attack on the stage. Incidentally it contains an enthusiastic tribute to John Dryden, of whom Churchill was a not unworthy scholar. In the *Rosciad* he had given warm praise to Mrs. Pritchard, Mrs. Cibber and Mrs. Clive, but no leading London actor, with the exception of David Garrick, had escaped censure, and in the *Apology* Garrick was clearly threatened. He deprecated criticism by showing every possible civility to Churchill, who became a terror to the actors. Thomas Davies wrote to Garrick attributing his blundering in the part of Cymbeline "to my accidentally seeing Mr. Churchill in the pit, it rendering me confused and unmindful of my business." Churchill's satire made him many enemies, and inquiries into his way of life provided abundant matter for retort. In *Night, an Epistle to Robert Lloyd* (1761), he answered the attacks made on him, offering by way of defense the argument that any faults were better than hypocrisy. His scandalous conduct brought down the censure of the dean of Westminster, and in 1763 the protests of his parishioners led him to resign his offices, and he was free to wear his "blue coat with metal buttons" and much gold lace without remonstrance from the dean. The *Rosciad* had been refused by several publishers, and was finally published at Churchill's own expense. He received a considerable sum from the sale, and paid his old creditors in full, besides making an allowance to his wife.

He now became a close ally of John Wilkes, whom he regularly assisted with the *North Briton. The Prophecy of Famine: A Scots Pastoral* (1763), his next poem, was founded on a paper written originally for that journal. This violent satire on Scottish influence fell in with the current hatred of Lord Bute, and the Scottish place-hunters were as much alarmed as the actors had been. When Wilkes was arrested he gave Churchill a timely hint to retire to the country for a time, the publisher, Kearsley, having stated that he received part of the profits from the paper. His *Epistle to William Hogarth* (1763) was in answer to the caricature of Wilkes made during the trial, in it Hogarth's vanity and envy were attacked in an invective which Garrick quoted as "shocking and barbarous." Hogarth retaliated by a caricature of Churchill as a bear in torn clerical bands hugging a pot of porter and a club made of lies and *North Britons. The Duellist* (1763) is a virulent satire on the most active opponents of Wilkes. in the House of Lords, especially on Bishop Warburton. He attacked Samuel Johnson among others in *The Ghost* as "Pomposo, insolent and loud, Vain idol of a scribbling crowd." Other poems are "The Conference" (1763); "The Author" (1763), highly praised by Churchill's contemporaries; "Gotham" (1764), a poem on the duties of a king, didactic rather than satiric in tone; "The Candidate" (1764), a satire on John Montagu, fourth earl of Sandwich, one of Wilkes's bitterest enemies, whom he had already denounced for his treachery in the *Duellist* as "too infamous to have a friend"; "The Farewell" (1764); "The Times" (1764); "Independence", and an unfinished "Journey."

In October 1764 he went to Boulogne to join Wilkes. There he was attacked by a fever of which he died on the 4th of November. He left his property to his two sons, and made Wilkes his literary executor with full powers. Wilkes did little. He wrote an epitaph for his friend and about half a dozen notes on his poems, and Andrew Kippis acknowledges some slight assistance from him in preparing his life of Churchill for the *Biographia Britannica* (1780). There is more than one instance of Churchill's generosity to his friends. In 1763 he found his friend Robert Lloyd in prison for debt. He paid a guinea a week for his better maintenance in the Fleet, and raised a subscription to set him free. Lloyd fell ill on receipt of the news of Churchill's death, and died shortly afterwards. Churchill's sister Patty, who was engaged to Lloyd, did not long survive them. William Cowper was his schoolfellow, and left many kindly references to him.

WILLIAM COWPER (1731-1800)

William Cowper (1731-1800) is notable as both a poet and a letter-writer. His poetry was among the most popular in England from the late eighteenth century to the mid-nineteenth century. The OED cites about 6,000 quotations from Cowper, over twice as many as from Wordsworth. And Gilbert Thomas suggests that among poets Cowper trails only Shakespeare as a source of common phrases and proverbs. But his reputation has declined. Though some of his Evangelical hymns still appear in Protestant hymnals ("O For a Closer Walk With God"; "There is a Fountain Filled With Blood"), and a few lyrics like "The Cast-Away" are regularly anthologized, his longer poems are less esteemed than they were during the first half-century after his death.

As a poet Cowper often is considered transitional between the neoclassic (Alexander Pope) and the Romantic (William Wordsworth). Cowper's first volume of poetry resembles Pope's: moral satire written in heroic couplets. Verbal and prosodic echoes of Pope abound. Furthermore, in his last ambitious project, Cowper attempted to "(contend) with Pope upon Homer's ground" (letter of 14 Jan. 1786) by translating the *Iliad* and the *Odyssey*.

On the other hand, he wrote many lyrics as well as longer poems in blank verse, and his poetry often anticipates the Romantic emphasis on common (as opposed to poetic) diction, descriptions of nature, and intimate self-revelation. Wordsworth knew Cowper's poetry well. He affirmed it in general and praised Cowper's "Verses Supposed to be Written by Alexander Selkirk" as "admirably expressed" and of great beauty because written in "natural language so naturally connected with metre" (de Selincourt, *Poetical Works* 2. 408). In 1835-37 Robert Southey published *The Life and Works* in 15 volumes.

Cowper's originality derives from his self-consciousness, his poetry's "confessional and psychodramatic elements", according to Vincent Newey (*Cowper's Poetry* 34). Occasionally Cowper celebrates the psychological struggle, and the person for whom, like himself, "contemplation is his bliss":

His warfare is within. There unfatigued
His fervent spirit labours. There he fights,
And there obtains fresh triumphs o'er himself
(The Task 6. 935-937).

Thus Newey credits Cowper with introducing "a new kind of lyric—peculiarly modern in its deliberate subjectivity, which . . . testifies to the sheer creative resilience of the self in isolation". That subjectivity encourages readers to turn to his biography (over thirty have been written), a life remarkable for his severe bouts of depression and his Evangelical beliefs. Both influence his poetry significantly.

Cowper was born in Great Berkhamstead, Hertfordshire. His father was a minister and his mother, Ann Donne, was the daughter of a wool merchant too impecunious to provide a dowry. Only two of six children, William and John, survived. Ann Cowper died when William was six, an event to which many attribute his recurring depression.

Cowper briefly attended local schools. Because he had problems with his sight, he was sent to live for a couple of years with Mrs. Disney, an oculist. He then went to

Westminster School (1742-1748). In 1748 he was admitted to Middle Temple to study law, a family tradition. Cowper's grandfather was Attorney General to the Prince of Wales and his great uncle, William, 1st Earl Cowper, was Lord Chancellor of Great Britain (appointed in 1707). Cowper was called to the bar of Middle Temple in 1754 and admitted to the Inner Temple in 1757. In the early 1750s he fell in love with his cousin, Theadora Cowper.

Cowper's practice of law apparently was casual. He served as Commissioner of Bankrupts from 1759-1765. His uncle, Ashley Cowper, arranged for him to be appointed to clerkships in the House of Lords, but when faced with an examination to qualify for the post of Clerk to the Journals of the House of Lords in 1763, he suffered a mental collapse during which he attempted suicide several times. In December of that year, his brother, John, committed him to an asylum, the Collegium Insanorum in St. Albans, run by Dr. Nathaniel Cotton, a student of Boerhaave's. In 1764 he was converted to Evangelicalism, a Calvinistic, morally stringent Christianity. Cowper gradually improved under Dr. Cotton's care and was released in June 1765.

He went to Huntingdon where he lodged with the Rev. Morley Unwin and his wife Mary. After Morley's death in 1767, Cowper continued to live with the Unwin family. They moved to Olney in 1768 in order to join the parish of John Newton, an Evangelical preacher. They later moved to Weston (1786 to 1795) and then East Dereham, where Cowper died in 1800. Mary may have offered the kind of maternal relationship the death of his mother had denied Cowper, as well as the stability and domestic peace that Cowper desperately sought. In 1773, urged by the perception of impropriety, the two became engaged, but Cowper's depression recurred, probably because he feared marital commitment. The betrothal was never renewed, but they lived in the same household until she died in 1796.

Cowper exemplifies melancholy as described by Robert Burton (*The Anatomy of Melancholy*). He suffered a series of severe depressions that correspond to his fear of commitment, rejection, or loss—of a cousin he loved, of a job, of his companion and surrogate mother, of close friends. But his deepest melancholy derived from his conviction that God had rejected him. In January 1773 Cowper heard a voice in a dream proclaiming him dead to God, after which he ceased attending church or praying for the rest of his life. But he continued to comfort others by reference to Evangelical tenets, though he could not comfort himself, according to John Newton.

Some of his most powerful poems record his despair, whose profundity is marked by "therefore" in the following passage ("Hatred and Vengeance, My Eternal Portion"):

Man disavows, and Deity disowns me:
Hell might afford my miseries a shelter;
Therefore hell keeps her ever hungry mouths all
Bolted against me.

Cowper's earliest poems were derivative; few survive. After his conversion he wrote devotional poetry, or hymns, attesting to God's presence and intervention in the believer's life. In 1771 Newton, as Cowper's spiritual advisor, proposed that they publish their hymns for use by other Evangelicals. (Newton wrote the famous hymn "Amazing Grace".) This project is variously described as contributing to Cowper's mental collapse or helping him respond to it. Whatever the case, the hymns were published in 1779 and went through thirty-seven editions by 1836 (James King, *William Cowper: A Biography* 83).

As he gradually emerged from his severe depression which had begun in January 1773, Cowper turned to gardening, carpentry, letter-writing, and poetry for distraction and amusement. In 1780 he began to write poetry more regularly, frequently responding to current events, and he published his first volume of poems in 1782. His first long poem, *Antithelyphthora,* contributed to an Evangelical controversy over polygamy, endorsed by his cousin Martin Madan and derided by Cowper. The titles of other poems suggest their Evangelical content: *The Progress of Error, Truth, Expostulation, Hope, Charity*. Others suggest his coping strategies: *Table Talk, Conversation, Retirement*. He affirms poetry's proper role as "the Giver's praise":

To trace him in his word, his works, his ways,
Then spread the rich discov'ry, and invite
Mankind to share in the divine delight (Table Talk 750-53).

After Cowper had completed his first volume of poems, his friend, Lady Austen, suggested he write about his sofa. He thus began to write what was to become his most celebrated work, *The Task*, a blank-verse poem in six books. He finished the poem in 1784, and published it the next year. According to James King, "*The Task* was immediately greeted by the critics as a masterpiece". It "was an overwhelming critical success", and "it remained the most widely read poetical text in England until about 1800".

The Task begins, "I sing the sofa," then moves on to meditations about his personal experience and life of retreat. His prefatory "history" of *The Task* suggests that he composed by means of local connections rather than a general outline: "having much leisure, he connected another subject with it [the sofa]; and, pursuing the train of thought to which his situation and turn of mind led him, brought forth at length, instead of the trifle which he at first intended, a serious affair—a Volume!" (*The Poems* ed. Baird and Ryskamp, 2: 113). The passage also exhibits Cowper's mildly humorous self-deprecation. It characterizes writing as a hobby (done during his "leisure" time), not a strong vocation, and ironically touts seriousness derived from heft—"a Volume!"

From the beginning readers have struggled to explain the poem's unity. In a letter to William Unwin (10 Oct. 1784), Cowper wrote, "If the work cannot boast a regular plan (in which respect however I do not think it altogether indefensible), it may yet boast, that the reflections are naturally suggested always by the preceding passage, and that except the fifth book, which is rather of a political aspect, the whole has one tendency; to discountenance the modern enthusiasm after a London life, and to recommend rural ease and leisure, as friendly to the cause of piety and virtue" (Wright, ed. *Correspondence* 2. 252-53).

Cowper's descriptions of nature are celebrated for their accuracy. Cowper usually depicts "nature in her cultivated trim / Dress'd to our taste" (*The Task* 3. 357-358)—in the garden particularly (gardening was one of his hobbies). As he himself claimed in the same letter to Unwin, "My descriptions are all from nature: not one of them second-handed. My delineations of the heart are from my own experience: not one of them borrowed from books, or in the least degree conjectural".

The Task is also notable for its confessional passages. In one of the most famous, Cowper describes himself as

A stricken deer, that left the herd
Long since; with many an arrow deep infixt
My panting side was charg'd, when I withdrew
To seek a tranquil death in distant shades. (The Task 3. 108-111)

This passage includes Cowper's recurring themes: his anguish which isolates him, drives him into retreat for safety, and leads him to seek resolution in death. He then attests that Jesus will minister to him (a hope that ultimately eludes Cowper). In *The Task* Book 6 he prays for "a safe retreat"—death—thanks to "some disease" operating "with gentle stroke".

Shortly after he had published *The Task,* Cowper began to translate Homer. He wanted to correct what he considered Pope's misconstrual of Homeric tone and style, and modeled his verse on Milton's. Besides being a literary enterprise, translating was therapeutic: Cowper wrote to Newton that writing had "become essential to my well-being", and that he had begun translating Homer "to divert attention" when he was "in such distress of mind as was hardly supportable" (3 Dec. 1785; *Corr.* 2. 393). "In Cowper's eyes, his Homer was the great undertaking of his life, and he became obsessively involved with every aspect of it". The translation of Homer was published in 1791. The reviews were mixed, but most of them were critical. Cowper's translation did not transcend Pope's.

Cowper then proposed to edit John Milton's poetry. Milton had always been an example for Cowper, who celebrates him in *The Task* as a "genius who had angelic wings" and affirms his early enthusiastic response to Milton's poetry. That project, however, never came to fruition.

Much of our knowledge of Cowper's life and personality comes from his letters. His letters, many of which were first published three years after his death, contain sprightly anecdotes, sincere expressions of gratitude and concern, honest accounts of his illnesses and bouts of depression, and playful irony. They reveal that he relishes the simple, sedate pleasures of life, revels in a rural existence, and enjoys a quiet conversation with a friend. The time he does not spend in his garden or greenhouse he devotes to a favorite hobby like cabinet making or tending to his pet hares, reading in the comfort of his study, or walking with a companion. Normally Cowper imparts news of a domestic nature: acknowledging a gift of fish or meat, arranging to send some delicacy like a cucumber, requesting money, describing a picnic, reporting on his health. From time to time he describes the joy he has derived from a walk, a prospect, the sounds of a rural morning, or a conversation. He also offers literary opinions and explains his own projects. Indeed, Cowper's epistolary style is conversational: "A letter is written as a conversation is maintained" (*Correspondence* 1. 222). The letters suggest why, in spite of his often debilitating melancholy, he established deep and lasting relationships with friends who provided emotional and financial support throughout his life.

Cowper's poetry is notable for its pastoral and domestic detail described in common language. As he writes, he is "enamour'd of sequester'd scenes, / And charm'd with rural beauty" (*The Task*. 3. 27-28). He celebrates "Domestic happiness" as the "only bliss / Of Paradise that has surviv'd the fall" (*The Task*. 3. 41-2). It is "the nurse of virtue" and offers "in the calm of truth-tried love, / Joys that her pleasure's stormy raptures never yield" (*The Task* 3. 56-57). His own life comprises "Friends, books, a garden, and perhaps his pen, / Delightful industry enjoy'd at home" (*The Task* 3. 355-356).

In *The Task* he describes reading newspaper accounts of politics and public events, deeming that "'Tis pleasant through the loop-holes of retreat /To peek at such a world" (4. 88-89) because

I seem advanc'd
To some secure and more than mortal height,
That lib'rates and exempts me from them all. (4. 94-97)

But he laments the instability of even a rural retreat: "The town has ting'd the country", and "The course of human things from good to ill, / From ill to worse, is fatal, never fails" (*The Task* 4. 553; 578-9).

Sometimes his sense of disintegration takes a comic turn, as in one of his most popular poems, "The Extraordinary and Facetious History of John Gilpin", which describes how a carefully-planned wedding anniversary celebration is ruined by a wild ride on a runaway horse. His first extant poem, "Written at Bath on Finding the Heel of a Shoe" (1748), reveals a similarly comic sensibility, though it also includes a moral lesson about vanity and the instability of human affairs.

Ultimately Cowper's melancholy prevailed. He ended his life feeling like a mariner cast overboard who cannot be saved:

No voice divine the storm allay'd,
No light propitious shone;
When, snatch'd from all effectual aid,
We perish'd, each alone:
But I beneath a rougher sea,
And whelm'd in deeper gulphs than he. ("The Cast-Away")

His poetry had offered only temporary respite from his mental anguish, though it attests to the pleasures that he frequently was able to derive from the support of loyal, loving friends in his rural retreat. For today's readers it offers some vivid descriptions of the English countryside of the late eighteenth century, a sense of Evangelical piety tempered by candid revelations of uncertainty and doubt, and the pleasures offered by quiet occupations and domestic tasks even to a man who suffers frequent, profound depression.

JAMES BEATTIE (1735-1803)

Beattie was born at Laurencekirk, a small town about thirty miles south of Aberdeen. He won a scholarship at Marischal College, Aberdeen, taught school, and studied for the ministry. From 1760 he held the chair of Moral Philosophy at Marischal College, and came forth as an orthodox opponent of the skeptical Hume, against whom he directed his *Essay on Truth* (1770). This work was much overpraised, and won for Beattie the patronage of Mrs. Montagu and others. Hume was so far superior in philosophic power that the pretensions of his critics now seem ludicrous. At Aberdeen Beattie was in contact with the exponents of the Scottish "common sense" school of philosophy, and with a school of rhetoricians and critics who exalted taste and original genius. Among his teachers was Thomas Blackwell; Alexander Gerard, author of *An Essay on Taste* (1759), was both teacher and colleague, and George Campbell the rhetorician was also a colleague. Beattie, always academic and docile, got from these men what we might call an official doctrine of pre-romanticism. While at work on his *Essay* he diverted himself by writing *The Minstrel,* which he thus described in 1768: "It is a moral and descriptive poem, written in the stanza of Spenser, but not much in his style. The hint of the subject was taken from Percy's 'Essays on the English Minstrels.'" In the preface to Book I (1771) he says: "The design was to trace the progress of a poetical genius, born in a rude age, from the first dawning of fancy and reason, till that period at which he may be supposed capable of appearing in the world as a *Minstrel,* that is, as an itinerant poet and musician." Beattie does not break fresh ground in this work; he does not, like Wordsworth, give us a study of the growth of a poet's mind, but puts his vaguely conceived young minstrel Edwin in the midst of sublime and picturesque scenery based to some extent on the Scottish landscape though not vividly localized. In Book II (1774) Edwin, under the instruction of a sage hermit, passes from the dreams of youth to a survey of moral duties, and is told at length of man's cultural progress. This didactic survey combines the idea of progress with the idea of the excellence of primitive simplicity. A similar pattern of themes occurs in Thomson, who influenced Beattie directly here. *The Minstrel,* now completely neglected, was once very popular because it set forth currently acceptable ideas and images in a smooth though undistinguished style. Though Beattie has a certain academic good taste, he falls far short of Thomson in imaginative and artistic power, and at the same time he lacks the scholarly enthusiasms of his friend Thomas Gray. Unlike his younger countrymen, Burns and Scott, he makes no significant use of the traditions of his native land.

James Macpherson (1736-1796) Edward Gibbon (1737-1794) James Boswell (1740-1795) Hester Lynch Piozzi (Mrs. Thrale) (1741-1821)

JAMES MACPHERSON (1736-1796)

Macpherson, the supposed translator of the once famous Ossianic poems, was born in southern Inverness-shire, in a remote region associated with the feuds of Highland clans and the rebellion of 1745. He grew up with a smattering of Gaelic, though without detailed knowledge of that difficult language. He was educated at Aberdeen and Edinburgh, and wrote mediocre verse. In 1759 he met John Home, who was moved to enthusiasm by a supposed translation of a fragment of traditional Highland poetry, *"The Death of Oscar."* Home and his scholarly friends in Edinburgh then encouraged Macpherson to publish *Fragments of Ancient Poetry Collected in the Highlands of Scotland, and Translated from the Gallic or Erse Language* (I760). There was already a well-defined idea that a great body of traditional verse had been preserved by the bards in Wales and the Scottish Highlands. John Campbell

Polite Correspondence (I741) had spoken of the heroic virtue and primitive enthusiasm of Celtic poetry, and suggested that "remains of this poetic spirit" should be sought in Wales, Brittany, and the Highlands. The "runic bards" in Collins *Ode on the Superstitions of the Highlands of Scotland* (written in 1749 and addressed to John Home) represent the same idea. A young schoolmaster, Jerome Stone, had published a letter on Gaelic poetry with a specimen translation in the *Scots Magazine* (I755-56). Macpherson was now virtually ordered by the Edinburgh literati to travel in the Highlands at their expense and find this primitive poetry. The Reverend Hugh Blair, Professor of Rhetoric and Belles Lettres at Edinburgh, was convinced that the fragments pointed to a Highland epic, and would be satisfied with nothing else. Macpherson was somewhat reluctant, but after two short Highland journeys he duly produced *Fingal* (I761, dated 1762), and *Temora* (I763).

Macpherson's later life is of no importance for literary history except for the long controversy that raged about the authenticity of the Ossianic poems. He cut a poor figure in these quarrels, and was never able to produce his alleged Gaelic originals. The question of the relation of *Ossian* to Gaelic literature lies outside the English field. The conclusion now is that Macpherson's work has a slender traditional basis but does not rest on traditional texts. What is denied, of course, is not the existence of traditional Highland poetry, but Macpherson's actual connection with that tradition. Quite apart from the question of authenticity, the enthusiasm with which the Ossianic poems were received and the influence they exerted throughout western Europe are historical facts of great importance. Ossian now seems to be merely bombastic and rhetorical prose, yet it could move a fastidious critic like Gray to write, "Imagination dwelt many hundred years ago in all her pomp on the cold and barren mountains of Scotland. . . . She reigns in all nascent societies of men." Gray and his generation were moved by preconceived ideas of early or primitive poetry. Macpherson succeeded because he gave what was expected, but gave it in a superficially novel way. His poetic prose is obviously influenced by the

Bible, and follows the parallel style of Hebrew poetry; his pseudo-simple style, with its stock similes and epithets, was taken to be Homeric. The Ossianic pieces have little concrete detail of character, manners, physical objects, or topography. In these respects they are the very opposite of Homer. Shadowy figures, such as Ossian, the great hero turned blind bard in his old age, and the young and tender Malvina move against a vague background of mountain, seashore, forest, and sky, the austere landscape of the Highlands. Simple feelings of regret, loyalty, tenderness, and heroism are expressed with pseudo-archaic simplicity and monotonous repetition. The generality and vagueness of Ossian gave an elevation which contemporary readers and critics found sublime.

But there is a complex fusion of moods here: the poetry of melancholy was already encouraging the somber-sublime, but also blended with softer emotions so cultivated for their own sake as to be sentimental. The narrative interest of Ossian is slight; the appeal is that made by graveyard poetry, the Gothic, and the sentimental cult of noble feelings. As Blair put it: "The general character of his poetry is the heroic mixed with the elegiac strain, admiration tempered with pity." The supposed historical significance of Ossian was also important; not only did Macpherson set up the Caledonian against the Irish, and thus appeal to Scottish patriotism—he appealed also to a cult of ancient simplicity and heroism. Even the historian Gibbon, though he was no primitivist and did not believe in the authenticity of Ossian, admired the contrast between "the untutored Caledonians, glowing with the warm virtues of nature, and the degenerate Romans, polluted with the mean vices of wealth and slavery." Perhaps it was this aspect of Ossian which later captivated Napoleon. The continental vogue of Ossian. as great as that of Richardson and Young, lies beyond our field. Cesarotti's Italian version and Le Tourneur's French version are only two among innumerable documents which attest the wide diffusion of Ossian. Goethe references in *Werther,* including a translation of the "Song of Selma," should be remembered.

EDWARD GIBBON (1737-1794)

English historian and scholar, the supreme historian of the Enlightenment, who is best-known as the author of the monumental *The Decline And Fall Of The Roman Empire*, often considered the greatest historical work written in English. "It was at Rome... as I sat musing amidst the ruins of the Capitol, while barefoot friars were singing vespers in the Temple of Jupiter, that the idea of writing the decline and fall of the city first started to my mind." However, Gibbon's first works were written in French.

Edward Gibbon was born in Putney in South London into a prosperous family. His father was a wealthy Tory member of Parliament who went into seclusion and left his son to the care of an aunt. Gibbon was a sickly child and his education at Westminster and at Magdalen College, Oxford, was irregular. According to Gibbon's own explanation he was too bashful to spend his time in taverns, but his studies ended anyway after one year: he was expelled for turning to Roman Catholicism - a decision which was undoubtedly directed against one of his intellectually lazy Anglican college tutors. In 1753 Gibbon was sent by his father to Lausanne, Switzerland. He boarded with a Calvinist pastor and scholar, who was very demanding in his teaching, and rejoined the Anglican fold. In Lausanne he fell in love with Suzanne Curchod, who eventually married Jacques Necker, a banker. Their relationship was ended by his father, and Gibbon remained unmarried for the rest of his life. Suzanne became the mother of the famous writer and early champion of women's rights, Madame de Staël.

From 1759 to 1762 Gibbon hold a commission in the Hampshire militia, reaching the rank of colonel. Before 1763 Gibbon had considered various subjects as worthy of the type of philosophical analysis that he wished to apply to history: the life of Sir Walter Raleigh, the history of Switzerland, and others. However, he felt that he had nothing original to say about Elizabethan politics and he could not read German.

In 1764 he visited Rome and was inspired to write the history of the city from the death of Marcus Aurelius to the year 1453. After his father died Gibbon found himself in some difficulties, but he was able to settle in London to proceed with his great work. The first volume appeared in 1776, with a certain amount of public reaction to Gibbon's ironical treatment of the rise of Christianity and the actions of early church fathers. Like Voltaire, Gibbon was himself a deist who had little appreciation of the metaphysical side of religion. He examined the secular side of religion as a social phenomenon - religion did not have for Gibbon special sanctity. But Christianity had a special role in the fall of the Roman empire: "... the church and even the state were distracted by religious factions, whose conflicts were sometimes bloody and always implacable; the attention of the emperors was diverted from camps to synods; the Roman world was oppressed by a new species of tyranny, and the persecuted sects became the secret enemies of their country."

Between 1774 and 1783 Gibbon sat in the House of Commons, and became a lord commissioner of trade and plantations, partly because he was considered a nuisance as a politician. In 1774 he was elected to Dr Johnson's Club. From 1783 Gibbon spent much of his time in Lausanne and in England with Lord Sheffield (John Baker Holroy) in his Sussex and London houses. After *Decline and Fall* Gibbon wrote a memoir. It went through many drafts and was not published during his lifetime. Lord Sheffield later prepared *Gibbon's Memoirs Of My Life And Writings* for publication (1796) and *Miscellaneous Works (1796).*

The last three volumes of *Decline and Fall* were published in 1788. The book was a bestseller, and offered the reading public a vivid narrative of the past instead of an antiquarian picture. "If he had been more vulnerable to the glittering abstractions of his age he might have become an English Montesquieu, writing for scholars of political thought. If he had sought historical laws or cycles or found some single cause, he might have been bedside reading no more than Vico or Marx." (Daniel J. Boorstin) Gibbon, who did not much value contemporary historians, developed his own approach and adopted influences from such diverse sources as the

"Protestant Enlightenment," Parisian philosophers, and the Scottish Enlightenment. Although Gibbon's conclusions have been modified, his masterful historical perspective and literary style have secured his place as the forerunner of English historiographers. On the other hand, his personal habits were peculiar - according to some contemporary comment Gibbon was so filthy that one could not stand close to him. How did Lord Sheffield manage to do so? Gibbon's devotion to routine was also a source of jokes - this harmless personal trait he shared with, amongst others, the German philosopher Kant and the Danish philosopher Kierkegaard. When Benjamin Franklin was visiting England he wanted to see Gibbon, who refused to meet him. It did not diminish Franklin's admiration of the historian and he promised to help Gibbon when he came to write the history of the decline and fall of the British Empire.

In *The Decline and Fall of the Roman Empire* (1776-1788) Gibbon himself was grateful to Jean Mabillon (1632-1707), Bernard Montfasucon (1655-1741), and Ludovico Muratori (1672-1741) for their collections of facts and documents. The work covers more than 13 centuries from the 2nd century AD to the fall of Constantinople in 1453. Christianity is dealt with in detail, he examines the encroachment of the Teutonic tribes who eventually held the Western Empire in fee, the rise of Islam, and the Crusades. Gibbon viewed the Roman Empire as a single entity in undeviating decline from the ideals of political and intellectual freedom that had characterized the classical literature he had read. For him, the material decay of Rome was the effect and symbol of moral decadence. "Many a sober Christian would rather admit that a wafer is God than that God is a cruel and capricious tyrant." With powerful narrative, fluid prose, and persuasive arguments the work has a remained a classic in historical literature.

"In the second century of the Christian era, the Empire of Rome comprehended the fairest part of the earth, and the most civilized portion of mankind. The frontiers of that extensive monarchy were guarded by ancient renown and

disciplined valour. The gentle but powerful influence of laws and manners had gradually cemented the union of the provinces. Their peaceful inhabitants enjoyed and abused the advantages of wealth and luxury. The image of a free constitution was preserved with decent reverence: the Roman senate appeared to possess the sovereign authority, and devolved on the emperors all the executive powers of government. During a happy period (A.D. 98-180) of more than fourscore years, the public administration was conducted by the virtue and abilities of Nerva, Trajan, Hadrian, and the two Antonines. It is the design of this, and of the two succeeding chapters, to describe the prosperous condition of their empire; and afterwards, from the death of Marcus Antoninus, to deduce the most important circumstances of its decline and fall; a revolution which will ever be remembered, and is still felt by the nations of the earth."

WORKS BY GIBBON

- *Essai sur l'étude de la littérature* (1761).
- *The History of the Decline and Fall of the Roman Empire* (Volume I, 1776; Volumes II and III, 1781; Volumes IV, V, and VI, 1788).
- *A vindication of some passages in the fifteenth and sixteenth chapters of the History of the decline and fall of the Roman Empire* (1779).
- *Mémoire justificatif pour servir de réponse à l'exposé, &c de la cour de France* (1779).
- *Memoirs of My Life* (1796, at the beginning of the posthumous *Miscellaneous Works of Edward Gibbon, Esq.* published two years after the author's death by his friend and literary executor John Holroyd, 1st Earl of Sheffield).

JAMES BOSWELL (1740-1795)

James Boswell was born on 29 October 1740, the eldest son of a distinguished judge known as Lord Auchinleck from his family estates in Ayrshire in what is now "Burns country" (they knew of each other but lived on different social planes and never met). James was conscious of family history and boasted that the blood of the Bruce flowed in his veins; he was distantly related to Prince Charles Edward, the Pretender, and the reigning monarch, George III. In politics, the father was a Whig; in religion a Presbyterian; in manner noted for his conservative Scottish speech and writing (though he was a fine classical scholar and built the smart neo-classical Auchinleck House). Much of James's early life consisted of reactions against the family's stern values and a search for alternative role models; there were signs of mental instability, even insanity among the Boswells; his younger brother was kept under supervision for most of his later life; and James himself suffered from bouts of melancholy.

At thirteen, Boswell went to University in Edinburgh, then in the early stages of the historical, philosophical and scientific revolution of the "Scottish Enlightenment", which made it one of the intellectual capitals of Europe. With a good grounding in arts, he took an interest in recent English literature as well as the prescribed Latin and Greek. Less predictable was his father's decision to send him next to Glasgow University, hoping that there might be less danger in the then quieter town from temptations such as theatre and an expansive social life. While Boswell was impressed in Glasgow by the lectures of Adam Smith on Moral Philosophy and Rhetoric, he was inflamed by an actress, went to London and seems to have converted to Catholicism. From this he was quickly dissuaded by his father's friends, who also helped restrain his military ambitions - Boswell had romantic notions of the independent life of a guards officer amid the pleasures of London. He devoted himself to several months of the city's delights as a civilian, with the minor author, Samuel Derrick. He consorted with the Duke of York, and commemorated a visit to the races in a doggerel poem, *The Cub at Newmarket* (1762); he met Lawrence Sterne, who had just published the first two volumes of his great novel, and was favoured with "A Poetical Epistle to . . . . Tristram Shandy";.

At this time Boswell tried his hand at miscellaneous versa and prose, gaining a reputation as a versatile if self-opinionated amateur. He compromised with his father and, passing his law examinations, was allowed back to London to try for a Guards commission. At this point his writing takes a new turning. For several years Boswell had been keeping brief diaries; now in 1762 he produced his first fully-written journal, relating to a Harvest Jaunt - or autumn tour. It shows his interest in himself, fluctuating in reaction to widely-varied events and people, recording the surface of life just as it strikes him.

The first of the full journals which became a central feature of Boswell's life, the London Journal of 1762-3, was only published in the mid-twentieth century, and became a popular if scandalous paperback. In this fairly self-contained unit, Boswell describes succumbing wholeheartedly to the pleasures of the metropolis. Although written with an eye on its reader, a student friend, it is fully composed, since Boswell, between social engagements, had little to do but wander the streets or write. His reasons for keeping the journal he sets down in rather stilted prose at the head:

It will give me a habit of application and improve me in expression; and knowing that I am to record my transactions will make me more careful to do well. Or if I should go wrong, it will assist me in resolutions of doing better. I shall here put down my thoughts on different subjects at different times, the whims that may seize me and the sallies of my luxuriant imagination.

The London Journal for 1762-3 shows an uncertain young man finding his bearings in a brilliant and extensive society. On a carefully-calculated budget, Boswell managed to base himself in modest lodgings in Downing Street and sally forth to whatever assemblies of the great he could penetrate, and to the public pleasures of the town - the theatres, taverns and executions. The genteel maker of virtuous resolutions lapses into the Boswell of legend, who takes his women as he finds them - in St. James's Park, up alleyways, on

Westminster Bridge. He records his affair with an actress; whatever the morality, it is a little comic masterpiece in which his awareness of his absurd situation is never quite clear; here he has just spent his first night with her:

> I got up between nine and ten and walked out till Louisa should rise. I patrolled up and down Fleet Street, thinking on London, the seat of Parliament and the seat of pleasure, and seeming to myself as one of the wits in King Charles the Second's time. I then came in and we had an agreeable breakfast . . . and calling a hackney-coach, drove to Soho Square, where Louisa had some visits to pay. So we parted. Thus was this conquest completed to my highest satisfaction. I can with pleasure trace the progress of this intrigue to its completion. I am now at ease on that head, having my fair one fixed as my own. As Captain Plume says, the best security for a woman's mind is her body. I really conducted this affair with a manliness and prudence that pleased me very much. The whole expense was just eighteen shillings.

Despite the triumphant comparisons to a Restoration buck, within a week Boswell, confronted with the symptoms of gonorrhea, is alternating between fear and rage. His last letter mentions a doctor's bill of five guineas and demands back money lent Louisa: "I neither *paid* it for prostitution nor *gave* it in charity . . . . Call not that a misfortune which is the consequence of your own unworthiness. I desire no mean evasions. I want no letters. Send the money sealed up. I have nothing more to say to you." At about this time too, Boswell recognized the folly of his military ambitions, and resigned himself to a law career.

At this unsatisfactory time, a great ambition was fulfilled: although he had met Sterne, Goldsmith and Macpherson, among leading writers, there remained a gap. On 16 May 1763, as he was drinking tea with the bookseller, Tom Davies,

> About seven came in the great Mr Samuel Johnson, whom I have so long wished to see. Mr Davies introduced me to him. As I knew his mortal antipathy at the Scotch, I cried to Davies, "Don't tell where I come from." However,

he said, "From Scotland." "Mr Johnson," said I, "indeed I come from Scotland, but I cannot help it." "Sir," replied he, "that, I find, is what a very great many of your countrymen cannot help." Mr Johnson is a man of a most dreadful appearance. He is a very big man, is troubled with sore eyes, the palsy, and the king's evil. He is very slovenly in his dress and speaks with a most uncouth voice. Yet his great knowledge and strength of expression command vast respect and render him very excellent company . . . . I shall mark what I remember of his conversation.

Although Boswell had previously jotted down friends' conversation, and stray dialogue from coffee-houses, the entry of Johnson into his life marks a new devotion to conversation unsurpassed in quantity and quality. Johnson, thirty years older, a public figure and apparently settled in his ways, was an effective reference point for the ever-doubting young Scot, A notable feature of Boswell's life is this desire to meet great men: partly out of sheer curiosity; but partly to measure himself against them, and try out various roles as the best expression of his own personality.

Immediately after London, he had a period studying law in Holland (which shared with Scotland a legal tradition rooted, unlike the English, in Roman law), and making the Grand Tour though France, Germany, Switzerland and Italy, in preparation for his return to the bar. He sought out in December 1764 two of the greatest men of the time: Rousseau and Voltaire. (A third - Frederick the Great of Prussia - was probably the only big fish not to take his hook.) Boswell set aside notes from third parties which could have gained him admittance to Rousseau; he preferred instead to catch the philosopher-recluse entirely on his own merits, sending a letter calculated to arouse interest

I present myself, Sir, as a man of singular merit, as a man with a feeling heart, a lively but melancholy spirit . . . . Your writings, Sir, have melted my heart, have elevated my soul, have fired my imagination . . . . Though I am only a young man, I have experienced a variety of existence that will amaze you . . . . Open your door, then, Sir, to a man who dares to tell you that he deserves to enter it. Place your confidence in a stranger who is different. You will not regret it.

The challenge was irresistible and Boswell was able to manage six interviews in five days, by haggling, cajoling, persuading. With Voltaire, whose presence was easier of access. he spent less time, but recorded some delightful details of their meeting:

At last we came upon religion. Then did he rage. The company went to supper. M. de Voltaire and I remained in the drawing-room with a great Bible before us; and if ever two mortal men disputed with vehemence, we did . . . . For a certain portion of time there was a fair opposition between Voltaire and Boswell. The daring bursts of his ridicule confounded my understanding . . . . He went too far. His aged frame trembled beneath him. He cried, "Oh, I am very sick; my head turns round," and he let himself gently fall upon an easy chair.

Encouraged by Rousseau, Boswell visited Corsica (1765), little known in detail but the focus of an independence struggle which he supported by political lobbying, arms- and fund-raising, and publications: His *Account of Corsica* (1768) – a combination of diary and description – at a stroke gave him a European reputation: "I had got upon a rock in Corsica and jumped into the middle of life.";

Boswell was now admitted advocate at the Scots bar, and endeavoured to build up his practice; his private affairs reveal several emotional tangles; and he joined in the famous controversy over the succession to the title of the Duke of Douglas, supporting one claimant with a Spanish tale *Dorando* (1767), a biased account of the background. After a spectacular fling at Garrick's famous Shakespeare jubilee celebrations at Stratford, where he appeared dressed as an armed Corsican chief and distributed copies of his own verses, he settled down as a professional man. In December 1769 he married his cousin, Margaret Montgomerie; in the subsequent years, we follow Boswell in his journal through the hard grind of legal practice with some sensational but many routine cases, punctuated by family discord largely due to his drunkenness and debauchery. He continually felt irked by the restricted provincial atmosphere of Edinburgh; he felt, too, that he was failing to make the career he deserved. So much the greater his relief when, at the end of the court session, he could head for the freer air of London, the beau monde, and the company of Johnson and The Club, including Burke, Garrick, Reynolds and Goldsmith; during these years he was filling his notebooks with the material of his great biography.

In 1773, he pulled off a personal coup by persuading the elderly and allegedly anti-Scottish Johnson to make a difficult journey up the east coast of Scotland and through the Gaelic-speaking island communities of the west, which had been in armed rebellion in support of the Stewarts only a generation before. Observing Johnson in almost laboratory conditions, he kept a detailed journal of sayings and doings that, aided by the critic Edmond Malone, he substantially reworked after Johnson's death (1784). Boswell's biographical method, first trialled in the *Journal of a Tour to the Hebrides* (1785), depended on copious detail, precise observation, verbatim recording of conversation, dramatically presented, and a greater degree of frankness than many contemporaries could easily accept. His work was a commercial but controversial success: widely serialized and debated in the press, but challenged by conservatives as to its social tact: Boswell came close to fighting a duel with Lord Macdonald in the dispute over criticisms of his highland hospitality, and entered a long feud with Johnson's former hostess Mrs Thrale-Piozzi. However the enduring success of the *Tour* justified his innovations and encouraged him in the six-year process of researching and writing the *Life of Johnson* (1791), again aided by Malone.

The *Life* has never lost its place as the greatest of English biographies: modern scholarship has supplemented our knowledge of Johnson's early career, but Boswell's uniquely detailed method of recording him, based on his own journals, together with the subject's idiosyncratic suitability for treatment, set the standard for vivid minuteness, dramatic presentation, inclusiveness, and frankness. Many well-disposed people felt that his recording of detail detracted from the idea of Johnson the philosopher, and that Boswell had betrayed his hero, himself, and acquaintances. But his consciousness of his art is shown in comments: "I draw him in the style of a Flemish painter. I am not satisfied with hitting the large features. I must be exact as to every hair, or even every spot on his countenance.";He talks of writing "Dr Johnson's life in Scenes"; "my readers will as near as may be accompany Johnson in his progress, and, as it were, see each scene as it happened." These remarks are sufficient to refute Lord Macaulay's thesis of unconscious greatness arising from Boswell's stupidity as Johnson's slave, idolater and parasite.

After Johnson's death, Boswell attempted to make a new career at the English bar from 1786, and then as the political protege of Lord Lonsdale, an influential peer; he became Recorder of Carlisle, but could not enter Parliament; the story of his last years is one of gradual disintegration: he died in London on 19 May 1795. Although a surprisingly prolific pamphleteer and essayist (";The Hypochondriack" ran for 70 numbers 1778-83 in *The London Magazine*), he was to his contemporaries a failed lawyer, to himself a failed politician. In the end, he is remembered for the various uses to which he put the originally private materials of his journals: the archives of diaries and letters that were preserved in his family only began to be made public in the twentieth century, and have greatly altered modern knowledge both of his private life and biographical methods.

HESTER LYNCH PIOZZI (MRS. THRALE) (1741-1821)

Mrs. Piozzi was born in Wales, very well educated and considered to be "half a prodigy". As a young girl she had sat at Garrick's knee and taught to recite passages from Paradise Lost by Quin, the actor.

In 1763 she married Henry Thrale, a wealthy Southwark brewer. It was a marriage of convenience, Hester not having been alone with Henry Thrale for more than five minutes before the ceremony. They lived in amity for seventeen years, had twelve children, four surviving to adulthood.

In 1764 a mutual friend, Arthur Murray, the playwright, brought Johnson to Streatham Park estate. This began a twenty-year intimacy. Johnson had his own rooms in the house and was treated as a permanent member of the family. He spent several days each week with them and accompanied them on trips to Wales and France. Many celebrities visited Streatham to meet Dr. Johnson and enjoy the Thrale's prodigious hospitality. Included among the recurring guests were Joshua Reynolds, Edmund Burke, David Garrick, Oliver Goldsmith, Sir Robert Chambers, Charles and Fanny Burney, James Boswell, etc. Thrale became a Member of Parliament representing his borough. He made poor business decisions resulting in his brewery being put into potential bankruptcy. Mrs. Thrale and Dr. Johnson became very involved in obtaining financial assistance and keeping the creditors at bay, ultimately saving the business. Thrale never recovered from this experience and finally killed himself with his uncontrollable eating behavior. Upon his death in 1781 the brewery was sold. Mrs. Thrale stated, "Johnson never left him, for while his health remained he still hoped." According to Johnson, "I felt almost the flutter of his pulse, and looked for the last time upon a face that for fifteen years had never been turned upon me but with respect and benignity."

Mrs. Thrale fell in love (for the first and last time) with Gabriel Piozzi, an Italian music master who had been employed by Henry Thrale to give lessons to their eldest daughter who had been nick-named Queeney by Dr. Johnson. Friends and family strongly disapproved. Newspapers and gossip mongers castigated her. Peter Pindar wrote eclogues about her. Boswell wrote a most derogatory poem. Johnson was bitterly opposed to the anticipated wedding resulting in a complete and permanent break between them. It was felt by mutual friends that Mrs. Thrale should have been willing to continue to care for Johnson who was now an old and ailing man. Marriage to a Catholic foreigner was considered beneath her. Her family finally relented when she became deathly ill and physicians feared for her life because of the constant vehement opposition. The relationship between mother and daughters never became closer than required by the rules of civility.

In 1784 Mrs. Thrale became Mrs. Piozzi. The marriage was a very happy one, "he being as much of an Englishman as a foreigner could expect to be".

After Piozzi's death in 1809, she returned to Bath, where having been once again accepted by much of society was described by Fanny Burney as "a very pretty woman still; she is extremely lively and chatty; has no supercilious or pedantic airs, and is really gay and agreeable". She died at age 80 and was buried next to her second husband.

Today she is mostly remembered for her small books, "Anecdotes of the Late Samuel Johnson, LL.D., During the Last Twenty Years of His Life" and "Letters To and From the Late Samuel Johnson, LL.D., to Which Are Added Some Poems Never Before Printed". These are considered to be second only to Boswell's Life of Johnson in providing an accurate portrait of the great moralist. Her diaries first published in 1942 under the title "Thraliana" give a fine insight into life as it was during the last part of the eighteenth century. Her letters have just been published in a six-volume edition.

Thomas Chatterton (1752-1770)
George Crabbe (1754-1832)
Robert Burns (1759-1796)

THOMAS CHATTERTON (1752-1770)

The brief career of Chatterton brings together two aspects of romanticism, the return to the Middle Ages and the escape of the individual from an uncongenial bourgeois world. The former makes his work of intense interest for the antiquarian movement of the time; the latter has made him for later times a symbol of martyred genius. Between the two it is hard to approach his work directly and estimate its value.

Chatterton's life centered in the neighborhood of the noble church of St. Mary Redcliffe in the great port of Bristol. His immediate ancestors had worked in or about the church. Thomas Chatterton, Senior, who kept a small school, died before his son was born, and the boy was educated at Colston's Hospital, a charity school, where he found the practical curriculum of writing and accounts very dull. His apprenticeship to the scrivener John Lambert was also dull, but gave him free time for his own strange studies. His imagination dwelt on local antiquities, the medieval architectural remains of Bristol, and he spent much time over some old parchments which his father had taken from a chest in the muniment room of St. Mary's. The documents he handled were legal, not literary, but they stimulated his imagination. By steps unknown to his biographers, he evolved a romance of fifteenth-century Bristol, centering about William Canynges, a merchant who became Lord Mayor and had been a benefactor of City and Church. About him Chatterton conjured up a group of learned priests, particularly Thomas Rowley of St. John's, whom Chatterton made a poet and antiquarian like himself. For the actual poems represented as those of Rowley and his circle he devised a vocabulary drawn largely from the dictionaries of Bailey and Kersey and from Speght's edition of Chaucer, and couched in elaborately archaic spelling. It was thus that he began to fabricate the "originals" of the Rowley poems.

In 1768, when the new bridge was opened in Bristol and there was a flurry of interest in local antiquities, Chatterton published his first spurious documents and was soon giving or selling his manuscripts to two Bristol antiquarians who repaid him with little sympathy or help. We cannot apply modern standards of literary honesty and historical accuracy to Chatterton; literary imposture was frequent in his time, from the fabrications of Macpherson and the later Shakespeare forgeries of Ireland down to the common practice of slipping modern pieces into collections of ancient literature. Scott himself may have planted a ballad or two of his own. Chatterton was indulging his poetic bent and his antiquarian enthusiasm, and resorting to a device to attract attention. In 1769, after an unsuccessful attempt to offer his wares to the bookseller James Dodsley, Chatterton sent Walpole a specimen, "The Ryse of Peyncteynge yn Englande." Walpole wrote a cordial answer, but on getting more Rowley material was warned off by Gray and Mason, and after some delay sent the manuscripts back with some good advice. He was justified in doing this, though when he was later blamed for Chatterton's disappointment and death he was goaded into an indiscreet defense. In 1769 and 1770 Chatterton turned suddenly to miscellaneous writings on current models,

African Eclogues after Collins, imitations of Ossian, satires in Churchill's style, and political letters on behalf of Wilkes. Many of his contributions appeared in the *Town and Country Magazine*, and when he left Bristol for London in April 1770 it was with the hope of earning his living as a hack writer. Despite enthusiasm and hard work he remained miserably poor, and in August he committed suicide in his London lodgings.

The controversy about the authenticity of the Rowley poems was soon settled in Tyrwhitt's edition (1777-78) and in Thomas Warton *History of English Poetry* (1778), though some people continued to argue that Rowley was too good to be written by Chatterton, just as Ossian had been considered too good to be written by Macpherson. The best of the Rowley poems stand on their own merit-the dramatic interlude of *Aella*, with its remarkable lyrics, the poem on freedom in *Goddwyn*, the *Bristowe Tragedy or the Dethe of Syr Charles Bawdin* (a ballad which is the only conspicuous example of the influence of Percy *Reliques* on Chatterton), and the last of the Rowley poems, *An Excelente Balade of Charitie*. Chatterton's skill in free and irregular meters and his quaintly simple diction, Elizabethan and Spenserian rather than medieval, influenced later poets, particularly Coleridge. His personal history and fate counted for much also. Every one knows the references to Chatterton in Wordsworth *Resolution and Independence* and Shelley *Adonais;* Coleridge *Monody*, an early sonnet by Keats, the dedication of Endymion to the memory of Chatterton, Alfred de Vigny drama Chatterton, and Rossetti's intense admiration should also be remembered.

GEORGE CRABBE (1754-1832)

Though Crabbe's life and work extend beyond our chronological limits, they are really of the eighteenth century. He has earned a secondary but important place in literary history by his effective use of the plain style of eighteenth century verse for the purposes of literal and disillusioned realism. Early experiences prepared him fot this approach to poetry. He was born at Aldeborough, a little seaport in Suffolk, where he saw and shared the struggles and troubles of the poor. He became a surgeon's apprentice, began practice in Aldeborough, and resolutely continued to educate himself by studying the classics, theology, and botany, and by trying to write poetry. A few months after he came to London in 1780 he was reduced to desperate straits, but he found a good patron in Edmund Burke, who helped him to publish a mediocre poem, *The Library* (I781), encouraged him to take orders and look for preferment in the Church, and soon got him a place as chaplain to the Duke of Rutland at Belvoir Castle. *The Village* (I783) justified Burke's faith in Crabbe and showed his full power. Here he makes a direct attack on the pastoral tradition, and sets over against the happy swains of the Golden Age the wretched inhabitants of Aldeborough. The artificialities of the pastoral convention had long been a commonplace of criticism, and in particular a favorite theme with Dr. Johnson, who read and admired the poem in manuscript and contributed a few lines (Book I, ll. 15-20). Crabbe attacks the whole sentimental concept of "the simple life that Nature yields," and his poem has often been taken as an answer to Goldsmith's *Deserted Village*. His work also connects with a tendency to minute and precise description in late eighteenth-century poetry. He approaches the naturalistic novelists of a later time in his grim transcription of physical detail and his picture of man bogged down in his own nature and his environment. He keeps his pity for the poor clear of sentimental idealization, and directness and surly honesty give him peculiar power.

After the publication of *The Newspaper* (I785) Crabbe printed nothing for twenty-two years, though he continued to write. In *The Parish Register* (I807) and *The Borough* (I810) he elaborates the theme of *The Village*, studying various phases of life and character within the same or a like community. *Peter Grimes*, one of the most powerful tales in *The Borough*, is the subject of a tragic opera by Benjamin Britten, successfully produced at Sadler's Wells in 1945. In *Tales in Verse* (I812) and *Tales of the Hall* (I819) Crabbe studies human character, particularly its limitations and disappointments, in simply plotted narratives with more widely varied settings. He was greatly admired by many readers and critics of the romantic generation, and has been praised by a minority of discriminating readers in later times. Thus the fastidious American poet Edwin Arlington Robinson pays tribute to Crabbe's "hard human pulse," his "plain excellence and stubborn skill."

ROBERT BURNS (1759-1796)

Few poets anywhere in the world can have acquired such unchallengeable status as national icons as Robert Burns: even readers who know nothing else about Scottish literature, or about Scotland at all, know that Burns is Scotland's national poet. Given the fact, as it incontrovertibly is, that Scotland in its long history has produced far more than a small country's fair share of gifted poets, the extent to which Burns has, in popular thought, dwarfed or eclipsed virtually all others is remarkable, not to say deplorable – it is no undercutting of his undoubted place as one of the great figures of European poetry to point out that several Scottish poets have approached his stature and a few have arguably equalled it (the names of Henryson, Dunbar and MacDiarmid come to mind) – and yet, the irresistible and inexhaustible fascination of both his poetry and his extraordinary personality exert a spell which none of his rivals can match.

Burns was the eldest of seven children born to William Burnes, a gardener (later a tenant farmer) from Kincardine, and Agnes Broun of Carrick, in Ayrshire. The cottage in which he was born and spent his early life (now a museum) was built by his father: on the night of the poet's birth the thatch blew off in a storm, forcing the family to seek shelter with a neighbour; an incident hinted at in the song "Rantin', Rovin' Robin":

Our monarch's hindmost year but ane
Was five and-twenty days begun,
'Twas then a blast o' Jan'war' win'
Blew hansel in on Robin.

Robert's childhood and youth were marked by poverty and hard labour, as a succession of crofts leased by his father chronically failed to provide the family with a living; and the poor health (stemming from a weakened heart) which marred his later life probably had its roots in the hardships of this period. Equally a part of his formative years, however, was a sound education, at the local schools and from a tutor named John Murdoch, hired by his father and other farmers to give their sons private lessons. This instilled in him an appetite for knowledge of all kinds, and an enthusiasm for literature: a frequent observation is that his poetry shows a unique mutual stimulation of the great English tradition of Shakespeare, Milton and the Augustans with the rich Scottish ballad and folk song heritage of which his mother was a living repository. The great tradition of Scots poetry of the mediaeval and Renaissance periods was very sparsely known in Burns's Scotland; but an important exception was the *Wallace* of Blind Harry, translated (virtually re-written) in 1722 by William Hamilton of Gilbertfield, which, as Burns was later to write, "poured a Scottish prejudice into my veins, which will boil along them till the floodgates of life shut in eternal rest." Much more important as influences on his poetic development were Allan Ramsay, already acknowledged as the seminal figure in the revival of vernacular poetry in Scotland, and to a still greater extent Robert Fergusson, the discovery of whose work persuaded Burns decisively to adopt Scots as his main literary medium. The status of those two great predecessors is reflected in frequent references not only by Burns but by several contemporaries: his friend David Sillar, following the publication of Burns's first volume of poems, used them as benchmarks in a tribute:

Brave Ramsay nou and Fergusson,
Wha hae sae lang while fill'd the throne
O' poetry, may nou lie doun
Quaet in their urns,
Since fame, in justice, gies the croun
Tae Coila's Burns.

On William Burnes's death in 1784, Robert and his brother Gilbert became joint tenants of the farm of Mossgiel: both brothers were later to recollect that Robert, though energetic and well-intentioned, had not the practical sense of the more down-to-earth Gilbert; though even he was later forced to rely on financial help from his by then famous brother to keep solvent as Mossgiel's sole tenant. Burns's work on the farm alternated with a lively social life: the Mauchline Debating Society, and Tarbolton Bachelors' Club, another debating society of which he and Gilbert were founder members, provided congenial diversion; and he participated enthusiastically in the popular culture of dances, fiddle music (he was a player of some skill) and convivial drinking. (That he was a habitual drunkard is a long-discredited myth: in fact the evidence suggests that he had a poor head for alcohol and was far from matching the bibulosity of many of his contemporaries.) His lifelong weakness for "the lassies" emerged in his adolescence: his first attempt at poetry —

O once I lov'd a bonnie lass,
An' ay I love her still,
An' whilst that virtue warms my breast,
I'll love my handsome Nell.

— was written at the age of fifteen, for a girl called Nelly Kilpatrick who had been his partner at a harvest celebration. (Of this aspect of Burns's life and character, it may be said that while his long list of amorous escapades and resulting illegitimate children — for all of whom he assumed full responsibility — is a biographical fact, so too is the cheerful effrontery with which he flaunted and exaggerated his sexual notoriety as a mark of defiance to the oppressive Calvinism of his community. His *A Poet's Welcome to his Love-begotten Daughter* (or *to a Bastart Wean* in some editions) places the verse:

What tho' they ca' me fornicator,
An' tease my name in kintry clatter:
The mair they talk, I'm kent the better:
E'en let them clash!

An auld wife's tongue's a feckless matter
To gie ane fash –

Among expressions of pride and tender affection for the child and her mother.

His literary gifts emerged early in his life; and it is worth noting that the writing and exchanging of verses was a remarkably important aspect of social life in Ayrshire at that time. Burns emerged from a highly literate culture in which books, pamphlets and broadsheets were bought, lent, copied and eagerly discussed. A loosely-constituted group of poets of varying talent, known collectively as the "Bardie Clan", provided mutual entertainment and stimulation by the practice of exchanging verse epistles: some of Burns's most characteristic work is found in his poems to John Lapraik, William Simson and David Sillar; and in a minor but amusing episode, a tailor named Thomas Walker wrote a solemn reproof to him for his immoral ways:

Ah Rab! Lay by thy foolish tricks,
An' steir nae mair the female sex!
Or some day ye'll come thro' the pricks,
An' that ye'll see!
Ye'll find hard livin' wi' Auld Nicks;
I'm wae for thee!

– to be rewarded with a mettlesome response:

What ails ye now, ye lousie bitch,
To thresh my back at sic a pitch?
Losh man! hae mercy wi' your natch,
Your bodkin's bauld,
I didna suffer ha'f sae much
Frae Daddie Auld.

(The Rev. William Auld, parish minister of Mauchline, had administered a public rebuke to Burns for fornication with Jean Armour, whom he was eventually to marry.)

Burns soon acquired local renown for the brilliance and the boldly satiric tone of his poems as they circulated among his Ayrshire acquaintances; but the publication of his first volume, the Kilmarnock Edition of 1786, had its immediate cause in a sequence of troubling events. Jean Armour, to whom he was betrothed (or possibly married by declaration, legal under Scots law) was forced by her father to repudiate the contract and sent to relations in Paisley. Burns, angry and injured, found solace with a girl called Mary Campbell (the "Highland Mary" of his poetry), and planning to emigrate with her to Jamaica, published his poems to raise the necessary money. This plan was frustrated by Mary's sudden death from typhus, the shock and grief of which affected Burns throughout his life. His *Poems, Chiefly in the Scottish Dialect*, however, were an immediate sensation. Travelling to Edinburgh to receive the plaudits of the literary public, Burns attracted enormous interest by his witty and accomplished conversation, and by the radicalism of his political and social views and the boldness and fervour with which he expressed them. The Edinburgh *literati*, expecting to find a "heaven-taught ploughman" were both fascinated and disconcerted by his erudition and his iconoclasm. A notable event of his time in Edinburgh was his romantic affair with Agnes (Nancy) Maclehose: the name "Clarinda", and that of "Sylvander" which Burns assumed for himself, were her affectations, and indicative of the sentimental nature of the relationship; but the poem with which Burns commemorated its ending is one of the most beautiful and most moving songs of parting in all literature:

Ae fond kiss, and then we sever!
Ae fareweel, and then forever!
Deep in heart-wrung tears I'll pledge thee,
Warring sighs and groans I'll wage thee.

Who shall say that Fortune grieves him,
While the star of hope she leaves him?
Me, nae cheerfu' twinkle lights me,
Dark despair around benights me.

I'll ne'er blame my partial fancy:
Naething could resist my Nancy:
But to see her was to love her;
Love but her, and love for ever.

Had we never lov'd sae kindly,
Had we never lov'd sae blindly,
Never met – or never parted,
We had ne'er been broken-hearted! ...

After spending the summer of 1787 travelling in the Borders and the Highlands, Burns returned to Edinburgh, where he became interested in a project of an engraver named James Johnson to compile a "Scots Musical Museum" or comprehensive anthology of Scottish folk song. Work on this occupied Burns's creative energies for the remainder of his life: only *Tam o' Shanter*, of his great poems, was written in his succeeding years, but the work which produced dozens of songs – some wholly original, others re-written or expanded versions of traditional lyrics (*Auld Lang Syne* is an example of the latter class), but all showing an exquisite skill in fitting words to the existing tunes – continued till a few days before his death.

Burns's fashionable popularity in Edinburgh was short-lived, a fact which he had been wise enough to anticipate; and he returned to the West in 1788, married his faithful and ever-patient Jean Armour (who had already borne him two sets of twins), and leased a farm at Ellisland, near Dumfries. The following year he took the post of excise officer, which brought him and his family a measure of financial security; and for a few years enjoyed an active and productive life. His collecting, adapting and writing of songs proceeded apace, helped now by his wife's fine singing voice and rich store of local ballads; and visitors to Ellisland are still shown the walk on which he composed *Tam o' Shanter*. In 1791 he left the farm and took a house in Dumfries (this too is now a museum). However, the long and strenuous journeys, often in inclement weather, which his duties as excise officer entailed, undermined his already failing health. A regimen of sea bathing and mineral water, prescribed in a woefully misguided attempt to restore his well-being, had the opposite effect; and his rapid physical decline, combined with anxiety for the future of his family, reduced him to extreme despondency. He died, after weeks of desperate attempts to maintain his social and creative life, on 21 July 1796. His ninth child by Jean Armour was born on the day of his funeral.

Which of the many aspects of Burns's poetic achievement entitles him to the status of Scotland's national bard? First, his skill in exploiting the Scots tongue is unsurpassed. The common speech of his time, with its rich vocabulary and fund of proverbs and aphorisms, is in his hands a medium of superb expressive power; and its resources are highlighted by his mastery of pointed rhymes and metrical effects. In particular, his dexterous use of the six-line stanza now generally known by his name (though inappropriately, since it had been established as a staple of Scots poetry long before) imparts an unforgettable sting-in-the-tail effect to countless verses. An ability to modulate between different registers of Scots, and between Scots and English, is a distinctive part of his technique: his satirical masterpiece *Holy Willie's Prayer* opens in the elevated style of the Presbyterian pulpit:

O Thou that in the Heavens does dwell,
Wha, as it pleases best Thysel,
Sends ane to Heaven an' ten to Hell
A' for Thy glory,
An' no for onie guid or ill
They've done afore thee!

— but soon evokes a colloquial tone suggestive of a behind-the-hand whisper:

O Lord! Yestreen, Thou kens, wi' Meg —
Thy pardon I sincerely beg —
O, may 't ne'er be a living plague
To my dishonour!
An' I'll ne'er lift a lawless leg
Again upon her.

Besides, I further maun avou —
Wi' Leezie's lass, three times, I trow —
But, Lord, that Friday I was fou,
When I cam near her,
Or else, Thou kens, Thy servant true
Wad never steer her.

That his English poetry is uniformly inferior to his Scots is of course an over-simplification; but there can be no question that Scots was more natural to him and gave greater scope to the full range of his skill.

That he wrote as a patriotic Scottish poet, too, is an integral part of his achievement. A frequently-quoted passage from *To the Guidwife of Wauchope House* states this:

E'en then, a wish (I mind its pow'r).
A wish that to my latest hour
Shall strongly heave my breast,
That I for poor auld Scotland's sake
Some usefu' plan or book could make,
Or sing a sang at least.

His poems depict and celebrate, with matchless energy and vividness, the life of the Scottish peasant class. Recurrently, and notably in the first poem in the Kilmarnock Edition, *The Twa Dogs,* he upholds the pride, self-sufficiency and convivial pleasures of the peasants, in contrast with the extravagance and affectations of their social superiors. *The Cottar's Saturday Night* emphasises the kindliness and mutual affection of the family depicted, and their religious faith (the ritual of family worship is a central episode in the poem); *Hallowe'en* both commemorates and affectionately mocks the ancient rituals and superstitions characteristic of rural life; the cantata *The Jolly Beggars* is a riotous celebration of the robust independence found among even the lowest orders of society.

Part of his individual genius, however, inheres in his ability to not only evoke but transcend his own local setting. An interesting recent development in Burns criticism has been a new emphasis on his political poetry, placing him in the context of near-contemporary English political commentators such as Blake and Wordsworth. On another level, his ability to depict and arouse a whole gamut of emotions and passions strikes a responsive chord with readers of any time and place. As poet of all aspects of love, seen through both male and female eyes, he is unsurpassed: the farcical comedy of *Duncan*

Gray, the celebration of a long and happy marriage in *John Anderson my Jo*, the fond recollection of an amorous tryst in *Corn Rigs are Bonnie*, the irresistible evocation of female flirtatiousness in songs like *The Braw Wooer* and *O Whistle and I'll Come tae ye, my Lad*: such poems illustrate the profound truth of his lines "My muse, tho' hamely in attire, May touch the heart". Conversely, his most brilliant and most scathing satires, including *Holy Willie's Prayer, Holy Fair* and *Address to the Unco Guid*, are in the first instance attacks on the narrowness and hypocrisy of the Church in his time and place; but in setting the morally and emotionally stunting ethos which it represented against the joyful affirmation of life and love to which his own inclinations prompted him he becomes a forceful proponent of universal human values.

Burns's humour whether light-hearted or ruthlessly satirical, his emotional intensity and intellectual keenness, his linguistic virtuosity, are together sufficient to earn him a place among the world's great poets. Yet a still more fundamental quality, and perhaps in the last analysis the ultimate reason for his universal appeal, is an indomitable conviction that the accidental and man-made evils which mar all life can, and eventually will, be overcome.

He'll hae misfortunes great an' sma',
But ay a heart aboon them a'.
He'll be a credit till us a":
We'll a' be proud o' Robin!

His prediction was exactly true of himself: his achievement is to make us believe that it can be true of mankind.

Minor Authors

CHRISTOPHER ANSTEY (I724-1805)

Anstey was a Cambridge wit, educated at Eton and King's College, and long resident at Trumpington, just outside Cambridge. After frequent visits to Bath, he took up his residence there and published *The New Bath Guide* in 1766. This is a series of verse epistles written by Simpkin Blunderhead and other members of his family, humorously describing life at Bath from various points of view. The device was taken over by Smollett in *Humphry Clinker*. The brisk and playful verse of the Guide and its light satire were immensely popular, and it ran through more than a score of editions up to 1800. Anstey wrote other light verse, and was one of the coterie that contributed to Lady Miller famous *Batheaston vase*, but he is remembered only for the *Guide*.

JOHN ARMSTRONG (I709-1779)

Armstrong, a Border Scot, practised medicine in London and gained some reputation by his *Art of Preserving Health* (I744), an example of somewhat pompous Miltonic blank verse applied to a didactic theme in a manner made standard by Philips *Cyder* and Thomson *Seasons*. As a boy Armstrong is said to have written independently of Thomson a blank-verse fragment on winter which aroused the admiration of

Thomson, Mallet, and their circle. This piece was first published in Armstrong *Miscellanies* (I770). His friendship with Thomson is also commemorated by a few stanzas contributed to *The Castle of Indolence.* He was a literary and personal friend of Smollett and for a time of Wilkes.

WILLIAM BECKFORD (I760-1844)

Beckford's eccentric literary career is unique, but may be treated under the general heading of prose romance. His immediate forebears were West Indian planters of great wealth, and his father was Lord Mayor of London. His private education and continental travels developed his brilliant vein of dilettantism, at once imaginative, sensuous, and playful. The oriental romance *Vathek* is the best-known expression of his amazing talent. It was composed in French in 1782. Beckford's tutor Samuel Henley published an unauthorized translation in 1786; variant French texts appeared at Lausanne (I786, dated 1787) and Paris (I787). The associated *Episodes of Vathek* remained unpublished until our own time. Beckford's vast fortune and his unrestricted whims led him into extravagant building projects centering about his modern Gothic Fonthill Abbey in Wiltshire.

APHRA BEHN (I640-1689)

The first professional woman writer in English drama and fiction is a rather mysterious figure. Doubts about the facts of her life are involved with the question as to the autobiographical basis of her famous story, Oroonoko, or the Royal Slave (I688). Her own account was that her father had been appointed lieutenant governor of the South American colony Surinam (British Guiana), and that she traveled thither and saw the slave rebellion which she describes. The best opinion now seems to be that she went to Surinam as an adventuress, and thus got some details which were used in her extravagant romance. Later she seems to have been a government agent in Holland. She began to write for the stage in the 1670's, and then turned to the writing of short pieces of fiction, called "novels," which tried to blend the loftiness of romance and the excitement of sensational drama with intense and facile sentiment and luscious love themes. Oroonoko represents also an attempt to heighten realism by the use of local color and the report of a supposed eye-witness. The story centers about an African prince who after an ardent love affair with Imoinda is sold into slavery and dies a bloody death in a rebellion in Surinam. The theme is not the horror of slavery, but the exaltation of this heroic and ferocious figure. His story is not primitivistic, though there is a primitivistic passage on the innocent natives of South America. Oroonoko was given a sentimental turn in Southerne's drama (I696), which remained popular through the eighteenth century.

SIR RICHARD BLACKMORE

Sir Richard Blackmore, physician and poetaster, incurred the contempt of Dryden and the other wits for his bad epics, *Prince Arthur* (I695) and *King Arthur* (I697), and for his campaign, somewhat parallel to Collier's, against literary immorality (*Satire against Wit*, 1700). But his *Job* (I700) and *Creation* (I712) earned him a place among serious religious poets in the estimate of Watts, Addison, Johnson, and even his old enemy John Dennis.

ROBERT BLAIR (1699-1746)

Robert Blair, a Scottish clergyman, is remembered for one poem, *The Grave* (I743), written independently of Young but published shortly after the first book of the *Night Thoughts*. The two poems were often published and read together, but there are considerable differences between them. Both, of course, indulge in religious and moral reflections inspired by the thought of death, and so may be said to belong to a "graveyard school," but Blair is much more interested than Young in painting "the gloomy horrors of the tomb." In a fairly terse and vigorous blank verse derived from Shakespeare and later tragedy he restates the commonplaces about death which come down from the tradition of Puritan sermon and elegy and religious treatise, and raises this popular religious vein to a somewhat higher literary level. *The Grave* was re printed more than fifty times in England and America before the end of the century.

HENRY BROOKE (I703-1783)

A cultured and benevolent Irish country gentleman who touched the literary life of his time at several important points. His *Universal Beauty* (I735-36), a long and turgid poem in heroic couplets, embodies much scientific detail for physico-theological purposes. The play *Gustavus Vasa* (I739), a manifesto of the opposition to Walpole and forbidden under the Licensing Act, deals with the struggle for liberty in ancient Sweden, and connects with the widespread doctrine that among the northern or "Gothic" peoples is to be found the origin of the free constitutions of Europe. *The Fool of Quality* is a long and confused novel, describing the education of the young hero in the principles of sentimental benevolism and mystical religious enthusiasm. This work was adapted by John Wesley and highly praised in the next century by Charles Kingsley.

TOM BROWN (I663-1704)

A clever, harsh, and dissipated Grub Street hack, who did much work in controversial pamphlets, translations, and miscellaneous literary adaptations. His *Amusements Serious and Comical* (I700) is one of the best of the realistic "trips" through London, and invites comparison with Ned Ward *London Spy* (I698-1700), a similar coarse and graphic piece. Another interesting work to which Brown was a principal contributor is *Letters from the Dead to the Living* (I702-03), in the tradition of the *Dialogues of the Dead* of Lucian and Fontenelle.

MICHAEL BRUCE (I746-1767)

A Scottish theological student born of humble parents in Kinross-shire, on the shore of Loch Leven. He died young. John Logan edited a posthumous volume of his poems in 1770, and has been accused of claiming some of Bruce work as his own, notably the fine *Ode to the Cuckoo.*

GILBERT BURNET (1643-1715)

A Whig bishop who was one of William's principal lieutenants. He belongs to political and religious history rather than to literature, but his partisan memoirs which appeared as *History of His Own Time* (1724-34) contain much spirited narrative and characterization.

THOMAS BURNET (1635-1715)

This learned clergyman is remembered for his *Telluris Theoria Sacra* (1681-89), translated as *The Sacred Theory of the Earth* (1684-90), an imaginative piece of cosmology written in elegant prose. Though opposed by many scientists, this work was admired by poets from Thomson to Wordsworth and Coleridge.

RICHARD OWEN CAMBRIDGE (1717-1802)

A witty and versatile country gentleman who wrote a heavy mock-epic the *Scribleriad* (1751), some excellent essays in the *World*, and some agreeable light verse, but is more noteworthy for his sociability and wide acquaintance, especially in the groups associated with Johnson and Walpole.

HENRY CAREY (1687-1743)

A struggling song-writer and music-teacher who did a good deal of work for the theaters. His burlesque *Chrononhotonthologos* (1734) has already been mentioned, and he also wrote a burlesque opera, *The Dragon of Wantley*. His poem *Namby Pamby* probably fixed this nickname on Ambrose Philips. Best known of all is his song *Sally in our Alley* (composed before 1719, first known publication in *Poems on Several Occasions*, 3rd ed., 1729).

THOMAS DAY (1748-1789)

A somewhat eccentric enthusiast for liberal and philanthropic ideas. He wrote against slavery and in favor of the American cause, and took some part in the Whig campaign for electoral reform, but his chief interest was in the application of the educational theories of Rousseau *Emile*.

Taking some hints from Brooke *Fool of Quality* also, he worked out his educational program in the story of *Sandford and Merton* (I- 1783, II- 1787, III- 1789), which became one of the most popular children's books in the language. Day opposed luxury and fashion and inculcated virtuous benevolism and rigorous simplicity. He was a good friend of the Lichfield group (Erasmus Darwin, Anna Seward), of the Birmingham scientists and inventors (Boulton, Priestley), and of the Irish philanthropist Richard Lovell Edgeworth, whose daughter, the famous novelist Maria Edgeworth, was influenced by Day's educational program.

JOHN DYER (1699-1757)

John Dyer was born in Carmarthenshire, in southern Wales; as a young man he studied painting under Jonathan Richardson, traveled in Italy, and about 1725 was a member of Aaron Hill's literary coterie in London, along with James Thomson and Richard Savage. In 1726 appeared three versions, one in Pindarics and two in Miltonic octosyllabic couplets, of his charming prospect poem *Grongar Hill.* Like his younger fellow countryman, the landscape painter Richard Wilson, Dyer no doubt came under the influence of the Italian picturesque tradition in painting, and carried over the results of these studies to poetry. He thus takes a modest but significant place in the history of the poetic treatment of landscape. Later he became a gentleman-farmer and eventually a clergyman. His *Ruins of Rome* (I740) invites comparison with Thomson *Liberty*; his *Fleece* (I757), an account of sheep-raising and the great British woolen industry, is one of the better descriptive-didactic blank-verse poems of the time, handicapped though it is by its subject.

SARAH FIELDING (1710-1768)

A sister of Henry Fielding and a member of Richardson's circle. These personal relationships are more important than her own novels, of which *David Simple* (I744) was the best known.

SIR SAMUEL GARTH (1661-1719)

A successful physician, a prominent member of the Kit-Cat Club, and an early friend of Pope's. His mock-heroic *Dispensary* (I699) attacks the apothecaries and their allies who opposed the opening of a free dispensary for the poor. The poem is loaded with allusions to this forgotten controversy, and though once popular is now neglected, yet it is a competent piece of work, one of the more rewarding of the secondary poems of the age. Pope respected and imitated Garth's command of the balanced couplet and the pointed line. *The Dispensary* occupies a significant place in the history of the English mock-epic: it largely imitates Boileau *Lutrin* and in turn passes on some features of style and method to *The Rape of the Lock;* equally important is its elaboration of the "stupidity" theme of *Mac Flecknoe,* which made it contributory to the *Dunciad.*

JOSEPH GLANVILL (1636-1680)

Joseph Glanvill, educated at Oxford and long rector of the Abbey Church at Bath, was eminent for his keen and fresh philosophical thought and his excellent prose. He was influenced by the Cambridge Platonists, Cartesian rationalism, and above all by the Baconian program of the Royal Society. In his *Vanity of Dogmatizing* (I661), called *Scepsis Scientifica,* or *Confest Ignorance the Way to Science* in the revised edition of 1665, and finally included in his *Essays* (I676), he commended "skepticism," not in the radical form of a denial of the possibility of knowledge, but as a tool to help man to attain well grounded knowledge. Skepticism cuts away mere speculation and "confidence in opinions" and insists on the test of experience. This is the anti-dogmatic and anti-speculative program of the Royal Society. Self-explanatory is the title of another of his works, *Plus Ultra, or the Progress and Advancement of Knowledge since the Days of Aristotle. In an Account of Some of the Most Remarkable Late Improvements of Practical, Useful Learning* (I668). In his religious thought, however, Glanvill kept to the Cambridge Platonists' exaltation of reason, and he argued vehemently, both on religious and scientific grounds, for the traditional beliefs in witches and apparitions (*Sadducismus Triumphatus*, 1681).

RICHARD GRAVES (1715-1804)

For many years rector of Claverton, near Bath, a close friend of Shenstone and Dodsley, and author of *The Spiritual Quixote* (1773), a satire on the Methodist movement which is also one of the most genial comic novels of the period.

MATTHEW GREEN (1696-1737)

A clerk in the London Custom House who diverted himself and his friends by writing verses. His posthumously published *Spleen* (1737) treats the somewhat hackneyed question of how to avoid ill health and boredom and live contentedly, but, as a friend remarks in the preface, it has a "peculiar and unborrowed cast of thought and expression." Green's work in the octosyllabic couplet is as fresh as Prior's, and his wit was deservedly admired by Gray, Walpole, and others.

GEORGE SAVILE, MARQUIS OF HALIFAX (1633-1695)

An eminent statesman and one of the wisest Englishmen of his generation. His public career belongs to history: though a Whig, he opposed Shaftesbury in the crisis of 1680; though he held office under James II, he warned the Dissenters against the King's pretended zeal for religious toleration (*A Letter to a Dissenter*, 1687; *The Anatomy of an Equivalent*, 1688). He was a leader in the Revolution, and as has been said above, expounded his political doctrine of compromise in his famous *Character of a Trimmer* (written 1685, published 1688). Like his celebrated *Character of Charles II*, this piece shows his mastery of the portrait-character as a literary form. His *Lady's New Year's Gift* (1688), addressed to his daughter, applies the practical ethics of compromise to the problems of married life; it assumes the domination of the husband, but urges the advantages of cleverness and good temper. Halifax was master of an urbane, clear, and witty style, strongly influenced by the French masters (La Bruyère, Montaigne); he avoided the affectations of fashionable

Restoration wit, and on the other hand he had much of the good sense of the eighteenth century without its pervasive sentimentality.

JAMES HAMMOND (1710-1742)

A protégé of Chesterfield's and a member of the literary group gathered about Frederick , Prince of Wales. His *Elegies,* closely imitative of Tibullus, were published in 1713. They seem to modern readers merely vapid and smooth, but probably had some part in helping to make the iambic pentameter quatrain standard for eighteenth-century elegy.

ELIZA HAYWOOD (1693-1756)

Following in the steps of Mrs. Manley, Eliza Haywood wrote short tales of intrigue and passion and "secret histories." Pope attacked her in the *Dunciad.* After the success of Richardson *Pamela,* she turned from the older forms to the novel of manners, in which she did mediocre work (*Betsy Thoughtless,* 1751; *Jemmy and Jenny Jessamy,* 1753).

JAMES HERVEY (1714-1758)

Though his position was not identical with Wesley's, Hervey was an ardent evangelical. His *Meditations and Contemplations* (I746-47), one of the most popular religious works of the century, is written in an inflated rhetorical prose. It is often put in the graveyard school, but the contents include not only "Meditations among the Tombs" but pieces on a flower garden, night, winter, the heavens, and a "Descant on Creation." Hervey quotes and imitates the poets freely, and follows the physicotheological treatises which use the new findings of science to glorify God.

WILLIAM LAW (1686-1761)

Law's best works are unfortunately buried among neglected religious treatises, but he was eminent for his piety, vigorous intelligence, and fine command of prose. As a Non-juror—that is, a Jacobite who refused to take the oath of allegiance to George I—he cut himself off from a career in university and Church. Yet he entered largely into the life of his time; he wrote against Hoadly in the Bangorian controversy, against Mandeville, against the corruptions of the stage, and against the deists; but he was not a mere controversialist, and his *Serious Call to a Devout and Holy Life* (1728), despite a title which suggests dreary piety, has the crispness, clarity, good taste, and wit of eighteenth-century prose at its best. "When at Oxford," said Johnson to Boswell, speaking of his early indifference to religion, "I took up Law's 'Serious Call to a Holy Life,' expecting to find it a dull book (as such books generally are) and perhaps to laugh at it. But I found Law quite an overmatch for me." His religious zeal influenced Wesley and the Methodist movement. In his later years he became increasingly enthusiastic and mystical, under the influence of Jakob Böhme. He was long associated with the family of Edward Gibbon, who pays him high tribute in his *Memoirs*.

CHARLOTTE LENNOX (1720-1804)

The one book for which Mrs. Lennox is remembered is *The Female Quixote, or The Adventures of Arabella* (1752), a satire on a romance-reading heroine which interested and amused a generation increasingly conscious of the claims of prose fiction. The works which turn Arabella's head are, however, the French heroic romances of the seventeenth century, not modern novels. The story was praised by Richardson and Fielding. Though comparatively obscure as a writer, Mrs. Lennox was highly admired by Dr. Johnson. Since she was born in New York, and lived in America until she was fifteen years old, she has some claim to be considered the first American novelist.

GEORGE LYTTELTON, BARON LYTTELTON (1709-1773)

Lyttelton was one of the group of young men connected by birth and marriage, including Pitt and the Grenvilles, who were led by Richard Temple, Viscount Cobham, in opposition to Walpole. In the 1730's Lyttelton was the chief political aide of Frederick Prince of Wales. He wrote *Letters from a Persian in England* (1735) in imitation of Montesquieu *Lettres Persanes*, a fine monody on the death of his wife (1747), *Dialogues of the Dead* (1760), and much else in verse and prose, but his chief claims to distinction were his cordial relationships with Thomson, Fielding, and other writers, including his Warwickshire neighbor Shenstone. Though sometimes derided for his seriousness and self-importance, as by Smollett, Lyttelton seems on the whole to have shown generosity and tact in combining literary patronage and personal friendship. Thus he helped Thomson to revise *The Seasons*, and to him Tom Jones is dedicated.

HENRY MACKENZIE (1745-1831)

Mackenzie was a genial and intelligent Scot who for two generations played a leading part in the literary life of Edinburgh. He showed talent with his excellent ballad imitations *Duncan* and *Kenneth* (1764 and 1765), but turned from the medieval revival to sentimental fiction, earning a reputation as an arch-sentimentalist by his famous *Man of Feeling* (1771). In this work he follows Sterne in writing "episodic adventures" keyed to moods and sentiments, but for Sterne's unpredictable humor and ingenuity he substitutes the somewhat banal delicacy and ethical commonplace of Shenstone. His other two novels, *The Man of the World* (1773) and *Julia de Roubigné* (1777) have recourse to the more violent stimuli of seduction and jealousy. In his essay-periodicals, the *Mirror* (1779-80) and the *Lounger* (1785-87) he does some of the best late eighteenth-century work in this form, writing sentimental tales, sympathetic humorous sketches, and at least one important piece of literary criticism in his essay on Burns (*Lounger* No. 97). His responsiveness to literary currents also appears in the paper on German literature which he submitted to the Royal Society of Edinburgh and which stimulated the young Walter Scott.

DAVID MALLET (1705-1765)

Mallet and James Thomson were fellow-students at Edinburgh, and belonged to the literary club which produced the *Edinburgh Miscellany*, where some of their earliest verses appear. When he came to London Mallet attracted attention with his ballad *William and Margaret* (written before 1723, published in Aaron Hill's *Plain Dealer,* 1724). Of his other miscellaneous labors, the best known was his edition of Bolingbroke's works (I754). He probably deserved the amusingly hostile sketch of his career, which Johnson gives in the *Lives of the Poets.*

MARY DE LA RIVIERE MANLEY (1672-1724)

Mrs. Manley, sensational and somewhat disreputable like Mrs. Behn before her and Mrs. Haywood after her, was notorious for her *New Atalantis* (I709) and its continuation *Memoirs of Europe* (I710), a scandalous chronicle of contemporary politics and society which jumbled fact, fiction, and gossip with intent to help the Tories, and was widely read, mere trash though it is. She was active as a political writer during the Tory régime of 1710-14, and was well known to Swift. References in *The Rape of the Lock* and *Spectator* No. 37 help to perpetuate her memory. Her best work is perhaps a piece of epistolary fiction published as Letters in 1696 and reprinted as *A Stage-Coach Journey to Exeter* in 1725. The romanticized autobiography *Rivella* (I714) is of some interest.

WILLIAM MASON (1725-1797)

Mason well represents the type of liberal and literary-minded clergyman who plays so prominent a part in eighteenth-century culture. His Miltonic, Spenserian, and Pindaric verses have little value; his dramas on the Greek model, *Elfrida* and *Caractacus,* though Gray took them seriously, are dull and wooden. *The English Garden* (I772-81) is an interesting document on its subject. His long friendship and correspondence with Gray resulted in his *Memoirs of Gray* (I775), a pioneer work in documented biography and thus an important forerunner of Boswell.

THOMAS PARNELL (1679-1718)

Parnell was an Irish clergyman, Archdeacon of Clogher, who became a friend of the Tory wits and a member of the Scriblerus Club, and was also on good terms with Steele and Addison. He contributed an *Essay on Homer* to Pope *Iliad.*

After his premature death Pope brought out his collected verse with a fine dedication to the Earl of Oxford (I722). Parnell was evidently fascinated by Pope's poetry, but his own work is of a somewhat different kind, including the once famous moral apologue *The Hermit*, meditative poems in octosyllabic couplet (A *Hymn to Contentment, A Night-Piece on Death*), the playful *Fairy Tale*, and some graceful lyrics.

AMBROSE PHILIPS (I674-1749)

Ambrose Philips, a very minor poet, is remembered chiefly because of Pope's hostility. The first four of his *Pastorals* were published in Fenton *Oxford and Cambridge Miscellany Poems* (I708); when all six appeared in the Sixth Part of Tonson *Miscellanies* (I709) they invited comparison with Pope *Pastorals* in the same volume. Pope thought they were overpraised in the Whig *Guardian*, edited by Steele, and contributed to that paper ironical praise of the weakest passages in Philips's pieces. This episode helped to bring to a head the feud between Pope and Addison Whig coterie at Button's, of which Philips was a prominent member. Gay *Shepherd's Week* may have been intended as a parody of Philips. Pope and Swift pursued Philips with their scorn, and Carey *Namby Pamby* (I725) satirized his pretty but sometimes mawkish poems to children, and thus fastened a nickname upon him. Philips spent the latter part of his life in Ireland as a Whig office-holder. Other works of his were an adaptation of Racine *Andromaque as The Distrest Mother*, praised by Addison in *Spectator* No. 335, and an essay-periodical called the *Freethinker* (I718-21). His editorship of *A Collection of Old Ballads* (I723-25) is very doubtful.

JOHN PHILIPS (I676-1709)

John Philips, educated at Winchester and Christ Church, Oxford, made an important contribution to eighteenth-century verse by showing how the Miltonic manner could be adapted to moderate or playful literary projects. His *Blenheim* (I705), planned as a Tory tribute to Marlborough's victory, unfortunately shows only the bombast of the misapplied Miltonic style. But he had already done better in

The Splendid Shilling, a humorous and skillful burlesque of Miltonic blank verse which appeared in three collections of 1701, in an unauthorized edition of 1705, and finally in an authentic text in that same year. Addison praised this piece as "the finest burlesque poem in the British language" (*Tatler* No. 249). In *Cyder* (I708) Philips uses the same style to treat the theme of the orchards of Herefordshire. This is an expository poem on the georgic model, but it admits the widest digressions, descriptive, geographical, historical, and personal, and so did much to set a model for the blank-verse descriptive-didactic poem. As exposition, it points forward to Dyer *Fleece* and many other poems of the kind; in its broad and leisurely style it points forward to Thomson *Seasons*. Thomson duly pays tribute to Philips when he hails him as

Pomona's bard! the second thou
Who nobly durst in rhyme-unfettered verse,
With British freedom sing the British song.
(Autumn, ll. 645-47)

JOHN POMFRET (I667-1702)

John Pomfret, a young clergyman with a Cambridge degree, wrote for the most part mediocre religious and philosophical verse (*Poems*, 1699; *Reason*, 1700), but won a place in all the anthologies and miscellanies by his poem *The Choice* (I700). This piece is an undistinguished but representative account of a way of life: the poet would have a small country house with pleasant grounds, a modest income, a library stored with classics, a small but well-stocked cellar, a few congenial friends, especially some "obliging modest-fair," "for I'd have no wife." The last stipulation got Pomfret into trouble with his bishop. Johnson, Southey, and Leigh Hunt all bear witness to the continuing popularity of *The Choice*.

RICHARD SAVAGE (I697-1743)

Savage wrote nothing of much importance, but his claim to be the illegitimate son of the Countess of Macclesfield and Richard Savage, fourth Earl Rivers, though stubbornly denied by his supposed mother, was generally accepted by the

London public, and helped the ne'er-do-well poet to get a precarious living. He was a sturdy literary beggar, always seeking pensions and patronage and airing his grievances. He had many literary friends, such as Dyer, Hill, Thomson, and above all the young Samuel Johnson, whose *Life of Savage* (I744) is a superb piece of biography and affords a remarkable view of the literary underworld of the time. Savage edited an important miscellany, *Miscellaneous Poems and Translations* (I726); his poem *The Wanderer* (I729) follows the trail of Thomson.

ELKANAH SETTLE (I648-1724)

Settle began to write heroic plays in the 1660's, and won much patronage with his*Empress of Morocco,* which succeeded both on the court stage at Whitehall and at Dorset Gardens (I671). It was notable chiefly for its elaborate staging and scenic effects; the engravings in the 1673 edition give important evidence about the physical stage of the Restoration. The preface attacks Dryden; Mulgrave and Rochester were evidently backing Settle against the greater poet. Shadwell and Crowne joined Dryden in a reply, *Notes and Observations on the Empress of Morocco* (I674), quoted at length in Johnson *Life of Dryden*. The quarrel was personal, and had little critical significance. Settle soon lost his patrons, but reappeared as a Whig partisan in the political crisis of the Popish Plot. He wrote an anti-Catholic play, *The Female Prelate* (I680), and a reply to *Absalom* and *Achitophel* called *Absalom Senior* (I682). He is the "Doeg" of Absalom and *Achitophel II*. But soon he was with the Tories again, finding himself on the losing side at the Revolution. From about 1691 Settle worked as "city poet," preparing pageants for the Lord Mayor's shows. He had already been engaged in the humble task of supplying drolls for Bartholemew Fair. He lived on to become a by-word in the Augustan period as a drudging rimester, and has a prominent niche in the *Dunciad*.

WILLIAM SOMERVILE (I675-1742)

A fox-hunting Warwickshire squire—not a Squire Western, however, but an Oxford man of considerable literary culture. In his best poem, The *Chace* (I735), he used the Miltonic blank verse and the digressive georgic pattern of Philips and Thomson to describe his favorite sport. His accurate knowledge of country life and his wholesome enthusiasms are set forth with considerable vividness in this artificial form. Another interesting blank-verse poem of his on country life is *Hobbinol,or the Rural Games*or the Rural Games (I740), though here the burlesque epic form is too elaborate for the theme.

THOMAS SPRAT (I635-1713)

Sprat, Bishop of Rochester, wrote inferior Pindaric odes in imitation of his literary master Cowley, and the important *History of the Royal Society* (I667), an official defense of the new science. The point of view is completely Baconian and practical: the coöperative gathering of experimental data is to take the place of speculation and hypothesis, and toward this end English diction and style are to become simple, objective, and clear. The whole program, he points out with patriotic pride, is particularly appropriate for an enlightened, practical, commercial people like the English.

THOMAS TICKELL (I685-1740)

The part Tickell's proposed translation of the *Iliad* played in the Pope-Addison quarrel has already been mentioned. Tickell was always prominent among Addison's Whig followers, and to his edition of Addison's works he prefixed the famous lines *To the Earl of Warwick on the Death of Mr. Addison.*

WILLIAM WARBURTON (I698-1779)

A self-educated scholar who by sheer weight of learning and arrogant will-power won a prominent place in the Church and the literary world, and became Bishop of Gloucester. His political and religious works are now forgotten (*The Alliance between Church and State, The Divine Legation of Moses*). He thought of himself as dominating the Christian apologetics and literary scholarship of his own time, and looked down on such contemporaries as Hume, Fielding, Richardson, Sterne, and even Johnson. But posterity has not taken him at his own valution. He is best remembered as Pope's friend, defender, and literary executor.

ISAAC WATTS (I674-1748)

Isaac Watts was born at Southampton and educated at a dissenting academy at Stoke Newington. The Independent congregations which had played such a prominent part in earlier religious and political struggles had now settled down to a quiet, prosperous, and relatively unenthusiastic existence. Cut off largely from political and professional interests, the middle-class Dissenter was likely to be a zealous man of business. Watts represents the best intellectual and spiritual interests of Dissent in the first half of the eighteenth century, and became the leading dissenting preacher and man of letters of his day. He held a theory of the religious inspiration of poetry illustrated in his *Horae Lyricae* (I706); he revolutionized the Protestant hymn, and some of his hymns are still sung throughout the English-speaking world; his *Divine Songs for Children* (I715) have gone through hundreds of editions. In terms of actual use and familiarity Watts may fairly be called the most popular English author of the century. His textbooks and educational manuals and his expositions of a moderate Calvinistic theology also had wide currency. Though he kept apart from the Methodist revival, much of his influence was concurrent with that movement.

GILBERT WHITE (I720-1793)

White was born and died at Selborne, Hampshire, and his whole life centered about that secluded village. His *Natural History and Antiquities of Selborne* (I789), which grew out of informal letters to interested friends, has become a classic for its accurate observation and charm of style. White's work as a field naturalist is of high scientific value, particularly his observations on birds, and his whole career shows us the cultivated English country clergyman of the eighteenth century at his best.

ANNE KINGSMILL FINCH, COUNTESS OF WINCHILSEA (I661-1720)

Anne Kingsmill was maid of honor to Mary of Modena (James II's Queen) and married Colonel Finch, later Earl of Winchilsea. She and her husband went into retirement after the abdication of James. Her verse, written under the name of "Ardelia" and circulated in manuscript in her own group, expresses at its best a fine observation of natural detail, and delicate, pensive, and devout feeling, though it includes much conventional work. Wordsworth laid the foundation of her modern fame by praising her "Nocturnal Reverie" in his Preface of 1815, and since then all the anthologies have included that piece and also her *"Petition.*

Index

C

D

E

F

I

J

K

L

M

N

O